MARK LEMON
FIRST EDITOR OF *PUNCH*

By the same author
Georgina Hogarth and the Dickens Circle

Mark Lemon
First Editor of *Punch*

ARTHUR A. ADRIAN

LONDON
OXFORD UNIVERSITY PRESS
NEW YORK   TORONTO
1966

Oxford University Press, Ely House, London W.1

GLASGOW   NEW YORK   TORONTO   MELBOURNE   WELLINGTON
CAPE TOWN   SALISBURY   IBADAN   NAIROBI   LUSAKA   ADDIS ABABA
BOMBAY   CALCUTTA   MADRAS   KARACHI   LAHORE   DACCA
KUALA LUMPUR   HONG KONG

Printed in Great Britain by
W. & J. Mackay & Co. Ltd., Chatham, Kent

For
VONNA

CONTENTS

LIST OF ILLUSTRATIONS

Half-tones

Line Illustrations

PREFACE

PAYING tribute to Mark Lemon shortly after his death in 1870, the *Athenaeum* speculated that he would 'be forgotten not many years hence', but held out the hope that some future literary historian might 'raise up a figure of a true, bright, and happy worker, under whose benignant eyes something new and valuable in journalism was produced in the middle of the nineteenth century'. Such an appraisal is long overdue. That England's greatest humorous magazine survived its early struggles, that its first writers and artists were fused into a loyal brotherhood dedicated to upholding the highest standards, that its published opinions on art, literature, and politics became a force to be reckoned with, must be attributed to the diplomacy and skill of Mark Lemon. With the approach of the 125th anniversary of *Punch* it is fitting, therefore, that its first editor be rescued from the neglect to which he has been too long consigned.

But it is not only as a pioneer in comic journalism that Lemon deserves consideration. As a minor dramatist and author of verse and fiction, an amateur actor and public entertainer, a member of important philanthropic circles, he typifies those Victorians driven by seemingly boundless energy to shape their careers. In short, he was a representative man of his time. The chronicle of his relationships with such prominent theatrical and literary figures as Benjamin Webster and Charles Dickens, of his galvanic stage impersonations (especially the immortal Falstaff), of his benefactions and civic enterprises, is rich in human interest and brings certain dimensions of Victorianism into focus.

In this biography I have not attempted a systematic history of *Punch*, for which the reader may turn to the comprehensive study by M. H. Spielmann and the more recent, and admirably compact, treatment by R. G. G. Price. My concern has been to concentrate on those aspects of the *Punch* story which reveal Lemon's genius as an editor: his penchant for attracting the highest talent, for moulding his staff into an efficient team in spite of personal friction, for gauging the tastes and interests of his readers.

For the sake of completeness I have felt justified in assessing Lemon's efforts at authorship, even though their literary merit is slight. His torrents of verse, drama, and prose attest to astonishing energy and industry. At the same time his published work reveals many of his idiosyncrasies and deep-seated convictions.

In assembling materials for this biography I have had the most gratifying support of Mr. Peter G. Agnew, managing director of the firm of Bradbury and Agnew. He has placed me heavily in his debt by showing me every courtesy and permitting me to transcribe and quote from unpublished materials at the *Punch* office, without which a life of Lemon could not have been undertaken. To Mrs. W. M. Ashton, the former librarian of *Punch*, I am grateful for directing me to these sources and answering numerous queries. Her successor, Miss Elizabeth Bower, and Mr. W. M. Walton, the assistant publicity manager, helped me further in collecting photographic material.

I am also indebted to the following for permission to examine and quote from unpublished letters and other documents: the Henry W. and Albert E. Berg Collection of the New York Public Library (particularly Dr. John D. Gordan), the British Museum, The Trustees of the Dickens House (especially Miss Doris L. Minards and Mr. Leslie C. Staples), the Edinburgh University Library (particularly Mr. C. P. Finlayson, keeper of MSS.), the Fales Collection of the New York University Library, the Garrick Club (particularly its secretary Commander E. S. Satterthwaite), the Haverford College Library, the Historical Society of Pennsylvania, the Houghton Library of Harvard University, Mrs. Humphry House, the Henry E. Huntington Library (particularly Dr. Herbert C. Schulz), the National Library of Scotland, Mrs. G. M. Palmer, the Parrish Collection of the Princeton University Library, the Philadelphia Free Library, the Pierpont Morgan Library, the John Rylands Library, the University of Texas Humanities Research Center, and the Library and the Enthoven Theatre Collection of the Victoria and Albert Museum.

For free access to secondary sources and indispensable records I am grateful to the Boston (Lincs.) Public Library (particularly Miss Bridget E. Robinson), the Cleveland Public Library, the Crawley Library (and its director, Mr. D. E. Plunkett), the Hammersmith Library (and Mr. K. G. Hunt, chief librarian), the Hendon Public Library (and its borough librarian, Mr. S. J. Butcher, and its reference librarian, Mr. John Hopkins), the Kensington Library (particularly Miss R. J. Ensing), the St. Marylebone Borough Library (especially Mrs. Ann Saunders), the Trinity College Library of Dublin, the Western Reserve University Library (for extended loans of rare books), and the Westminster Borough Library (particularly Miss Mary Dunbar).

To others who have suggested valuable sources of information I acknowledge my indebtedness: Mr. F. P. Beck (headmaster of Cheam School), Mr. R. J. L. Bell, Mr. R. A. Brimmell (Rare Books, Hampton Hill), Mr. W. J. Carlton, Professor David B. Green (Bryn Mawr College), Mr. W. H. Hart (British Railways), Mr. E. Kersley, Mr. Roger M. B. Micholls, Miss Winifred A. Myers (Autographs Ltd.), Professor Noel Peyrouton (Emerson College), Mrs. A. J. Ritchie, the late General Sir Cecil Romer, Mr. R. N. Rose (*The Field*), Miss E. M. W. Sikes, the late Dr. Percy E. Spielmann, Mr. T. L. Stevens, Mr. A. H. Taylor (borough treasurer, Boston, Lincs.), Professor Carl Woodring (Columbia University), Mr. Maurice Woolf, Mrs. J. Varley (archivist, Lincolnshire), the Reverend C. C. Welch (St. Mary's, Hendon), and the Reverend T. C. Williams (St. Margaret's, Ifield). My special thanks are due to Professor J. L. Bradley (University of South Carolina) for sharing with me his findings on Lemon's relations with Henry Mayhew; to Miss Daisy Warren, Arundel, for invaluable historical material on Crawley; to Mr. Eric Jeffcott, director of Highgate Library, for consulting many records bearing on Lemon's early years in London and his later residence near Gordon Square; to Mr. Arthur G. Clarke, chairman of the Mill Hill and Hendon Historical Society, for interesting details and several photographs of old Hendon; and to Mr. Arnold U. Ziegler, treasurer of the Boston (Mass.) Dickens Fellowship, for repeatedly sending me valuable books and clippings from his library.

I gratefully acknowledge the timely aid which enabled me to conduct my research. Two generous grants from the American Philosophical Society and one from the American Council of Learned Societies made it possible for me to gather the larger part of my material in Great Britain during a sabbatical leave from Western Reserve University in 1962. Several grants from the Graduate Research Fund of Western Reserve University helped me to acquire valuable unpublished letters and other documents.

To Mr. R. G. G. Price I am especially indebted for directing me to important primary sources and for reading an early draft of my manuscript. To my wife, Vonna H. Adrian, who read my final draft and suggested numerous revisions, I am deeply grateful for working with me during the early stages of my research and for helping me to bring this biography to its conclusion.

Finally, I take pleasure in acknowledging my heavy indebtedness to the present descendants of Mark Lemon, especially his grand-daughter, Mrs. Sidney Matthews of Crawley, Sussex, and her daughter Phyllis. From the first my undertaking has had their fullest endorsement, reinforced by press cuttings, photographs, and a wealth of family lore preserved through several generations. Mrs. Adrian and I cherish happy memories of visits to the Matthews home, where we gathered around the tea-table with other Lemon descendants and listened to fascinating anecdotes about 'Grandfather'. I sincerely hope that my portrait has done justice to the rich materials with which they have entrusted me.

Western Reserve University
12 April 1965   A.A.A.

KEY TO ABBREVIATIONS IN THE FOOTNOTES

References to individual works give the author's surname, the title (generally shortened), and the page.

Adrian MS.	=	Letters owned by the author.
B.D.	=	Manuscript diaries of Shirley Brooks (for 1869, 1871, 1873) in the London Library.
Berg MS.	=	Letters in the Berg Collection of the New York Public Library.
B.M. MS.	=	Letters and other documents in the British Museum.
Dick.	=	*Dickensian.*
Dick.H. MS.	=	Letters in the Dickens House, London.
Ed.U. MS.	=	Letters in the Library of Edinburgh University.
Fales MS.	=	Letters in the Fales Collection, New York University.
Harvard MS.	=	Letters in the Houghton Library of Harvard University.
Haverford MS.	=	Letters in the Haverford College Library, Pennsylvania.
Hunt. MS.	=	Letters in the Henry E. Huntington Library, San Marino, California.
Morgan MS.	=	Letters in the Pierpont Morgan Library, New York.
Mr. and Mrs.	=	*Mr. and Mrs. Charles Dickens. His Letters to Her.* ed. Walter Dexter.
Nat. Lib. of Scot. MS.	=	Letters in the National Library of Scotland, Edinburgh.
Nonesuch	=	*The Letters of Charles Dickens.* ed. Walter Dexter.
Pa.H.S. MS.	=	Letters owned by the Historical Society of Pennsylvania.
Palmer MS.	=	Letters owned by Mrs. G. M. Palmer, the Old Rectory, Doynton.
P.O. MS.	=	*Punch* Office Manuscript.
Ports. MS.	=	Letters in the Dickens Museum, Portsmouth.

Silver   =   Manuscript diary in which Henry Silver of the
                     Punch Table recorded the conversations at the
                     weekly staff dinners from 4 August 1858 to 23 March
                     1870. Since this document is not to be published
                     and will remain, therefore, generally inaccessible,
                     my citations do not include dates.

Trinity MS.   =   Letters owned by Trinity College, Cambridge.

U. of T. MS.   =   Letters in the Humanities Research Center, Uni-
                     versity of Texas, Austin.

V. and A. MS.   =   Letters in the Victoria and Albert Museum Library,
                     London.

Punch

1868 — 1882
1886 — 1889

(the Paper)

up to
1882
[Atlan 2:840 (T. B. Fox)
?Westm. 38:265 (Phil. of)
~~Lond. Soc. 28:49-511~~ (J. Hatton)
~~29:127-438~~ (True Story of)
~~30:57-554~~

1882 —
1886
~~So. Lit. Mess. 35:54~~ -hist. in
?Fortn. 46:49 { 1841-1854 }
?Liv. Age 150:323 {
~~?Fortn. 46:737~~ { " 1851-1861 }

~~34:591~~ (why not an amen.?

82)
P96

8 2) ³
P9696

customs -942,08
H138

741,5 ³

(9696

82).08
P9696

823
T 32wo
v. 11/12

823
1321i

'THE DAYS OF GLORY'

LONDON, 25 October 1809, the Royal Jubilee of George III: a day of official thanksgiving. It dawned with the peal of church bells, proceeded through a morning sermon at St. Paul's Cathedral, gathered momentum with marching bands and noisy demonstrations, and culminated with the dazzling night illumination of all important buildings. The City celebrated with a dinner at the Mansion House. And at the King's Theatre, where the stage had been 'converted into a Grand Saloon, forming an Imperial Chinese Pagoda', guests sat down to an English supper, featuring, according to *The Times*, 'all kinds of poultry (cold), Beef, Ham, Raised and other Pies, Shell-fish, etc. together with Sherry and Port (Vintage 1804)'.

London's lavish holiday mood was not reflected, however, in the manufacturing centres of the North, where the working classes were suffering from a renewal of the war with France. With shipping lanes threatened or cut off by the enemy, England's trade declined drastically. Textile mills closed down; hundreds of labourers lost their jobs; the price of bread kept rising. The poor braced themselves for a hard winter.

But to London's theatre-goers the war with France was of less concern than the prices at Covent Garden. The trouble began when Kemble, the manager, raised admissions by one shilling in the boxes and by sixpence in the pit. With the added income he hoped to pay off his debt on the handsome new Doric building, erected at a cost of over one hundred and fifty thousand pounds. His action provoked furious rioting. Night after night, from all parts of the theatre, came barking, groaning, catcalls, and cries of 'Off! Off! Old prices!' The demonstrators were determined to riot at every performance so long as Kemble held out. Displaying the letters 'O.P.' (Old Prices) on their hats and coats, they laughed, sang, and chanted to the accompaniment of horns, bells, and watchmen's rattles. Placards

displayed warnings: 'Mr. Kemble, lower your prices; for no evasion /
Will suit John Bull on this occasion.' At the climax of the rioting
came the O.P. Dance, a stamping of feet alternating with the chanting
of 'Old prices' in noisy and monotonous cadence. An item in *The
Times* nearly five months after the opening of the new building gave
little assurance of an early end to the disturbances: '*Covent Garden.*
Uproar returned to this theatre last night [29 November] . . . and
interrupted the last of the Opera of the *Exile*, so as to spoil the whole
effect. . . . The O.P. dance was given in time and tune with the
finale dance and the chorus.'

Of an event the following day, the birth of Mark Lemon, *The
Times* was silent. But it is significant that the news this autumn—
the social inequalities displayed in the lavish Jubilee as against the
poverty of the labouring classes, and the fortunes of the popular
theatre—foreshadowed the lifelong major interests of the child born
on 30 November 1809. For as editor of *Punch*, Mark Lemon was ever
to protest at the oppression of the poor, and to endorse liberal
causes; as minor dramatist and amateur actor he was ever to occupy
himself with theatrical matters.

The birth took place in a small house in Oxford Street, near
the site now occupied by Peter Robinson's department store. The
parents, Martin and Alice Collis Lemon, had been residents of
the neighbourhood at the time of their marriage in St. Marylebone
Church on Boxing Day the previous year. The baby's paternal grand-
father, also named Mark, and grandmother (*née* Grace Denyer) had
likewise been married in this church in 1784 and had lived in Oxford
Street before moving some seven miles north-west to a farm at
Hendon. This elder Mark was a man of considerable substance.
According to his will, in which he called himself a 'Dealer in
Horses', he owned real estate ('Messuages or Tenement Closes,
Lands, and Hereditaments') in Finchley, Dunsfold, Wembley,
Harrow, and Neasden.

Young Mark's mother also came from a prosperous household.
Her father, Thomas Collis, had brought his family to London from
West Haddon, Northamptonshire, and, according to the rate-books,
was living at 194 Oxford Street when his grandson was born near by.
A son, also named Thomas, became a prominent hop and timber
merchant in Boston, Lincolnshire, where he served as mayor from
1839 to 1840. Later, with the expansion of his firm, he divided his
business between London and Boston.

Nowhere in this ancestral history is there evidence to support published statements that Mark Lemon was of Jewish extraction. According to Maurice Woolf (*Jewish Chronicle*, 15 August 1958), it was Edmund Yates, 'hostile to Lemon', who started the 'myth' by asserting in his reminiscences that Mark 'was a Jew, as his *prénom* and surname sufficiently testify'. Mr. Woolf properly considers this the 'thinnest evidence', pointing out that ' "Mark" is apostolic . . . and more often than not is of non-Jewish usage'. But even before Yates's statement there were hints that Mark might be of Hebrew lineage. As early as 1849, after he had appeared at Bow Street Police Court to prefer charges against a pickpocket for an attempted robbery, some verses entitled 'Ballads of Bow Street' appeared in *Chat*, an old paper. Insisting that 'for hall the world [Lemon] looked unkimmon like a Jew', the author added supporting detail:

> His 'air it ung in corkscrew curls,
> He had a heagle look;
> His chin it vos a double vun,
> His nose it vos a hook.[1]

It should be pointed out that the editor of *Chat*, G. A. Sala, was not on friendly terms with Mark and may well have written these unsigned lines. Apparently Mark's appearance was chiefly responsible for the conjectures, though Mr. Woolf sees features in his portrait 'more Falstaffian than Jewish—almost like a bearded Chesterton with a great head of hair'.

That Mark himself was aware of the speculations about his alleged Semitic origin is borne out by his own testimony: he told friends that once, in preliminary questioning before serving as court witness, he had given a decisive 'no' when asked whether he was Jewish.[2] So far as he knew, certainly, there was no Jewish strain in his immediate forebears, all of whom belonged to the Anglican communion. For generations, moreover, his father's family could trace their descent from Cornish yeomen. (That the dark complexion, crisp wavy hair, even the aquiline nose, may have been handed down through the Iberian strain in his Cornish ancestors seems worthy of mention.) But hints of a Jewish background persisted. A few months after his death a literary historian commented: 'Whether Mark Lemon, as we shrewdly suspect, be of that ancient race which gave kings to Judea

---

[1] Reprinted in the *Dickensian*, XVI (June 1920), pp. 91–92.   [2] Silver.

and prophets to the world, it boots not to inquire.'[3] Unchallenged, such surmises were in time to pass from the realm of rumour to the area of unsupported belief, to be repeated as accepted fact in later published sources.

Whatever the truth, as a boy Mark was unconcerned about his background. An only child, he enjoyed the advantages of a middle-class home with moderate comforts and freedom from worry. Seated beside his mother in her carriage, he often accompanied her on calls to fashionable addresses in Wimpole Street or Cavendish Square.[4] Though there are gaps in the information covering this period, his early childhood was apparently happy and agreeably punctuated by visits to his paternal grandparents in rural Hendon.

When Mark, less than two months beyond his eighth birthday, was left a half orphan by the death of his father, he went to live with these grandparents. At this time Hendon was a peaceful village with roughly three hundred and fifty homes and a population of three thousand. An agricultural community, it was noted for the quality of its wheat and hay. In all directions, outlined by high hedges, stretched a patchwork of cultivated fields and meadows, broken occasionally by woodland. From the centre of the village spread Grandfather Lemon's acres. Church Farm House, his home, was a three-gabled building dating from 1650, one of the show places of the neighbourhood. (Today it is a museum.) Next door stood the old Greyhound Inn, built about 1776, which served both as a meeting-place for church and parish business and as a house of refreshment. Here the elder Lemon, an overseer of the poor, went at intervals to present, and swear to, his accounts before the justices. In handwriting of thin strokes he recorded such disbursements as '3s. to a woman for sitting up with the sick in the workhouse', or '£2. 2s. to Mr. Black for curing Mary Heath's head'.[5]

Years later Mark immortalized this favourite grandfather in a pen portrait: '[He] had a face as rosy as a peony, and usually wore a red waistcoat; his wavy hair was surmounted by a broad-brimmed hat, which threw out the colours of his face strongly.' Mark remembered, too, the old man's pride in his two-hundred-acre farm: 'The stack-yard was near the house, and the roads about it were neatly gravelled, the hedges clipped, and the grass carefully mown. The house and

[3] Friswell, *Modern Men of Letters*, pp. 49–57.   [4] Ibid.
[5] For these details I am indebted to Mr. A. G. Clarke, chairman of the Mill Hill and Hendon Historical Society.

garden were always in "apple-pie order" . . ., and nothing delighted him more than to get a few friends to come down and admire and be most hospitably treated.' Jogging along the country lanes in a 'one-horse shay', little Mark sat for safety between his grandfather's 'dear old mahogany-top-boots' and was often allowed to hold the reins in the belief that he was 'driving old Jack'.[6] Later he blended this experience into one of his earliest poems, 'My Grandfather's Boots':

> These boots were my grandsire's (a better ne'er strode
> A hunter or hack, in the field—on the road—
> None more true to his friend, or his bottle when full,
> In short you may call him a thorough John Bull).

During the country rides Grandfather Lemon told stories of his own boyhood. There was, for example, the oft-repeated tale of how he had run away from home because of his father's harshness. Exhausted after walking all day along the highway without any clear idea of his destination, he rested beside a gate. Before long a man rode by and asked him whether he could read and write. Would he like a job? Invited to come along, the runaway was soon employed by this new friend. Later he fell in love with his master's daughter and married her. On the death of his father, who had forgiven him for running away, he inherited a considerable fortune. Some years later he met a sailor in another village and recognized him as his brother Robert, who had also run away from home. This great-uncle of Mark's was to advance from midshipman on board *H.M.S. Liverpool* to chief clerk of the Record Office in the Tower of London, a post he held from 1766 till his death in 1813.

A public footpath wound past the Lemon farm, with several seats conveniently placed on the higher ground for those who wished to stop and admire the view. Here, on sunny afternoons, young Mark could see Edgware, Great Stanmore, Wembley, Harrow, and Kingsbury, as his eyes ranged over the route of the Romans. Here, too, he often watched the red-coated hunters mount in front of the Greyhound Inn and set off across the fields. All his life he was to be fond of riding, a pleasure which his occasional spills could never mar. Among his keener recollections was the time when, a lad of eleven, he had shared a horse with one 'sweet Kate'—he at the reins, she holding on behind.

Church End Farm, the Greyhound Inn, St. Mary's Church next

[6] See 'What Firkin Picked Up on the Road' in *Tom Moody's Tales*.

door—these three shared the crest of the hill and dominated the village as they were to dominate Mark's early memories. But it was chiefly the venerable church, a landmark visible for miles around, that nurtured the boy's sense of history and helped to waken his social conscience. The main structure, a blend of red and soft yellow sandstone, flint, and freestone, dated from 1220; even older were parts of the foundation of the Lady Chapel, said to go back to 950. Though the clock on the square tower had struck the hours only since 1759, the weather vane, a lamb and flag, served to remind the boy of the ancient badge of the Knights Hospitallers of St. John of Jerusalem.[7]

Before entering by the recessed west doorway with its pointed arch (since bricked up when the church was enlarged), Mark might pause beside his father's grave, only a few feet away, and ponder the newly cut inscription: 'Life how Short, Eternity how Long.' Once inside he was fascinated by the tower, with its ringing-room, clock chamber, and belfry, later to figure in 'The Old Bell-Ringer's Story', one of his Christmas tales.[8] 'The church-yard of H——abutted on my grandfather's garden,' Mark recalled, 'and it was the old gentleman's custom on village festivals to send to the ringers certain jorums of harvest beer . . . which never failed to set more clappers than those of the bells in motion.' At this period there were six bells, and he remembered how he had 'more than once been allowed to call the peal' from the numbers chalked on the belfry door. On Christmas Eve, after 'the ale had been freely distributed', the church tower was 'kept in a continued state of tremulousness by the clanging of the bells, until the hour of midnight had passed, and the last peal had been rung'. Weary from their exertions, the ringers sat in a group and finished their pitcher of ale as they talked about past Christmases. One of the most attentive listeners was young Mark.

On Sunday mornings, as he went with his grandparents to their pew in the Gothic chancel, he must often have noted the inscriptions on the plaques under the belfry. Bold letters commemorated the good works of one Elizabeth Parsons, who had died on 24 April 1751, bequeathing 'unto the Vicar and Church Wardens' one hundred

---

[7] One Hendon historian has suggested, however, that the lamb had no connexion with the Knights Hospitallers, but represented the sacrificial lamb.

[8] In *A Christmas Hamper*.

pounds for 'the Poor of this Parish'. There also Mark could admire the record of a still earlier benefactor, Robert Daniel, a seventeenth-century London merchant who had left a legacy 'to Build an Alms house' and insure the 'Maintenance and Cloathing of six poor Men and four poor women of the age of 50 upwards'. Such testimony of past generosity, together with the presence in the galleries of the charity school children, wards of the Church, could but nurture young Mark's sense of social responsibility—particularly as he sat in the pew beside his grandfather, an active overseer of the village poor.

When the boy allowed his mind and eyes to wander during the service, he could scarcely have avoided fastening them at times on a brass plate in the aisle to the left of the altar. There a two-hundred-year-old epitaph testified not only to the virtues of its subject but to the crude powers of some local versifier:

> By power Death hath of Every Mortal Wight
> Hath Robert Nuttinge to heaven tooke his flight
> Trew friend to peace an enimy to strife
> Liveinge fifty and seven A happie life
> Wher of his marriage years were thirtie seaven
> Had Children like the olive plants of heaven
> Blessed the dead that in the Lord do ende
> They rest from labours and their workes assend

Whether or not these artless lines helped to arouse in Mark the poetic fancy that led to his own simple songs and ballads, it is certain that an epitaph in the churchyard did inspire a later composition. Among the more recent graves was that of one Robert Thomas Crossfield, once accused and acquitted of plotting to assassinate George III. Buried in 1802, Crossfield had written his own 'Epitaph as truly characteristic of himself':

> Beneath this stone TOM CROSSFIELD lies,
> Who cares not now, who laughs or cries;
> He laughed when sober and when mellow,
> Was a Harum-scarum heedless Fellow;
> He gave to None designed Offence;
> So 'Honi soit qui mal y pense.'

Only slightly altered, this epitaph appears in one of Mark's tales based on his Hendon recollections.[9]

[9] See 'What Firkin Picked Up on the Road' in *Tom Moody's Tales*.

Another early link in the chain of influences leading to Mark's literary and journalistic career was undoubtedly his acquaintance with Theodore Williams, the vicar of St. Mary's, a cultivated man who built up an excellent library at the vicarage and enriched his sermons with literary allusions and quotations.

But more important to the boy's education was the period spent at Cheam School in Surrey. One of the oldest private schools in England, it catered for gentlemen's sons. Its nineteenth-century exclusiveness is illustrated by the story of a tradesman's son who had to leave when his father's name was discovered over an old-established cutlery shop in London. (Ironically, Mark's mother was earning her living as a milliner in London while her son was pursuing his studies at this select school.) Some idea of the *prestige* of Cheam may be gathered from a list of its alumni, who include Dr. Charles Davenant, son of the poet, in the seventeenth century; Henry Addington (later Sixth Viscount) in the eighteenth century; Lord Randolph Churchill in the nineteenth century; and, more recently, Lord Louis Mountbatten (1910), the Duke of Edinburgh (1930–3), and Charles, Prince of Wales (1957–8). The main building, with lofty, airy rooms, stood on the high street of a village with a population of approximately eight hundred.[10] Since the records before 1855 are no longer extant, it is unfortunately impossible to determine the length of Mark's attendance or the quality of his work. From the surviving school journals of a period slightly later than his, however, we may form some idea of the curriculum. The emphasis was on the classics and Greek and Roman history, with English poetry and the Holy Scriptures next in importance. Though there is little mention of mathematics, Mark is known to have studied arithmetic under the eminent Charles Butler, author of several learned treatises. The headmaster was James Wilding, a graduate of Magdalen College, Oxford, who also served as curate of Cheam. He educated his boys on the Pestalozzian system.

At Cheam, Mark had an unforgettable experience which he eventually wove into his second novel, *Loved at Last*. Recognized by his schoolfellows for his inventiveness, he entertained them at night

---

[10] In the twentieth century Cheam School was moved to Headley, Newbury, Berkshire. Today its earlier site is occupied by a block of flats, Tabor Court, named after the headmasters in control from 1855 to 1920. Only its original chapel remains. For this information I am indebted to Mr. F. P. Beck, headmaster of Cheam School.

with stories in their dark bedroom, long after 'the rest of the household lay wrapped in deep slumber'. But there came a time when he lost his hold on his listeners. In an effort to recapture them, he hit on the idea of a mock trial: a court to inquire 'into the proceedings of the day, and to pass sentence upon the misdemeanours recorded'. Mark himself was to preside as judge. A nightgown over a black suit for his judicial robe and a bolster with 'flapping ends for a wig', he conducted several trials by the light of a lantern, while the 'higher court below stairs' remained unaware of these sessions. One evening as he was summing up the case of a boy on trial for stealing marbles from another's desk, he observed the startled faces of the jury. Turning round, he froze as he saw the headmaster. Without a word Mark was marched downstairs, 'nightgown, bolster and all', and into the drawing-room, where guests were celebrating the birthday of Wilding's daughter. Brought before her, he was 'gravely' and in a loud voice introduced as Judge Lemon. 'O Lord! What agony I suffered!' he recalled as a man in his fifties. 'The good-natured girl pitied my horrible confusion, and entreated her father not to prolong it. But the schoolmaster enjoyed the joke. He presented me with a glass of wine, and made me drink to the health of the company, and then released me, amid roars of laughter.' After retreating to the dormitory, Mark hid his 'diminished head' under the bedclothes, ignoring all questions from the boys, who had anxiously awaited word of his fate.

For this humiliation he apparently harboured no hard feelings against Wilding. Quite the reverse, for the sound instruction and guidance given him at Cheam far outweighed the brief embarrassment of that one episode. In his fifty-third year, learning that his old headmaster was living in Cherbury, he poured out his gratitude in a letter. 'So many recollections of kindness and benefits received from you crowded upon me', he wrote, 'that I have ventured, even at the risk of being forgotten by you, to say how grateful I am still for your teachings in school and church.' Declaring that these precepts had 'conduced to all the good I have known throughout my life', he asserted further: 'Had it been my good fortune to continue under your care I should have been a better and wiser man. As it is, I have often been thankful to God, that He gave me such a friend and instructor as yourself.' Since he was writing this letter only nine days before Christmas, he added that he had before him his first Cheam Christmas prize, *The Life of William Stevens*.

And he subscribed himself 'your unworthy but attached friend'.[11]

Like all schoolboys, Mark welcomed any holiday respite from study. On such occasions he was sometimes lured to his favourite attraction in London, the bazaar in Exeter Street, whose millionaire proprietor, one Thomas Clarke, had once offered young Mark a glass of wine. Over the bazaar, its entrance barred by an imposing beefeater, were the quarters of the renowned wild-beast show. On the outside, huge paintings advertised the spectacles within. Here Mark could watch spellbound as an enormous elephant crushed a mangel-wurzel underfoot or with its trunk picked up a penny from an iron box.[12]

Such schoolboy diversions would have been out of place, however, during the Christmas holidays of 1820, which were shadowed by the death of Grandfather Lemon on 12 December. As eleven-year-old Mark stood by the new grave in the family plot at St. Mary's, he may have been dimly aware that an era in his life was about to end. At any rate, there would be no more story-telling on country jaunts in the 'one-horse shay'.

But before the privileged days of the Hendon period came to a close Mark was to experience the most colourful, the most dramatic event of his boyhood: the ceremonies attending the Coronation of George IV in 1821. As the date (19 July) suggests, the occasion must have barely preceded the close of a school term, and it is thus possible that he witnessed events with Cheam companions fortunate enough to be entitled to coveted points of vantage. That at least one other boy shared the experience with Mark is evident in the account given in his late fifties, when he still recalled each thrilling detail: how he was sent to bed early on the 18th, but slept hardly a wink before being roused at midnight to dress in his plum-coloured suit with a white shirt collar turned back over his shoulders; how he went by coach to Palace Yard. From Westminster Hall to the Abbey stretched a vast platform. Dancing lights from many fires played on the fretted work of the buildings. Around the fires sat soldiers in their greatcoats, their glittering arms piled up and catching the light. Led into a house fronted with scaffolding, Mark finally entered a room dimly illuminated by candles. Though warned to keep quiet, he could hardly control his excitement. At five in the morning, on the recommendation of another boy, he had a glass of sherry, only

[11] Reprinted in *London Society*, XXIX (Feb. 1876), p. 132.
[12] Related by Mark Lemon in *Up and Down the London Streets*, pp. 256–7.

to find his head humming like a top when he went outside. He had a horrible fear of not being able to watch the proceedings. Fortunately, he got over his dizziness in time to witness an historical encounter: twenty lifeguards, their breastplates decorated with laurel and their swords drawn, met the discarded Queen Caroline as her carriage approached. Asked for her ticket to enter the Abbey, she retorted, 'I need no ticket; I am the Queen.' Repulsed, she drove away cursing, while the crowd groaned and shouted.

An impatient interval—the ancient rite was proceeding inside the Abbey. Finally lines of red-coated soldiers took their places beside the platform. The tempo of expectancy increased: trumpets and drums; officers on horseback, beefeaters, heralds; dukes, earls, barons, all in Elizabethan costume, with slashed trunks and side cloaks. At last—His Majesty under a canopy of gold, his velvet train gold-embroidered and carried by pages with feathers in their hats. Even heavier now than in 1809, when Leigh Hunt had called him a 'bloated Adonis, fat at fifty', the King bulged beneath his diamond-studded crown. Behind him came Lord Castlereagh in plumed hat. Next, in polished armour, the Champion of England on a white charger rode into Westminster Hall to throw down the traditional gauntlet. Altogether it was a story-book day in a schoolboy's life, a day to be relived again and again.[13]

Just how Mark was occupied during the months following this memorable July is conjectural. Perhaps it was then that his public-school days ended. Certainly the phrasing of his letter to Wilding ('Had it been my good fortune to continue under your care') hints that his schooling at Cheam was interrupted—perhaps after his grandfather's death. Family deaths among the Lemons had a way of recurring at approximately three-year intervals, just far enough apart for the boy to adjust himself to the changes each one brought. At the age of eight he had lost his father; at eleven, Grandfather Lemon; and at fourteen he was to see Grandmother Lemon laid beside the other two in St. Mary's churchyard. With this third bereavement Mark's boyhood in Hendon came to a close.

During his six years in Hendon his mother had remained in London. Though she had earlier enjoyed driving about the West End in her own carriage, she faced the harsh realities of widowhood by opening a millinery shop at 336 Oxford Street, where she specialized

[13] The material for this and the preceding paragraph has been drawn from Lemon's *Up and Down the London Streets*, pp. 256-7.

in straw bonnets. With most of her time given to business she must have realized that an adolescent boy needed more attention than she could devote to him. Moreover, and in spite of his legacy from his grandfather (an eighth of the estate), it was time Mark prepared himself for earning a living as soon as possible. His next home, therefore, was in Boston, Lincolnshire, with his mother's brother, Thomas Collis, under whose guidance he was to learn the hops business.

The provincial environment of the North provided a sharp contrast to Mark's former life. At this time Boston, a town of not more than eleven thousand inhabitants, consisted mainly of one long curving line along the east bank of the River Witham. In the flat coastal area, appropriately named Holland, Boston was a centre for fen and marsh farmers, who enlivened the community on Wednesdays and Saturdays by bringing their stock, poultry, grain, butter, eggs, and fish to the market-place.

A rival to the market-place was the fifteenth-century Gothic Guildhall, where Mark could inspect the iron cages which had confined the Pilgrim Fathers who sailed to America in 1620. More fascinating still was the notable parish church of St. Botolph, with its tall lantern-topped tower, visible on clear days for forty miles, and generally referred to as Boston Stump. One can picture Mark groping his dim way up the three hundred and sixty-five steps to the lantern in order to emerge into air and light for a wide view of sea and marsh.

For all these attractions, however, Boston lacked amenities when he lived there with his uncle in South Place. There were no water pipes, and regiments of women lined up at Pump Square to fill their pails. And the streets were only dimly lighted by a few flickering oil lamps. There were compensations, however. The natives were genuinely friendly, and Mark formed some close attachments with the young people. 'When I was here among you,' he told a Boston audience during one of his visits in 1856, 'almost every young man had a sweetheart.'[14] The extent of his own involvement is not revealed, though there are hints that he was attracted to the local beauties as he approached manhood.

Perhaps one of his youthful infatuations inspired a story in *Tom Moody's Tales* (occasionally autobiographical in content), 'How I and

[14] As reported in the Boston and Louth *Guardian*, and Lincolnshire *Advertiser* for 5 and 12 Mar. 1856.

Davy Handey Lost Our First Loves'. Captivated by the ravishing Anonyma, whom he had met at a fox hunt, the narrator confides his feelings to his uncle's servant. 'Davy, I'm about as miserable a young party as you can find anywhere,' he complains. 'For three weeks I've thought of nothing but her; dreamed of nothing but her.' With Davy's help the love-lorn young man sends Anonyma sentimental notes. Encouraged by her smiles, when he sees her again at a meet he boldly follows her. He is enraptured when her groom slyly motions to him and places a pink note in his hand. Tearing it open, he reads: 'Sir,—I will trouble you not to rite to me no more, or foller me about in the field, or I shall leave the naybor-hood.'

If indeed Mark had such an experience with one of the rustic beauties, he could have found solace in a favourite diversion, the local theatre. Here he could be thrilled by the performances of actors like Pemberton, whose powers Bostonians considered equal to Kean's or Macready's. In addition to Shakespeare, there was the crude dramatic fare typical of the time. The triple bill for 7 April 1829, for instance, consisted of *A Bold Stroke for a Husband*, followed by a 'new entertainment' entitled *The Green-Eyed Monster*, and concluding with the drama *Anaconda, or the Serpent of Columbia*.[15] Soon Mark himself would be writing similar pieces.

For typical music-hall shows he might visit the great annual fair, which offered, in addition to the customary farmers' exhibits, equestrian troupes and arrays of giants and dwarfs, monkeys, and crocodiles. According to the bills there were also peep-shows whose 'bloody histories' were embellished with 'appropriate horrors'. And in the market-place a local lad might jostle 'ballad mongers, dying speech makers, and wandering vagabonds'.

What Mark saw in Boston of rural customs was to prove useful to him later. Always a close observer, he stored up details to enliven his future fiction. So in his first novel, *Wait for the End*, he could write from personal acquaintance that 'the small British farmer of other days was a dull fellow enough [who] knew nothing of phosphates, and all the other great agents of agricultural chemistry, and would as soon have thought of threshing by steam as going up in a balloon to catch larks'. It was this farmer, with his idiosyncrasies, native shrewdness, and industry, whom Mark sketched to the life in one of his best portraits:

[15] Ibid., 7 Apr. 1829.

He brightened up greatly on market days, whether he was buyer or seller, and it was difficult to dip your fingers into his leathern money bag more deeply than was conducive to his own interests. He worked hard for his money, and generally knew how to keep it. But he was brightest at sales, where he always made up his mind to get a bargain if he could, and approached the object he desired very charily, taking sly looks at it, and never closely examining into its merits so long as a possible competitor was at hand. . . . His bids were always made with winks, and when the offers of others had nearly reached the limit of his estimate, he would thrust his hands into his pockets and take a few turns to keep down his rising anxiety. . . . When fortunate to have been the purchaser, he usually gave his name with a blush, as though he were ashamed of his bargain, or had been detected in an act which reflected upon his prudence, and would expose him to the small wit of the market-table.

During his Boston days Mark had ample opportunity to indulge in his favourite rural sport, riding. This was the period of his hunting exploits, his horse-breaking, his races across the fens. In later life he amused his friends by recounting one of these experiences: how he had mounted a horse never before saddled, had been whisked over a hedge and gate before he knew it, and had stuck on as the trees streaked past. Another time, however, the day before his twenty-first birthday, he fell under his mount, was dragged for a distance, and had to lie in bed for three months. While recovering from this mishap he relieved his boredom by dashing off verses, one piece bearing the punning title 'Accidental Stanzas':

> Precious is rest to the worn and spent,
> (Unstringing the bow too long unbent,)
> Creation's self doth loveliest seem
> When first awoke by the morning's beam;
> Rest glads the joyous and soothes the wretch
> But O! it is tiresome three months at a stretch.[16]

As soon as he could get out of bed he was dancing on crutches. Shortly after, he was back in the saddle again.[17] 'The love of the chase is an enduring passion,' he declared years later in *Loved at Last*, for an aged and infirm sportsman can still be 'mounted on Old Memory to cheer on the hounds'.

[16] Later published in *The New Sporting Magazine* for Oct. 1835.
[17] Silver.

In his fifties Mark often rode Old Memory back to his idyllic childhood in Hendon, his adolescence and early manhood in Boston. When family and professional responsibilities weighed heavily, he could always retreat temporarily to the past. His eyes would twinkle as he repeated, 'The days of our youth were the days of our glory.'

2

HOPS, CHOPS, AND PLAYBILLS

⟶ ꞅ∘◉∘꞊ ⟵

JUST when Mark left his uncle's home in Lincolnshire and struck out for himself is not a matter of record. By 1836 he was almost certainly living in London, for a letter of his dated 12 March that year gives his address as 6 Macclesfield Street, Soho.[1] According to the rate-books a tailor kept a shop on these premises from 1834 to 1848. Had Mark found temporary employment there, or was this only an accommodation address? In any event, he did not stay there long. By 1837, as is borne out by another letter, he had found work in a brewery in Mansfield Place (now Holmes Road), Kentish Town.[2] Having learned the hops business in Boston, he was a good man for the job. John Verey, a brother of his mother's second husband, managed the place.

The story of Alice Lemon's remarriage forms part of the family lore that has survived. As previously stated, Mark's widowed mother had opened a millinery shop, which she operated in partnership with Betty Lemon, her unmarried sister-in-law. Courting this spinster came one Henry Verey, a hosier with a shop at 135 Strand. When he discovered that the hat business belonged to the widow, he transferred his affections and secretly married her. Not until shortly before the birth of their daughter Alice, Mark's half-sister, was the marriage made public. However the jilted spinster responded to the situation, she continued as joint manageress of the millinery shop until its close in 1858. Through his stepfather, presumably, Mark got his post at John Verey's brewery.

While at work in Kentish Town, Mark found time to continue his attempts at authorship, the sketches and verses with which he had been bombarding the publishers for several years. That some of these unsolicited offerings never saw print is shown by the following

[1] P.O. MS., Lemon to Collier, 12 Mar. 1836.
[2] Hunt. MS., Lemon to Planché, 27 Apr. 1837.

notice in *Leigh Hunt's London Journal* for 3 September 1834: 'To Correspondents. We should be glad to hear, on other subjects, from MARK LEMON. Those of the two papers sent us do not happen to suit our journal.' Undaunted by such setbacks, Mark persisted and found a place for some of his light verse and semi-sporting sketches in Robert Surtees's *New Sporting Magazine*. Bearing the signature 'Tom Moody', they appeared between 1834 and 1837. There were acceptances, too, from *Bentley's Miscellany*. Illustrated by Cruikshank, the earliest of these pieces, 'Some Passages in the Life of a Disappointed Man', appeared in September 1837 and brought Mark six pounds. In this first-person narrative one Theodosius Wise, having been sued for breach of promise and ruined by a sharper, plunges yet deeper into disaster and is about to be hanged, only to wake up and find that he has been dreaming, 'the result of having eaten a hearty supper of pork chops much underdone'! A stock-in-trade device with Mark, the dream ending was to reappear in a number of his later stories. Trivial as it is, the sketch shows promise of what were to become the distinguishing traits of his writing: a lively humour and a flair for close observation.

In January 1838 Mark's second paper appeared in *Bentley's*: 'The True History of the Celebrated Wedgewood [*sic*] Hieroglyph, Commonly Called the Willow Pattern.' This account of the faithful lovers who were transformed into a pair of doves, 'those emblems of love and gentleness which have so long occupied such a conspicuous position in . . . "The Willow Pattern" ', fetched a mere three pounds and seven shillings. Though only another slight piece, it again exhibits some of the tendencies of Mark's later work. There is, first of all, the discreet handling of a situation which might violate Victorian propriety. When, for instance, a father surprises his daughter and her lover at their tryst, the author intrudes: 'But, like the modest painter of Greece, let me draw a veil over this part of the picture.' (This device Thackeray was to use later in handling Becky Sharp's moral laxity.) Another feature, already observed in Mark's earlier sketch, is the broad humour. Not for him the quiet laughter of the mind, the subtle innuendo: his was chiefly the forthright, sometimes ludicrous, fun.

Also published in *Bentley's* (July 1838) was one of Mark's early effusions in verse, a ten-stanza piece entitled 'The Song of the Fire-King'. Picturing flames feasting uncontrollably on 'gilded wood and chisel'd stone', the poem concludes:

Down with the roof to the blacken'd ground!
Shout like the thunder one loud hurray!
Wave your dark mantles of smoke around,
Spirits of fire, away! away!

Full of exclamation marks, as was much minor verse during this period, these stanzas show, nevertheless, evidences of craftsmanship in the regular metre and the rhetorical parallels.

It is of passing interest that these contributions to *Bentley's* appeared while Charles Dickens was the editor (2 January 1837 to 4 February 1839). Whether Mark ever addressed any correspondence to him at this time or even referred to this period when they became close friends later is not known. Since these were the years, however, when Dickens was frantically winding up the monthly parts of one novel while keeping those of another going, it is unlikely that he would have recalled, after a decade, the names of writers who had supplied him with material for his first editorial venture.

As a playwright Mark found another creative outlet. Even before the publication of his early pieces in *Bentley's Miscellany*, he had already seen his first farce (*The P.L.; or, 30, Strand*) produced at the Strand Theatre on 25 April 1836. Called by the *Morning Post* a 'smart bagatelle', *P.L.* traces the manœuvrings of one Stamper Jingle, the poet laureate of Warren's Blacking Warehouse. In a rapid succession of episodes, freely interspersed with verse and song, he restores domestic tranquillity to the quarrelling Snarlings and gets their consent to a match between their ward Lucy and his friend Dick. Though marred by cumbersome exposition and obvious attempts at humour, the dialogue keeps up a lively tempo. It is interesting to speculate whether Dickens ever learned of this farce and confided to its author the details of his own boyhood association with Warren's Blacking Warehouse.

A few months later, in July, the Surrey Theatre staged Mark's first melodrama, *Arnold of Winkelried; or, The Flight of Sempach*. According to a contemporary notice in the *Theatrical Observer*, this performance was expected to 'signal quite an epoch in theatrical affairs', because a legitimate drama had been produced on the 'boards at an illegitimate theatre with the most thrilling and triumphant success'. (Only Drury Lane and Covent Garden were considered legitimate before 1834.) Using as his source for this five-act blank-verse play Holberg's account (in *Travels Through Germany*) of the famous victory won by three hundred confederates at Sempach against the much larger army of Leopold, Duke of Austria, Mark concentrated on Arnold's self-sacrifice to bolster the morale of his men. The curtain line is the hero's impassioned dying speech:

> Friends, let this day
> Be memorial in your hearts; that should a tyrant
> Again attempt to chain ye, ye may know
> The way to check his power.

What may have been Mark's own experience as he gained a foothold in the theatre can be gathered from an episode in his earliest novel, *Wait for the End*. The hero, an aspiring dramatist, watches the rehearsal of his first play. Viewing the disarray of sets and properties backstage, he is 'surprised and disappointed . . . to find himself surrounded by objects the most incongruous and unattractive imaginable'. All sense of magic evaporates as he sees the 'rude daubs of colour', the large rollers, wheels, and ropes overhead, and the 'lantern on a pole' which will do duty for the moon. Turning a windlass over which a strip of blue cloth has been stretched, a 'grimy man' tries to simulate a waterfall. The harsh 'glare of light' on the 'rough carpenter's work and the backs of dingy canvases' destroys the illusion of 'costly splendours'. The rehearsal itself is equally disillusioning. 'The frequent interruptions occasioned by changes of position, arrangements of the business of the stage, and trivial attractions of dialogue' nullify the 'passion and humour of the scene' and make it impossible to imagine how out of 'this apparent chaos' can emerge 'the perfect chrysolite' which 'partial critics [have] declared to be waiting the acceptance of the British public'.

Discouraged by such unpromising beginnings, the young author anxiously waits for the reviews of his play after the opening night. The plaudits exceed his fondest hopes. The plot is called 'ingenious', the language 'fresh and scholarly', the moral 'undeniable'. As for the acting, the male in the leading role has never been 'more successful' and the 'others of inferior merit' have been 'most satisfactory'. Encouraged by this response, the manager sends the author a heartening note: 'I congratulate you most sincerely on the reception of your drama, and enclose your cheque for £100, being quite contented to bear any future risk.' Here Mark the novelist overreached himself: though he occasionally sold a play for a hundred pounds, it is doubtful whether any manager ever underwrote him to the extent of 'bearing any future risk'.

ML–C

At opera, too, he tried his hand while still at Verey's brewery. Collaborating with him was a young actor and composer, Frank Romer, who prepared the scores. One of their earliest joint efforts, *The Corsair* (based on Byron's work), was sent to the manager of Drury Lane, only to be returned after four days as unsuitable.[3] On 7 July 1838, however, they won recognition at the Theatre Royal, English Opera House, with *Rob of the Fen*, which Mark had translated from the German *Das Falkners Braut*. It enjoyed a run of eleven nights.

Mark's association with the young composer soon brought an introduction to the rest of the Romer family. John, the father, was a jeweller. His daughter Emma, the most accomplished member, made regular appearances in opera. An older sister, Helen (Nelly), also had an excellent voice and sometimes sang offstage for her. It was Nelly, eight years younger than he, to whom Mark found himself drawn. Now approaching thirty, he felt the need for a home of his own. In spite of his low wages at the brewery and his uncertain earnings from his writing, he and Nelly were married at Holy Trinity Church, Sloane Square, Chelsea, on 28 September 1839. The register of marriage gave his occupation as brewer. Tradition has it that he undertook his new responsibilities on a borrowed five-pound note.

Notwithstanding this precarious beginning, the marriage was a success. For one thing, Mark shared with the Romer family a common interest in music and drama. Besides, he respected and liked them, and came to share their family traditions. In a lecture delivered in his fifties, he was to recall with mingled pride and amusement that Nelly's grandmother had once poured out seventeen cups of tea for Dr. Johnson. 'The cups were small china ones,' he explained, 'and the Bohea was 38*s*. a pound.'[4]

Having hitherto lacked the security of life in a single continuing household, Mark became a most appreciative and affectionate husband. He remembered his wife's birthdays, liked to have her accompany him as later success brought numerous social engagements, and gave her considerable freedom in managing the household. At no time, apparently, did serious friction mar their partnership. One secret of such harmony may well have been Mark's

---

[3] P.O. MS., Lemon to Collier, 12 Mar. 1836.
[4] Lemon later published this lecture as part of *Up and Down the London Streets*, p. 215.

tolerant firmness. A true Victorian, he believed in being master of his own household. That he was not, however, the mythical heavy father is evident in his tongue-in-cheek remark: 'I never argue with my wife; I say "no" twice, and then hold my tongue.'[5] In short, the realist in him admitted that a man may be master in his home—up to a point.

Evidently Nelly responded with matching tolerance. During an age when many a fastidious wife sent her husband to the garden or cellar to enjoy his pipe or cigar, Mark puffed away happily after dinner in the dining-room or drawing-room. Like the heroine in his *Loved at Last*, Nelly 'valued her husband's society more than her curtains, and thought that the bread-winner had a right to select his own form of relaxation and enjoyment'. She realized that 'a wife had better present him with a cigar than a latch-key'. Happy were the evenings Mark spent at home, when Nelly sat at the piano and sang in her sweet voice some of his favourite songs, like 'Wapping Old Stairs':

> Why should Sal, or should Susan, than me be more prized?
> For the heart that is true, Tom, should ne'er be despised.
> Then be constant and kind, nor your Molly forsake;
> Still your trousers I'll wash, and your grog, too, I'll make.

Beating time with his pipe, Mark listened admiringly.[6]

Not without considerable economic strain, however, did he and Nelly get through the first years of their marriage. Almost immediately came threats of disaster when Verey's brewery closed down early in 1840, leaving Mark without regular income.[7] Through one of Verey's customers, fortunately, he was soon put in charge of the Shakespeare's Head, a tavern at 31 Wych Street, Drury Lane. Once the gathering place of the Club of Owls (so named because the members kept late hours), it became, under Mark and Nelly, the haunt of actors, playwrights, poets, artists, and journalists. As this Bohemian group assembled in an upstairs room, Mark, rubbing his hands and beaming at his guests—he preferred this term to 'customers'— would call out reassuringly, 'More steaks, gentlemen! coming

[5] Silver.
[6] Hatton, *With a Show*, pp. 69–70.
[7] According to the rate-books John Verey was the proprietor of the brewery from Jan. 1837 to Feb. 1840. The premises stood vacant after that until Sept. 1841.

directly!' Meanwhile the pleasant little man at the bar, known familiarly as Pat, filled the trays with glasses of brandy, whisky, rum, and gin from the four pulls at his counter. On shelves behind him miniature barrels advertised their contents in golden letters: 'Old Tom', 'Spruce', 'Peppermint', 'Shrub'.[8]

Situated not far from the sites of the famous Elizabethan taverns, the Devil and the Mermaid, the Shakespeare's Head was also near Johnson's alamode beef-house in Clare Court, where Charles Dickens, while employed as a boy at Warren's Blacking Warehouse, would sometimes stop to get a plate of hot beef to eat with his bread. Wych Street, which was eliminated with the construction of Kingsway early in the twentieth century, once led from St. Clement's, Strand, to Drury Lane. Though gone now from the face of London, it is immortalized in Mark's fifth novel, *Golden Fetters*, as a narrow thoroughfare lined by buildings whose windows 'were continually obscured by the mud bespattered on them by passing cabs and other vehicles' and whose occupants 'were in a state of *tremulando* all day from the rumbling of coal and other waggons'.

Stimulated by the theatrical and literary gossip of the 'guests' who came for their chops and beer, Mark continued to write for the stage. Nelly encouraged him, for she always felt that he had a future as an author. Certainly it soon became evident that he had no future as a tavern-keeper. With income lagging dangerously behind expenditures, his business, for all the *bonhomie* of the nightly gatherings, failed. And a further financial liability came with the arrival of his first child, a son. Born at humble lodgings in Newcastle Street, Strand, on 20 October 1840, the baby was christened Mark at St. Paul's Church, Covent Garden, 'the actor's church'. By the year's end the parents were no longer connected with the tavern in Wych Street. The rate-books for 1841 show another name for the proprietor.

Again without a steady income, how was the young father to support his family? His one recourse was to sell more plays. But to do so he had to gauge the public taste. What fare were the theatregoers of the mid-nineteenth century demanding?

'It's not as if the theatre was in its high and palmy days,' observes Mrs. Curdle, a character in Dickens's *Nicholas Nickleby*. 'The drama

[8] The details of this paragraph are a blend of information drawn from the following sources: Yates, *Fifty Years of London Life*, pp. 316–17; and Athol Mayhew, *A Jorum of Punch*, pp. 59–60.

is gone, perfectly gone.' This is an accurate appraisal of the stage when Mark began writing. Never had English authors produced so few theatrical pieces of real merit; never had the scenes degenerated into such spectacle and extravaganza; never had popular taste sunk so low.

Several conditions contributed to the decline of the stage once graced by Shakespeare, Jonson, Congreve, Dryden, Goldsmith. Chief of these was the lack of good dramatists. The better authors devoted their efforts either to poetry, where they could earn prestige at the sacrifice of income, or to the novel, where the returns were fairly lucrative. This left only those writers who, without any illusions about their place in literature, were content to exploit the popular taste for immediate gain. Often they looked abroad for inspiration. Foreign plays were reworked for English audiences: plots were appropriated, particularly from the French, and freely adapted. Contemporary English novels also fell prey to unscrupulous authors. The action, characters, and much of the dialogue could be lifted for hasty staging. There was little original drama of genuine merit; the springs of inspiration had gone dry.

It is doubtful whether good drama could have flourished in an age when the public had so little discernment. With the rise of the great middle class, which had yet to learn how to make wise use of its growing power and new wealth, the prevailing temper was materialistic and coarse. To satisfy this class, comprising the majority of theatre-goers, producers concentrated on the spectacular and sensational. There was a demand for plays with action, ludicrous and absurd situations, and moral sentiment. All subtleties of dialogue and all restraint would, of course, be lost on such an audience. The emphasis of an evening's entertainment was on quantity rather than quality. The triple bill, beginning at six-thirty or seven and continuing until well after midnight, called for a three-hour drama, a farce, and a pantomime.

For the rise of entertainment exploiting a debased public taste the monopoly theatres were initially responsible. By virtue of the patent rights granted in 1660 to Killigrew and Davenant, only Drury Lane and Covent Garden were permitted to present legitimate drama. These two houses jealously guarded their rights, sometimes through litigation, and held on to them until 1843. Since they alone could present spoken drama—any form of dialogue was technically defined as legitimate drama—the minor theatres were forced to confine their efforts to entertainment in which nothing could be spoken without musical accompaniment. As a result of such limitations these lesser playhouses were obliged to attract audiences by a variety of spectacular entertainments. On their stages appeared all manner of dancing, pantomime, dialogue to instrumental accompaniment—a play punctuated by occasional tinklings on the piano was technically a musical piece—burlesques, and extravaganzas. Once these had become standard theatrical fare, even Drury Lane and Covent Garden turned to such entertainment to satisfy the popular taste.

Paralleling these changes in early nineteenth-century drama were the physical alterations in the theatres themselves. In general the managers and audiences favoured showy furnishings. The Surrey, for instance, was decorated in gold and velvet, with a Genoa curtain covering its stage; the Coburg boasted a splendid looking-glass curtain. By 1822 the picture-frame stage had come to stay. Gas illuminated realistic settings. Smoke and mist were suggested by gauze, ingenious contraptions provided offstage sound effects, and actors wore rich authentic costumes.[9]

With the conventions of early nineteenth-century drama firmly established, Mark merely observed contemporary practices as he worked in the prevailing media. Of these melodrama was perhaps easiest to compose. The formula called for stock characters and situations: a heroine in distress, a noble hero to the rescue, the machinations of a pitch-black villain—often against a background of attempted seductions, false accusations, treasured secrets, hidden identity, unknown parentage.

A sampling of Mark's early pieces will show his awareness of this pattern. In *The Ancestress* (City of London Theatre, 27 April 1837)[10] a young robber, while resisting capture, mortally wounds a count, his own father. Kidnapped as an infant, the son had grown up in ignorance of his own family. In *Self-Accusation; or, A Brother's Love* (Lyceum, 10 September 1838) a last-minute confession by a degenerate character absolves the hero of a false murder charge and enables him to rescue his beloved and her brother, who have been

---

[9] The preceding summary of nineteenth-century drama is based on the following sources: Nicoll, *A History of Early Nineteenth Century Drama, 1800–1850*; and Watson, *Sheridan to Robertson*.

[10] The references in parentheses will indicate the place and date of the first performance.

reduced to abject poverty by the villain. The latter meets death at the hands of a disgruntled accomplice. *The Three Secrets* (Olympic, 9 June 1840), an adaptation from the French, revolves around the surreptitious efforts of a noble wife to rescue a young man whose father has been ruined by the loss of a purse containing a thousand francs. She hopes to atone for the wrong committed by her husband, who had found the purse, but failed to return it. With *The Demon Gift* (English Opera House, 29 June 1840) Mark introduced a startling stage effect: a dream vision in which an alchemist conjures up Mephistopheles behind a shimmering red fire. Mark's melodramas abound in explicit stage directions: diagrams indicate the positions of characters for a final tableau, and repeatedly 'the curtain falls upon the picture'. Such concluding effects were a further manifestation of the Victorian delight in the spectacular.

Like his melodramas, Mark's farces have all the characteristic weaknesses of the period: forced humour and atrocious puns parading as wit; thin plots and ludicrously bad exposition; bustling action and rough language. The farce was designed to provoke laughter, and Mark geared his low comedy solely to this end. Commenting on his *M.P for the Rotten Borough* (Lyceum, 27 July 1838), a contemporary review in the *Town* noted the 'somewhat overdrawn' incidents, interlarded with puns that 'keep the table in a roar'. That Mark recognized this defect is apparent from a line in the play itself. 'I hate puns,' declares Jerry Chance, one of the characters; 'they're like ginger beer, all froth, but without stamina.' Having expressed his contempt for this form of humour, Mark apparently felt free to invent egregious examples for the amusement of his audience. Equally poor is the exposition as characters overload their asides with information intended solely for the audience.

One of the most successful of Mark's early farces was *Fashionable Arrivals* (Covent Garden, 29 October 1840). According to his own story, he dreamed this play, got up immediately on waking, sketched it, and caught a violent cold. But he was amply rewarded for his trouble: he sold the piece for a hundred pounds and got an additional thirty for its lyric, 'Lovely Night',[11] whose final stanza provides the languorous, melting sentiment typical of the popular song in the Victorian theatre—and after:

[11] Silver.

Lovely night! lovely night!
Tho' thy dews may be thy tears,
Yet how bright, yet how bright!
From thy grief the world appears.
The flowers that before the noon,
Had faded with the sun's warm ray,
But smiled on by the gentle moon,
Revive to bless the coming day.

Set to music by Tully, this song made a hit. So did the lavish setting
in the second act: a conservatory whose roof covered the stage, a
vista of trees, Chinese lamps, a mosaic pavement, and a drawing-
room viewed through an opening at the back. The farce itself,
concerned with the complications arising when a well-meaning
bachelor tries to patch up the matrimonial differences of three
couples by inviting them to his home for a visit, uses such stock
devices as mistaken identity and eavesdropping. 'A piece of bustle,
intrigue, and repartee,' *The Times* called it, 'one of the best that has
been produced for a long time.'

In addition to a steady succession of farces Mark turned out a
number of burlettas. Originally musical pieces with dialogue, this
genre later used rhymed couplets extensively and added a few songs.
During the monopoly it could be produced legally if it had only
three acts—five constituted legitimate drama, included at least five
lyrics, was accompanied at intervals by piano tinklings, and went by
the name *burletta*. Mark's most successful venture in this medium
was *The Ladies' Club* (Olympic, March 1840), a great favourite with
the public. Its highly entertaining situation revolves around a company of wives who, neglected by their club-lounging husbands,
decide to form a club of their own. Shocked by what several spies
have learned about male practices, they organize with the strictest
decorum, draw up lengthy resolutions, and cast their ballots with
coloured balls of cotton. Only after their husbands have agreed to
'more home, and less club', do they return to their households. The
piece was acclaimed for its 'constant succession of novelties' that
answered the 'end of creating a laugh'. Interspersed at frequent intervals, witticisms like the following kept the audience in an uproar:

'I was the principal accountant to the theatre. (*Aside*) I delivered the bills.'

'In great families, when bills are more plentiful than means to dislodge them, it's the duty of a good servant to supply prompt lies instead of prompt payment.'

'Franklin was perfectly right when he said that matrimony was like a bagful of snakes, with only one eel in it.'

It would be a mistake to misconstrue this burletta as a plea for women's rights, a topic soon to have the serious consideration of William and Mary Howitt, F. D. Maurice, and John Stuart Mill. Actually, as he was to do in his prose later, Mark injects occasional sentiments that make the crusading wife appear slightly ridiculous. Admittedly, as man's partner she deserves consideration, but her position is definitely secondary to that of her husband. This Victorian attitude Mark held all his life.

In the casting of his pieces he was fortunate, for the players included some prominent actors and actresses of the time. Appearing in his *Fashionable Arrivals* at Covent Garden, for instance, were the managers themselves, that well-known pair, Madame Vestris and her husband, Charles Mathews. Another outstanding actor, William Farren, who had distinguished himself as Peter Teazle, played numerous roles in Mark's dramas. So did the popular Mrs. Julia Glover and Mrs. Ann Stirling. For celebrated comedians there were Benjamin Wrench and Henry Compton, the Shakespearian clown of the stage. Mark praised them extravagantly. But of all those who impersonated his characters, he valued most Benjamin Webster, whose encouragement had helped him through some early difficulties and later kept him in production. Webster staged and acted in Mark's farce *Out of Place* (19 October 1840) and followed this with more of his pieces.

During the five years following the staging of his first play in April 1836, Mark loosed a torrent of theatrical entertainment. 'It is impossible that anything less than a bundle of quills could write so many pieces', declared *The Times* (27 June 1840) in a review of his *Ins and Outs*, a burletta. In spite of his productivity, however, it is doubtful whether his earnings provided more than the bare necessities for his family. Only rarely could he count on such a windfall as the hundred and thirty pounds for his *Fashionable Arrivals* and its lyric. Generally fifty pounds was a good price for a melodrama, with short farces bringing considerably less. Forced to invest heavily in elaborate decorations and costly costumes and to pay their star

actors prohibitive salaries, the managers had little left for the dramatists, especially for beginners of no reputation. So it was that Mark,
in spite of his zest for the theatre, might have found in the 1840s
only drudgery and dismay, had not a great new avenue opened
before him just then.

3

PUNCH IS BORN

'COME to town—here's a man with a notion for a comic paper, and he has £2,000 to lose.' So, in the early summer of 1841, wrote Henry Mayhew, journalist and minor dramatist, to Mark Lemon, who was then staying at the seaside.[1] Journalism appealed to Mark. He had already thought of launching a paper under the title *Pen and Palette*, to be made up of contributions from his guests at the Shakespeare's Head. For lack of capital, however, this project had never got beyond the stage of reading aloud and discussing at weekly meetings the pieces that had been signed with pseudonyms and left in a special box. It is quite likely that Mayhew, who ten years later was to publish his monumental *London Labour and the London Poor*, had often associated with the Bohemian set at the tavern in Wych Street.

The events of this period have been obscured by a haze of conflicting reports, but in early June, at his lodgings in Newcastle Street, Strand, Lemon almost certainly met Mayhew and Joseph Last, a printer. It was Last who had introduced Mayhew to Ebenezer Landells, the proposer and prospective backer of the comic journal. The paper was to be a weekly modelled on Philipon's Paris *Charivari*, though with a distinct English flavour. Moreover, it would avoid the scurrilities and indecencies of such short-lived predecessors as the *Satirist*, the *Scourge*, the *Ass*, the *Wasp*, the *Scorpion*, the *Town*, and *John Bull*. Recognizing the possibilities of Landells's proposal, and assured of his support, Mayhew turned to the immediate business of finding a staff. For this he wanted Mark's advice.

The meeting in Newcastle Street was followed by others: at the Edinburgh Castle Inn, Strand; at Landells's home; and at the Crown Inn, Vinegar Yard. Eventually a definite plan emerged. At first the editorial responsibilities were to be shared by Mark, Mayhew, and Stirling Coyne, a minor Irish dramatist. (Before long

[1] Silver.

Coyne was dismissed for plagiarism.) Last was to be the printer, Landells the engraver, and W. Bryant the publisher. Among those writers approached for contributions were W. H. Wills, later Dickens's sub-editor; Douglas Jerrold, dramatist and journalist; Gilbert à Beckett, a minor playwright; and Percival Leigh, a young surgeon. Archibald S. Henning, a skilful draughtsman and caricaturist; Birket Foster, a landscape artist; and John Leech, a medical student, were among those chosen to supply the early drawings.

While recruiting the staff, the founders had to decide on a name for their paper. At first, taking their cue from Philipon's Paris *Charivari*, they chose *The Funny Dog; or, The London Charivari.* That this title was altered at the last minute is shown by the manuscript of the prospectus, where 'The Fun' has been crossed out and changed to 'Punch'. During the meeting at the Edinburgh Castle Inn, where light-hearted talk often interrupted the business discussions, someone remarked that a humorous magazine, like good punch, needed Lemon. 'A capital idea!' exclaimed Mayhew. 'Let us call the paper *Punch*.' If this was indeed the origin of the name, Mark did not confirm it in later years. 'Why was it called *Punch?*' a friend once asked him. 'Because the title was short and sweet,' he replied, 'and Punch is an English institution; everyone loves Punch, and will be drawn aside to listen to it. All our ideas connected with Punch are happy ones.' As for the name of the person who had invented the title, that he could not remember.[2]

To Mark fell the assignment of preparing the *Punch* prospectus.[3] On blue foolscap paper he drafted his preliminary advertisement. 'This guffawgraph', he announced, 'is intended to form a refuge for destitute wit—an asylum for the thousands of orphan jokes—the superannuated Joe Millers—the millions of perishing puns, which are now wandering about without so much as a shelf to rest upon!' Planned to make its first appearance on 17 July 1841, *Punch* was promised weekly thereafter, and would include such departments as politics, fashions, police, reviews, fine arts, music and drama, and sporting. This prospectus, printed as four pages, featured at its conclusion a woodcut of dogs in various modes of male and female

[2] *London Society*, XXVIII (July 1875), p. 56.
[3] The charge that Mark was the amanuensis only and actually composed little of this prospectus may be dismissed as a fabrication by Edmund Yates, who was hostile to Mark.

attire, with the caption 'Funny Dogs with Tales!' Thousands of copies were circulated.

Having given their projected paper widespread publicity, the collaborators were determined to bring out the opening number on the date announced. Douglas Jerrold, then in Boulogne, was to furnish the leading article. For this Mark waited in vain until the last possible moment. Finally he was forced to write it himself.[4] Entitled 'The Moral of Punch', it told the readers what to expect of the new journal. 'Our title may have misled you into a belief that we have no other intention than the amusement of a thoughtless crowd, and the collection of pence', Mark began. Insisting that the paper had a 'higher object', he promised 'pleasant instruction'. He called attention to the obvious association between this new venture and the Punch and Judy show, where he regretted hearing 'the ring of the bars mingling with the song'. Offenders must be corrected, he admitted, but why should such 'generous and kindly beings' go to prison for 'poverty and misfortune'? In this humanitarian spirit, which was to inform *Punch* in its early years, he also inveighed against capital punishment. 'Destroy the principle of evil by increasing the means of cultivating the good,' he advised, 'and the gallows will then become as much a wonder as it is now a jest.' Finally, he assured the readers that *Punch* would intersperse its pages 'with trifles that have no other object than the moment's approbation—an end which will never be sought for at the expense of others, beyond the evanescent smile of a harmless satire'.

Punch was born in Crane Court, Fleet Street, where Joseph Last kept his press. On 17 July 1841 the first number was distributed as scheduled from the premises of the publisher, Bryant, at 13 Wellington Street, Strand. George Hodder, a journalist and occasional contributor to the early *Punch*, and Mayhew spent the afternoon in walking up and down the Strand from Wellington Street to St. Clement Danes, repeatedly dropping in at Bryant's office for the latest word on the sales. 'I smell lots of tin thereabouts,' Mayhew remarked after *Punch* had made a start, 'but our Lemon requires a great deal of squeezing.' And it took squeezing to get at least five columns out of Mark for each of the early issues. For this his pay averaged only a guinea.[5] Even so, the publication costs soon ran far ahead of the proceeds. During the early months of *Punch*, while its

4 Silver.
5 Ibid. Mark told Silver that he was paid only a guinea for five columns.

pages sparkled with quips and jests in a simulated mood of light-hearted gaiety, a heavy shadow of mounting debt and threatened bankruptcy hung over the paper. For those who had invested heavily in this venture these were anxious days.

Indeed, for the entire nation they were anxious days, the hungry forties having brought suffering and oppression, fear and bitterness, violence and crime. In a land of unprecedented wealth, overproduction had brought a glut on the market. Thousands of exploited labourers, underpaid, underfed, and miserably housed, soon found themselves adrift, with the workhouse their only alternative. Warehouses overflowed with shirts, yet many backs were bare. 'Paupers sitting enchanted in the sun', willing to work, but with no work provided for them, commented Carlyle in 1842. He deplored the paradox of England's simultaneous wealth and shocking poverty. 'We have more riches than any Nation ever had before,' he observed in *Past and Present*; 'we have less good of them than any Nation ever had before.' Were these the fruits of the much-heralded Reform Bill of 1832? 'Liberty, I am told, is a divine thing', wrote Carlyle. 'Liberty when it becomes the "Liberty to die by starvation" is not so divine!' He demanded 'new definitions' for liberty.

So did the labouring classes. Decrying the maladjustments of the social order, disappointed in their expectations from the Reform Bill, convinced of the indifference and inhumanity of the factory-owners, they agitated for a six-point charter: manhood suffrage, vote by ballot, equal electoral districts, annual parliaments, payment of members, and abolition of the property qualifications. In mass meetings, street demonstrations, and conventions they pushed their demands. Ominous rumblings threatened violence.

Further disturbances followed the birth of the Anti-Corn Law League. Established in 1838, it had gained ground rapidly in its battle against the Corn Law of 1815, whose provisions had kept the price of grain artificially high by restricting imports of wheat. For the poor, consequently, the cost of bread had become prohibitive. A vigorous campaign conducted against the landlords, dubbed 'aristocratic plunderers', produced blasts of oratory against the selfishness of the rich and threats of strong measures to force repeal.

In this climate of unrest, in this 'bleak age', it took no little courage to initiate a comic journal. All too soon Mark and Mayhew realized that they had been too sanguine in their expectations. With income from the early circulation unable to keep pace with the mounting debt, Landells and Last saw little prospect of returns on their investment. Had Mark not sold a two-act domestic drama (*The Silver Thimble*) for thirty pounds and turned the money over to the publisher, the third number of *Punch* would not have gone to press.[6] A few months later he produced a farce at the Strand Theatre and again used the proceeds to keep the paper going. Entitled *Punch* (later revised as *Star of the Street*), the piece was noticed in *The Times* as a 'very merry little entertainment' whose 'renowned hero' had 'lately added a pen to his stick' to launch 'a smart little periodical'. But one of the performances skirted disaster when a parrot in a prominent part had to be replaced by a substitute. Ignoring the prescribed lines, the bird galvanized the audience by croaking obscenities.[7]

In addition to pouring the income from his plays into *Punch*, Mark contributed a lively serial to the weekly issues between August and November of 1841. Entitled *The Heir of Applebite*, it chronicled the experiences of Agamemnon Applebite—his bachelorhood, subsequent marriage, honeymoon, and the birth of his first son. For knowledgeable readers its plotless series of episodes must have been reminiscent of Dickens's 'Boz' period. Unpretentiously successful in its realistic detail, portrayal of human nature, and mild satire, it demonstrated what Mark could achieve easily and well when he did not try to overreach himself. In sketches based on close observation and sparkling with humour and whimsy he was at his best. One of the characters, a Mrs. Pilcher, the monthly nurse who looked after the Heir, anticipated Dickens's Sairy Gamp by some dozen years.

In spite of Mark's resourcefulness and his industrious attempts to keep *Punch* alive, it did not prosper. For one thing, it had to overcome considerable initial hostility because its printer and engraver had once been connected with such a ribald comic paper as the *Town*.[8] It suffered, moreover, from dissension within the ranks. On Saturday, publishing day, when the staff usually gathered in some tavern to look over the new number, endless squabbles arose, every writer finding fault with articles published in preference to his own. And the financial picture worsened; it became so grim, in fact, that the proprietors met at the Edinburgh Castle Inn and debated whether they should go on.[9] Finally, after the printer had sunk six hundred pounds in the venture, the proprietors decided that the only hope lay in the discovery of a financial backer.

[6] Tinsley, *Random Recollections*, II, p. 87.　　[7] Silver.　　[8] Ibid.　　[9] Ibid.

They found him in the firm of William Bradbury and Fred Evans, who were at first engaged as printers to replace Joseph Last. Soon Mark, Mayhew, and Douglas Jerrold suggested that Bradbury and Evans take *Punch* and all its assets over by paying its debts, some eight hundred pounds. Long afterwards, as he recalled the negotiations, Evans described how Mark had been the 'chief conspirator', how it had been his 'eloquence alone that induced us to buy *Punch*'. He remembered that Jerrold had not said much, except to support Mark. 'They talked us over very easily,' he concluded, 'and I need not now confess that it was a glorious day for Bradbury and Evans when they succeeded in their mission.'[10]

The sole owners of *Punch* by December 1842, Bradbury and Evans reorganized the staff. To Mark they gave the editorship; for Mayhew they made a place as suggestor-in-chief. Never happy about the reorganization, Mayhew, feeling that he had been unfairly ousted from a project initiated by him, severed his connexions in 1845. Much later, when asked what had happened, Mark explained, 'The editorship *became* centralized.'[11] He could have added that a friendship had ended, that the earlier intimacies with Mayhew had given way to bitterness and recrimination.

Just why Mayhew lost ground in the reorganization is not clear. That he was a person of remarkable ability cannot be denied. Witty, full of schemes for advancing the fortunes of the paper, always prolific with his pen, he seemed to be cut out for comic journalism. Eighteen years after he had left, some of the original *Punch* staff still quoted his definition of a Whig as 'a false thing attached to the crown'. It may be that Bradbury and Evans, advised by Mark, considered him too unstable for the editorship. Though clever and imaginative, he had no head for business. Douglas Jerrold, his father-in-law, occasionally had to straighten out his muddled affairs. 'I must be in London on Saturday and sometime on Monday,' he wrote to John Forster in July 1850, 'in re Mayhew, whom God make wiser!'[12] Years later Mayhew still had not overcome his instability, as was demonstrated when he walked out of his performance of *Punch on the Platform* at the Town Hall, Brighton, because he had

[10] *London Society*, XXVIII (Aug. 1875), p. 160.
[11] Burnand to Spielmann, 9 Jan. 1895, quoted in Price, *History of Punch*, p. 29.
[12] V. and A. MS., Jerrold to Forster, 18 July 1850, quoted in Renton, *John Forster*, p. 176.

been embarrassed during his opening lines by recognizing his father in the front row.[13] In the middle sixties, when he tried to launch a rival to *Punch*, his plans did not materialize for lack of practical management. Mark, who had seen his prospectus, complained that the projected journal would be 'vulgar and abusive'. It was to be printed in black and red—'the only thing that will be *read* in it', he punned.[14]

In addition to feeling that he had been unfairly pushed out of *Punch*, Mayhew may have had a further grievance. This came out when he testified in the bankruptcy court on 11 February 1847 that the debt of two thousand pounds which he had contracted between September 1845 and July 1846 could have been met if Mark had honoured an agreement, entered into ten years earlier, to share with him the proceeds from certain plays: *The Ladies' Club*, *Grandfather Whitehead*, and *Gwynneth Vaughan*. Whether Mayhew had actually collaborated in these pieces has not been established. But for another of Mark's plays, a farce entitled *The Gentleman in Black* (Olympic, March 1840), the evidence does support Mayhew's claim to authorship. Actually an adaptation of his prose tale *Mr. Peter Punctilio*, it shows only slight changes from the original, like the occasional cutting of a word or phrase (especially all 'damns'). For the most part the dialogue has been taken over bodily from Mayhew's work. Such practice was common at the time, of course, Dickens, for one, suffering from this kind of literary piracy. It would be difficult to excuse Mark on this score, though, especially if he had agreed to share the income from a piece whose language and plot were largely Mayhew's. Although the two men were never to resume their earlier friendship, reports on Mayhew did occasionally reach the *Punch* office. In 1862, for example, he was rumoured to be in Germany, living on three hundred pounds a year.[15]

* * *

During Mark's editorship *Punch* was to move its headquarters several times: from 13 Wellington Street, Strand, to 194 Strand in 1843; to

[13] Beale, *The Light of Other Days*, I, p. 275.
[14] Silver.
[15] For an account of Mayhew's testimony see *The Times*, 12 Feb. 1847, p. 8. I am indebted to Professor J. L. Bradley for bringing this item to my attention. The rumour about Mayhew's living in Germany is reported by Silver.

92 Fleet Street in January 1845; to 85 Fleet Street in March 1845; to 27 Bouverie Street in 1864. For nearly thirty years the fortunes of this weekly were to be Mark's chief concern. With his instinctive knowledge of human nature, his eye for talent, his genius for translating the special aptitudes of his men into work of the highest standards, and his consummate skill in moulding his disparate staff into a brotherhood of the strongest loyalties, he brought a new era to comic journalism. Above all, he had an unfaltering faith in his mission. 'I was made for *Punch* and *Punch* for me,' he used to say in later years; 'I should never have succeeded in any other way.'[16]

For his success he was indebted in part to his proprietors, Bradbury and Evans. His relationship with his backers was more than a business arrangement: it was a partnership based on mutual admiration and respect, and it ripened into the deepest friendship. Linking his arms in theirs as he walked between them to a near-by eating-place at lunch-time, Mark, jovial and more Falstaffian in figure with the years, appeared to be taking his intimates out on a spree. He was treated as an equal, not as a mere employee. Only once did he have to assert his editorial prerogative—and that fairly early in his career: when his proprietors asked him to puff some railway stock they were interested in, and further insisted that he publish a certain article which he considered libellous. He refused. Still Bradbury and Evans persisted in their demands. Finally, certain that all his staff would back him, Mark, rising as if to leave, called out, 'Boys, follow me!' The proprietors yielded. Thereafter Mark had no difficulty in enforcing his policy of non-interference.[17]

His right-hand man, Douglas Jerrold, was perhaps the most important member of the early *Punch* staff. It was his contributions that boosted the circulation. As a champion of the labouring poor and a caustic critic of the Tories in his 'Q Papers', a tender philosopher in 'Punch's Letters to His Son', a scathing satirist of cant and hypocrisy in his 'Jenkins' and 'Pecksniff' papers, a moving and earnest narrator in his 'Story of a Feather', and an exuberant humorist in 'Mrs. Caudle's Curtain Lectures', he put his stamp on the paper for over a decade. His deep sympathy for the underdog, more than any other influence, was responsible for the early liberalism of *Punch*.

A self-educated man, he had successively tried the Navy, printing, and writing. His play *Black-Eyed Susan* had already scored a success

16 Hatton, *With a Show*, p. 148.
17 Silver; Spielmann, *History of Punch*, p. 264.

before he came to *Punch*. In any group he stood out with his striking appearance. A massive head with mane of hair swept back looked top-heavy on his slight body, which was, nevertheless, charged with nervous energy. From under shaggy brows blue eyes shot piercing glances at an adversary or twinkled with amusement during an animated conversation. His irrepressible wit could be harmless or trenchant to suit the occasion. Thus, at the wedding of W. H. Wills he greeted the bridal couple with 'Bless you, my children, go make your Wills.' Of someone eating calf's-tail soup he remarked, 'Extremes meet.'[18] Toasting Mr. Punch at dinner, he declared, 'He will never require spirits while he has good Lemon-aid.'[19] For those whom he disliked, however, his humour carried a sting. He had no use for Albert Smith, an early contributor, who, to the general relief of the staff, left after a few years. Mark had become disgusted with Smith for showing his proofs at the Cheshire Cheese and for submitting as his own work adaptations from the French.[20] Looking at the 'A.S.' with which Smith initialed his pieces, Jerrold grunted, 'Only two-thirds of the truth.'[21] For Thackeray, with whom he frequently sparred, he also had his acid quips. Hearing him say that the natives had tried to make a Roman of him during his visit to Rome, Jerrold muttered, 'They should have begun with your nose.' Hypersensitive, he had reasons for clashing with Thackeray, who had once accused him of eating peas with a knife and being, therefore, not fit company.[22] This slur on his background hurt Jerrold. The son of a printer, he had struggled every step of the way to win, through wit and persistence, recognition as a journalist and dramatist. Quite outside his range was Thackeray's gentlemanly standard with its 'gently nurtured men and women of the Anglo-Saxon race'. Thackeray used to say, 'It takes three generations to make a gentleman.' Jerrold obviously could not qualify. Hence his suspicion of Thackeray, of whom he once complained: 'He is the most uncertain person I know. To-day he is all sunshine—tomorrow he is all frost and snow.'[23]

William Makepeace Thackeray, a towering six feet three inches, must have made Jerrold feel inferior in physique as well as in literary reputation. When he began contributing to *Punch* in 1842 he

[18] Silver.   [19] Spielmann, *History of Punch*, p. 75.
[20] Silver; Spielmann, *History of Punch*, p. 305.
[21] Spielmann, *History of Punch*, p. 304.
[22] Silver.   [23] Mackay, *Forty Years' Recollections*, II, p. 285.

had already been a free-lance writer for *Fraser's*, *The Times*, *Bentley's Miscellany*, and the *New Monthly Magazine*. And he had three serials to his credit: *The Yellowplush Papers*, *Catherine*, and *A Shabby Genteel Story*. His early papers in *Punch*, 'The Snobs of England by One of Them', probably helped to confirm Jerrold's suspicions of his arrant cynicism. A further source of friction doubtless was the growing rivalry as Thackeray won popularity with the *Punch* readers. 'Let's see what Master Douglas has this week,' he would tease as he began to look through a new number. Jerrold bitterly resented, moreover, Thackeray's upper-class sympathies; these, he felt, betrayed the liberal spirit which *Punch* stood pledged to champion. Even Mark, who tried to be on the friendliest terms with all his staff, was conscious of a psychological barrier between himself and Thackeray. 'I never felt quite at home with him,' he confessed; 'he was always so infernally wise. He was genial; but whatever you talked about, you felt he would have the wisest views upon the subject. He seemed too great for ordinary conversation.'[24] Fresh from his hops and tavern connexions, still clownish and boisterous in his antics, full of puns and ridiculous word play, Mark would naturally have found Thackeray's keen-edged wit chilling, at least during the first decade of *Punch*. For Thackeray could make his colleagues look foolish. Occasionally, bent on amusing himself at someone else's expense, he would begin, 'I've written a little poem today: "The mouse lay cosy in her hole and nothing could be snugger." ' Then, as if perplexed, he would exclaim, 'For the life of me I couldn't find a rhyme to it.' If some unsuspecting victim suggested the obvious word, Thackeray would fire back, 'Dear me, yes, of course, I never thought of that!' Once he announced, 'There's no rhyme for *Babbage*.' Caught off guard, Mark insisted, 'Yes, *cabbage*', and was 'sold'.[25]

Now and then Thackeray fell short of his weekly commitments to *Punch*. 'I must beg you to excuse me,' he would inform Mark by note, 'for I've worked just as much for you as though I had done something.' But so brilliant were his contributions when he did send them, like his first-rate parodies in '*Punch's* Prize Novelists', that his shortcomings could be overlooked. Not to be condoned, however, was his shabby conduct on one occasion. Even while slacking on his work for *Punch* and criticizing its policies in letters to Dickens (yet

[24] *London Society*, XXIX (Feb. 1867), pp. 255–6.   [25] Silver.

all the while drawing his regular salary), he was planning a rival journal, to be called the *Pen*. At this point the proprietors debated whether his pay should continue. And Mark, however much he might defer to superior wit and intellect, now assumed his sternest editorial dignity and, charging Thackeray with treason, made him blush.[26] Later, as Thackeray was forced to devote more time to his novels, his contributions to *Punch* appeared irregularly. Finally, in 1854, disapproving of the paper's abusive attitude toward Prince Albert and Louis Napoleon, he severed his official connexion with it,[27] but continued for the rest of his life a frequent visitor at the weekly dinners.

Another of the early *Punch* writers, Gilbert Abbott à Beckett, was valuable to Mark not only as a regular contributor but also as a collaborator on several plays. A person of many talents, he had already started a number of comic journals in his twenties, had been called to the Bar as a young man, had held posts as Poor Law Commissioner and Metropolitan Police Magistrate, and had written leaders for *The Times*. Week after week Mark could count on him for a steady succession of columns in *Punch*. Like his articles, his poems were witty and clever. The intensity of his literary activity was matched by the gusto with which he enjoyed his food.[28]

Other early *Punch* writers on whom Mark depended were Percival Leigh, Tom Taylor, and Horace Mayhew. Leigh, a medical student whose *Comic Latin Grammar* had already gained attention, abandoned plans for a career as a physician and turned to journalism. Scholarly in his interests, he had made a speciality of Shakespeare and the classics and was, therefore, generally referred to as 'the Professor'. Taylor, a one-time holder of a Trinity Fellowship at Cambridge, began writing for *Punch* in 1844. He was remarkably versatile: from practice at the Bar he had gone to a Professorship of English Language and Literature at London University, then to an important post as a Civil Servant. Generally quite loquacious, he could talk with authority on a great many subjects, from high art to Low Dutch. He had a facile pen and could knock off a poem in an hour or two.[29] Horace Mayhew, Henry's brother, gravitated to the *Punch* circle in 1843 after a period of study in Germany. Until Mark decided to manage his editorial duties alone, Horace served briefly as messenger between draughtsmen and writers. In this connexion he

[26] Ibid.   [27] Spielmann, *History of Punch*, pp. 323-4.
[28] Silver.   [29] Ibid.

earned the nickname 'Ponny'.[30] A handsome man of distinct Jewish type, he was a flashy dresser, kept late hours, and excited considerable speculation about his amorous exploits. At the age of fifty-two he ended his bachelorhood by marrying a woman of forty-four. The event was facetiously hailed as a blow to London's night houses. 'Now, I suppose he will purge and live cleanly', one of his friends wrote in a letter to Mark.[31] At one of her birthday parties his wife was overheard to say, 'I don't care how many children you give me, 'Orace.' 'Don't be impatient, my dear,' he admonished her.[32]

Believing that cartoons should be important features in a comic journal, Mark took special pains to encourage his artists. Of these John Leech, who began contributing in 1842, was for more than two decades his most valuable man. For many readers he made the paper, and Mark recognized his gifts fully. A friend of Thackeray's since their schooldays together at Charterhouse and a former medical student like Leigh, Leech had given up medicine to devote himself to art. Though his first cut was late and sent the circulation down,[33] his subsequent work soon repaired the damage. He could execute a cartoon with amazing speed, sometimes in an hour or two, while Mark, smoking a cigar, sat beside him and waited until it was finished. Extraordinarily prolific, in twenty-three years he did three thousand drawings, at least six hundred of them cartoons. So apt was he in delineating contemporary styles in dress that women too far from London to observe fashions modelled their wardrobes on his illustrations. In 1862 Mark, much interested in a new lithographic process, got Leech to exhibit enlarged copies of his most distinguished *Punch* drawings at the Egyptian Hall.

Another of Mark's gifted draughtsmen in the first decade of the paper was Richard Doyle. He had demonstrated his talent while still a boy, drawing comic illustrations to Homer at twelve and completing his *Comic English Histories* at fifteen. Shown his youthful work, Mark recognized his talent and had him taught woodengraving by a *Punch* craftsman. Once he had become a regular contributor, Doyle used a 'dicky bird' as the distinguishing feature of his monogram signature. It was his cover design that Mark finally adopted for the journal. In 1849, when England waged a campaign

[30] An alternative explanation attributes the nickname to his having written a poem on Poniatowski. For this information I am indebted to Mr. R. G. G. Price.
[31] Palmer MS., Brooks to Lemon, 8 July 1868.   [32] Silver.   [33] Ibid.

against papal aggression and *Punch* became too outspoken in its attack on the Pope and Catholic doctrine, Doyle, a devout Roman Catholic, gave notice that he could not countenance such blatant disrespect to his Church. Late in 1850, seeing no let-up in the anti-Catholic campaign, he resigned and left Mark with some unfinished blocks of drawings.

*　　*　　*

Looking back over his first ten years with *Punch*, Mark had every reason to pride himself on his achievement. Once Bradbury and Evans had put the paper on a sound financial footing and had made him the sole editor, its progress had been steady. To be sure, for a time there had been struggles to meet the weekly publication date, and Mark had often worked late in an upper-story room of his lodgings at Newcastle Street with Horace Mayhew beside him. In shirt-sleeves, scissors in hand, the two men had cut and pasted away desperately as the deadline for the make-up of the journal approached.[34] But they always managed to get each issue out punctually.

For the continuing success of *Punch*, Mark was largely responsible. He had brought together men of diverse talent and had set them off against each other, even while he shaped them into a cohesive team dedicated to keeping the paper strong. Not that this had always been possible without friction, for sharply opposed views had inevitably produced clashes. Jerrold, the champion of the underdog, naturally insisted on a policy of liberalism. But Thackeray and Leech, Carthusians devoted to the cultural tradition, balked him as they tried to steer *Punch* toward the upper classes. Leech actually professed some antipathy to the working man. Mark, though of decided liberal convictions himself, wisely let each man write as he chose, subject, of course, to editorial supervision. *Punch*, he felt, should hit low as well as high. And he insisted, even though derided by other comic journals, that writers be paid well. If men were treated properly, they would work together and try to please.[35]

But for all his generosity, his good humour, and his efforts to maintain staff harmony, he must at times have sensed that some of his writers and artists were condescending toward him, even as they gave him their best work. Jerrold, with his incisive wit and vigorous

[34] Spielmann, *History of Punch*, p. 256.　　[35] Silver.

intellect, could not conceal his contempt for Mark's often crude humour. His suggestion that Mark's *Prose and Verse* be called 'Prose and Worse', though put as a joke, doubtless expressed his convictions. And Leech and Thackeray, considering themselves several cuts above a former tavern-keeper, even went so far as to twit him as 'mine host'. At staff meetings, moreover, he was not always able to control the noisy arguments. He had brought *Punch* safely through the hungry forties, but it would be another decade before he acquired sufficient polish and social stature to command the respect of all his men.

4

'FROM STREET CORNER TO DRAWING-ROOM'

DURING the next two decades, as *Punch* came of age, new names added lustre to its already impressive list of regular contributors. Of these Shirley Brooks was to become Mark's valued friend, adviser, and never-failing source of inspiration. They made perfect partners. To Lemon's exuberance, volubility, and diplomacy were added Brooks's cultivated taste and literary background. His nimble wit could always supply the *bon mot*. But what he enjoyed in mental agility he sometimes lacked in judgement, and it was here that Mark's shrewd common sense filled the gap.

Brooks joined the staff under unusual circumstances. Once a steady contributor to the *Man in the Moon*, a rival journal which Albert Smith had launched in 1846 after being sacked by Mark, he had indulged zestfully in diatribes against *Punch*. Chief of these was 'Our Flight with Punch', an accusation in verse that the wit once distinguishing Mark's paper had degenerated into mud-slinging and boring attempts at humour. After reading these gibes at his own gauche jokes, Mark told his colleagues, 'That man is formidable; he must be sought as an ally.'[1] Douglas Jerrold suggested that the way to silence 'this uncommonly sharp and clever dog was to treat him according to the well-known recipe of Mrs. Glasse's cookbook: "first catch" your Shirley Brooks and then serve him up for the Punch table'.[2] It remained for suave and affable Mark to win him over. By the end of 1851 this had been accomplished, and Brooks wrote his first piece for *Punch*. This was followed six months later by the weekly instalments of his novellette *Miss Violet and Her 'Offers'*.

Trained in law, Brooks had early switched to literature and journalism. For this he was admirably endowed. With his facile pen he could produce a poem or an article in an hour. In the past he had

[1] Layard, *Shirley Brooks*, p. 43.
[2] *Pall Mall Magazine*, XXIX (Feb. 1903), pp. 262–3.

also reviewed plays, including Mark's *A Loving Woman*, on its appearance at the Haymarket.[3] He was not worried at having to write to the clock, and he filled his columns with entertaining matter up to the last possible minute. 'Shirley's pen is the gracefullest in London,' Mark would declare. His best-known contribution to *Punch*, based on an idea entirely original with him, was his 'Essence of Parliament', conducted weekly over a twenty-year period whenever Parliament was in session. It is a witty and humorous record of considerable interest to present-day historians.

Occasionally, when Mark was ill or away on business, Brooks, as his right-hand man, would take over the editing of a number. But only after completing a probationary period did he rise to such a position of trust and esteem. Like all new-comers to *Punch*, he had originally done piece-work and had been paid by the column. After nearly two years of this he wrote to Mark, inquiring whether 'an opportunity of being more useful to *Punch*' would not, in fact, make him so. 'I believe I could serve *Punch* far better', he explained, 'if, without reference to the mere quantity of copy sent in, I were desired to regard it as my business to be generally useful to the best of my power, instead of merely handing in an outsider's contribution, the value of which, to myself, depends on its length. For writing, for one to whom it is bread and cheese, hardly allows him to please himself, as he would gladly do, by giving a day to his elaboration of work at a guinea a column.' In brief, he hoped to be placed on a regular weekly salary of five guineas. 'I have named a sum which I believe I am right in supposing considerably below that received by any of my fellow labourers,' he continued, 'but I do so remembering, of course, your kind assurance that in the event of a change, I stand for promotion.'[4]

Another of Mark's valued acquisitions, the artist John Tenniel, began contributing at the close of 1850, after the sudden resignation of Richard Doyle. Left in the lurch, Mark invited Tenniel to submit drawings. A book and magazine illustrator, he had attracted attention in 1848 with his plates for an edition of *Aesop's Fables*. At first he was taken aback, almost outraged, at being asked to draw for a comic journal. No idle spoofing for him! His domain was high art. But with characteristic blandishment Mark got him to change his mind. And it was fortunate that he did, for in time Tenniel's illustrations,

[3] *Illustrated London News*, LVI (4 June 1870), p. 573.
[4] Adrian MS., Brooks to Lemon, Lord Mayor's Day, 1853.

especially the political cartoons, elevated *Punch* from a mere comic journal to a paper of general interest, a national institution. He was particularly adept at handling high comedy and tragedy. Though he had sight in only one eye, having lost the other in a fencing accident, he never allowed this to interfere with his work. By conviction a conservative, he did not agitate for a cause or seek to correct social injustice at a time when *Punch* was known for its strident liberalism. It was for others to suggest ideas for cartoons; as a draughtsman he merely executed them, though he did so superbly. At the *Punch* office he was generally referred to as 'Jackides', a nickname which Mark had given him during one of the staff dinners by jocularly quoting the burlesque line: 'No longer Jack, henceforth Jackides call.'

Mark added another important artist to his staff during this decade, Charles Keene. Once a fellow student of Tenniel, whose disapproval of *Punch* liberalism he shared, Keene had strong Tory sympathies. He began submitting sketches and drawings in 1851, marking them only with a mask to hide his identity. Not until three years later did he begin affixing his initials. During the period of his anonymity Mark recognized his genuine talent and repeatedly called for more drawings. Keene was a draughtsman of the highest order, meticulously exact in detail and with a gift for capturing arrested action.

When, after a long probationary period of nine years, he finally became one of the regulars, he was usually quiet and inconspicuous at staff meetings, though respected by all and affectionately known as 'Carlo'. He seldom suggested ideas for cartoons, and occasionally excited considerable merriment because of his inability to see the point of a joke. Now and then, though, he would try to contribute to the badinage by injecting some humour of his own. Such was his riddle: Why is a schoolboy after a flogging like a man who gives support to one of the Royal Family? Answer: Because he carries the prints of Wales on his back.[5] In telling a joke, he would conclude with a wink, achieved by raising the lower eyelid.[6] His most appreciated contribution to staff merriment was the singing of old English songs, especially 'The Three Ravens'.[7]

Henry Silver, a friend of Keene's, also began sending work to *Punch* in the fifties. In 1857 he became one of the regulars. A bachelor during his early years on the paper, he would blushingly

[5] Silver.   [6] Price, *History of Punch*, p. 78.   [7] Silver.

and with sheepish grins acknowledge Mark's sly hints about possible amatory exploits. Shy and often the butt of good-natured digs from his colleagues, he would, Chaucer-like, cast his eyes downward, at the same time observing every bit of by-play with unsuspected vigilance. He often regretted his ineptness at repartee, complaining that his 'staircase wit' supplied an appropriate retort only after he had left the room.[8] His *forte* was straight journalism, which he could turn to advantage whenever the editor needed an article on a specific topic or current happening. But today, of greater interest than his pieces in *Punch* is his diary for the years 1858 to 1870, in which he recorded with astonishing frankness all that occurred at the weekly staff dinners.

In the sixties, as *Punch* entered its third decade, Mark engaged another of his leading artists, George du Maurier, who, with Leech, Tenniel, and Keene, constituted the zenith of illustration in comic literature. Parisian born, he had studied art in France after an unsuccessful effort in England to prepare for a career in science. During his student days he was called 'Kiki', a nickname that he carried with him through his long term with *Punch*, for 'kicky' he was: his feet were never still. Like Tenniel, he had sight in one eye only—the result of illness—and lived in constant dread of blindness. (It was sometimes remarked that they had one pair of eyes between them.) With his faculty for spotting talent, Mark at once recognized du Maurier's promise, but told him to check his '*youthful* and generally aggressive tendency'. 'A young fellow like you is always for pitching into somebody or something,' he warned him, 'but if you want to get on you must put the kicking strap to your dander and offend nobody.'[9] At first Mark thought him 'cocky, as a young fellow with hair should be',[10] but eventually he shaped him into one of the paper's great assets, an artist specializing in the gracefully amusing rather than the blatantly absurd. His *Punch* drawings documented the age with their authentic portrayal of contemporary manners and fashions. Especially striking were his tall women.

Generally jovial and expansive, always prepared to offer sound advice where needed, occasionally stern and fiery, Mark knew not only how to pick his men but also how to help them to give their best. So when in 1864 du Maurier became a *Punch* regular, and at times allowed relaxation to interfere with his duties, Mark's threats

[8] Ibid.　　[9] Du Maurier, *The Young George du Maurier*, p. 97.
[10] B.D., 8 Jan. 1873.

of dismissal brought results. But some relaxation was permitted during the staff discussions of politics, when 'Kiki' would pull up a chair for his legs, cover his face with a handkerchief, and immediately fall asleep.

Of the writers who came to *Punch* in the sixties, F. C. Burnand made the greatest impact. A Roman Catholic, he had once studied under Cardinal Manning for an ecclesiastical calling. Finding himself unsuited for the priesthood, he turned to the stage, then for a brief period tried law, and finally settled on play-writing and journalism. After a short probationary period Mark added him to the staff in the middle of 1863. His serial 'Happy Thoughts', whose narrator counters life's trying experiences with a cheerful philosophy, captivated *Punch* readers by its graceful fooling with serio-comic overtones. Good-humoured teasing about his religion he parried with agility. And he promptly quashed any suggestions for cartoons disrespectful to Catholicism. But he did not take some of its restrictions too seriously, as when he announced one day, 'Can't rehearse on a fish diet: must ask for a dispensation.'[11]

*   *   *

Such were the supporting pillars of *Punch* as Mark built it during the three decades of his editorship: Jerrold, Thackeray, Horace Mayhew, Leech, and Doyle in the forties; Brooks, Tenniel, Keene, and Silver in the fifties; du Maurier and Burnand in the sixties. On intimate terms with them all, both as friend and colleague, Mark knew their idiosyncrasies and weaknesses, but at the same time valued their talents. 'All better men than I am,' he used to say. 'But is not his judicious editing a talent that they can't show an equal to?' argued Silver. Such it was, for, without Mark Lemon, *Punch* might never have been heard of after its first issues. Born in the hungry forties, nourished by ridiculously small capital, barely hanging on from week to week, it had seemed unlikely to survive its infancy. With unflagging dedication, however, Mark had kept it going until, backed by Bradbury and Evans, it had outgrown its perils. But more than financial success was required to keep *Punch* growing. That it did not go the way of its short-lived predecessors, that it met the challenge of would-be rivals, that it captured public interest at no sacrifice of quality must be credited to the wisdom and shrewdness of its editor. Recognizing the potential of his clever writers and

[11] Silver.

artists, Mark suggested, cajoled, and, when necessary, demanded in order to get from them the contributions that distinguished his paper. With an instinctive knowledge of men and the ability to excite their enthusiasm, he could maintain the highest standards. At the same time he had a genius for holding his brotherhood of turbulent wits together.

Mark was a born editor. His administrative ability, his faculty for gauging public opinion, his skill at handling personal relations— these won him the esteem of his men. Though Thackeray and Leech had once twitted him about his earlier role as a potboy, they respected his editorial talents and acknowledged his authority. His was the sole responsibility for all appointments, for the make-up of the paper, for what was accepted or rejected.

Two or three times a week he was in the editor's room to see after his business. 'But if business were ever combined with pleasure,' Shirley Brooks recalled later, 'it was in the hands of Mark Lemon. . . . He did everything in the cheerfulest way—approved the article, amended the paragraph, and paused over and passed or condemned the epigram, transposed the initial pictures, tossed a laughing remonstrance at a peccant contributor or a tremendous compliment at one who had done his duty, [and] suggested the cigar as a substitute for a visitor's talk when the printer wanted instruction.' Time and again he interrupted his work to tell a joke or anecdote, but would be back at his task before the laugh had died away. Once he had made the important decisions for the next issue of *Punch*, he 'shut up books and drawers in the most thunderous manner, and with the sternest glance'. Then, 'affecting to unbend from royal state', he called out, 'Some light refreshment.'[12]

Each week Mark devoted a full day to calling at the homes of his artists, to check the progress of their illustrations for the next number. In addition to using this opportunity to encourage his men individually, he wanted to make sure that all cartoons and sketches would be ready on time, for his paper was never late (except for the issue that had carried Leech's first drawings). On these trips of inspection he travelled in a hansom, always using the same cabman. To go by omnibus would have been unthinkable. Having grown stouter with the years, he was not one to force his way through umbrellas, baskets of greens and clothes, and bulging parcels, only to squeeze himself into a tight place beside a mother nursing her

[12] *Illustrated London News*, LVI (4 June 1870), p. 574.

infant. As it was, his ample proportions completely filled the seat of his cab. But here he was free from horrible odours, draughts, fear of infection, and crying babies. His cabby once built him a special hansom, and for decoration suggested the figure of Mr. Punch on the panels. Mark discouraged such ostentation.

Though not a draughtsman himself, he had a knowing eye for detecting artistic promise where others saw only mediocrity. And he could inspire the beginner: with a pat on the young man's head, a kindly chuckle over the genuinely amusing, unstinted praise for the deserving sketch. At the same time he had definite ideas of what was right for *Punch*. 'You may try your hand at a large drawing,' he once told a young artist. 'But let it be broad fun. We don't want any more ladies and pretty children.'[13] He was especially happy over a cartoon showing a toper in profound sleep, while a spider had found time to spin a web from the imbiber's nose to the bottle on the table.[14] Keenly interested in the mechanics of art-reproduction, Mark recognized the possibilities of photography, and himself devised a technique for reducing or enlarging blocks made from india-rubber.[15]

With his authors he always avoided dictation; he merely reserved the right of correction. Each man was to write what he liked, subject only to editorial supervision. 'This has the benefit of a variety of minds,' Mark explained, 'unfettered by my own.' Variety, he declared, was essential, even at the risk of including a certain amount of mediocrity. In the final analysis *Punch* would always be guided by common sense. Actually only two requirements were laid before the staff: to write economically and to get all contributions in early.[16] Since the paper went to press on Saturday, all copy must be ready for the printer by Friday evening. Not always, though, did Mark have the full co-operation of his men on this score. Sometimes a writer might fail him or several of the staff be away on holiday, so that he found himself short for the next issue. On one occasion Brooks related how Mark 'made a jolly row the other day, for he was reduced to his last shred of copy to make up a number, and was indeed I believe driven to write himself, while I was gorging at the Albion in Aldersgate Street. This touched my heart, so I cut away, as you will see.'[17]

During their probationary period the *Punch* writers were paid

---

[13] Spielmann, *History of Punch*, p. 538.   [14] Ibid., p. 415.
[15] A Beckett, *The à Becketts of 'Punch'*, p. 76.   [16] Silver.
[17] Layard, *Shirley Brooks*, pp. 167–8.

only for contributions accepted. Once they were appointed to the staff, however, they received a regular salary. This was an arrangement Mark insisted upon—it reduced jealousy among the men, he felt, and gave them a sense of security. The actual number of columns submitted by each writer had always to be recorded in an office book, the Day Diary. If he lagged behind for one or more issues, he was expected to close the gap in subsequent numbers. Though Mark held his men to rigid minimum requirements, he was the first to insist that they should be rewarded according to their merits. 'Don't you think that Tom Taylor's salary might be made £5.5.0?' he suggested to the proprietors in 1851. 'I think he wd not object to it and he works earnestly.'[18] Quick to recognize inequities, he demanded fair treatment for all.

How much did Mark himself actually write for *Punch*? In addition to supplying fill-up material occasionally, he liked to put his own literary stamp on the paper from time to time despite the heavy demands of his editorial post. He was always careful, however, not to set aside another's work to make room for his own. His contributions were really not considerable: except for *The Heir of Applebite* in 1841, they were generally short items, entered in the Day Diary as 'Editor's Copy'. And many of these may have been sent in by correspondents. But he did, now and then, print some of his own articles and poems, an early series of his verses being entitled 'Songs for the Sentimental'. These lilting stanzas feature a serious build-up followed by an anti-climactic twist in the punch line. Though not one of the series, Mark's 'Sonnet' (8 April 1843) illustrates the device: a surprise ending in startling contrast to the misleadingly solemn opening.

> She took the veil,—'twas at the vesper hour,
> When day was gently melting into night,
> When Earth's fair features fade from human sight,
> 'Twas then she took the veil—farewell her bower,
> Farewell home, friends—as some transplanted flower
> In a lone vase pines for the garden bright,
> So she is reft from every dear delight,—
> Shut from Love's sunshine, Joy's refreshing shower;
> She took the veil; nor did she shake nor blench—
> She saw not him who fixed his glaring eye
> Upon her every motion anxiously;

[18] P.O. MS., Lemon to Bradbury and Evans, Monday, n.d. 1851.

ST. MARY'S CHURCH, HENDON. *From an engraving by T. Bonner in Brayley Britton's* The Beauties of England and Wales, *1816*

CHURCH FARM HOUSE AND THE GREYHOUND INN, HENDON

THE
'MAHOGANY
TREE,'
In the Punch
Dining-room
at 10 Bouverie
Street

> Silently awhile she stood. She took the veil!
> Then loud he cried, 'Policeman, here's a wench
> Shoplifting, take the customer to jail.'

One of Mark's effusions in verse, the satirical 'Ballad for the Delectation of All True Sportsmen' (1 February 1845), formed part of the *Punch* campaign against Prince Albert when England still regarded him as a foreigner. Jeering at his poor marksmanship, it impudently suggests that Albert shot his game only after his keepers had maimed it:

> Each keeper raised his stick and struck
> The hare upon the head;
> The Prince he shot, the keepers knocked,
> Until each hare was dead.

'A fine thing for a hare/ By Princely hand to die,' is the final taunt:

> 'Twas this perhaps the game inspired
> To court their Prince's aim,
> They died to give Prince Albert sport,
> And therefore they died game.

Mark's more serious efforts often had a social emphasis. Such was his 'Pauper's Christmas Carol' (23 December 1843):

> Bright and blessed is the time,
> Sorrows end and joys begin,
> While the bells with merry chime
> Ring the Day of Plenty in!
> But the happy tide to hail
> With a sigh or with a tear,
> Heigho!
> I hardly know—
> Christmas comes but once a year!

The awakening of England's social conscience was to become increasingly important for Mark: much of his energy went into championing the destitute.

He followed the same theme in some of his prose contributions to *Punch*. In 'Substance and Shadow' (13 July 1843) he observed sardonically that 'there are many silly, dissatisfied people in this country, who are continually urging upon ministers the propriety of considering the wants of the pauper population under the impression that it is as laudable to feed men as shelter horses'. Such an 'act of folly' might well embarrass the Chancellor of the Exchequer, with his 'balance of the budget . . . triflingly against him', and with such 'righteous and paramount claims upon him as the Duke of Cumberland's income, the Duchess of Mecklenburg Strelitz's pin-money, and the builder's account for the Royal stables'. It would appear, concludes Mark, 'that ministers have adopted the very best means to silence this unwarrantable outcry. They have considerately determined that as they cannot afford to give hungry nakedness the substance which it covets, at least it shall have the shadow.' The final sentence is a slashing rebuke of the Government: 'The poor ask for bread, and the philanthropy of the State accords—an exhibition.'

Mark aimed his most withering sarcasm at those scoundrels who built their fortunes on the wretchedness of the poor, like the 'slop-seller Moses' of Tower Hill, whose inhumanity had been publicized by *The Times* (25 October 1843). In order to buy bread for herself and her two starving children, Biddell, a miserable widow, had pawned some trousers on which she had been sewing. 'Moses' had her prosecuted. In his testimony he swore that she had stolen out of sheer viciousness, that she earned a 'good living'. This, under questioning, he admitted to be only seven shillings a week. Outraged by such callousness, Mark loosed his barrage at 'Moses' in 'Famine and Fashion' (*Punch*, 4 November 1843).

Seven shillings a week! One penny—not the value of the pestiferous cigar which Moses' man puffs in the faces of passers'-by, from the threshold of his master's door—one penny only, for an hour's ceaseless labour at tasks that if long pursued will shut out the blessed light of heaven, and make the sweet air a torture to the ulcerated lungs of the poor living wretch who devotes herself to such self-sacrifice, 'in order to provide dry bread for herself and infants;' and yet this jackanapes . . . dares to call such a pittance a good living for a mother and her two infants. We would that Moses and his class were doomed to walk the streets of London arrayed in their choicest 'slops' (blood-stained as the shirt of Nessus, but without its avenging qualities,) branded

SEVEN PENCE,

that men might know how they gained their sleekness!

Mark insists that 'Moses' is worse than a cannibal, who '*slays* his victim before he commences his revolting feast', for he 'refines such cruelty, and banquets day by day on some throbbing nerve, or wasting muscle'. The rebuke concludes by directing the readers to 'Moses and Co.' for bargains in clothing, 'made by a shivering wretch too fond to die—cheap as pauper life':

> For every garment help'd to break a heart.
> Then hasten all who mindful of the purse,
> For Moses' bargains brave the poor man's curse.

While *The Times* and Mark were denouncing 'Moses', Thomas Hood, investigating the pay of seamstresses, learned that they got only five farthings for making a shirt and had to supply their own needles. Shortly afterwards he recorded his protest in his immortal humanitarian poem, 'The Song of the Shirt'. But he found no immediate publisher: three papers rejected it in rapid succession. Finally he submitted it to Mark, apologizing that it was hardly suitable for *Punch* and leaving him free to throw it into the waste-paper-basket. Mark consulted his staff, who recognized its merits, but unanimously advised against publication, because the subject was too painful for a comic journal. Still he decided to use it. Appearing anonymously in the Christmas number, 1843, in the same issue as his own 'Pauper's Christmas Carol', it tripled the circulation and was quoted in newspapers throughout the country.

This was not the last time that popular approval justified Mark's judgement. Another of his fortunate decisions led to the publication of a piece by Burnand, who was then writing for *Fun*, a rival journal. One of his manuscripts having been rejected by the proprietor, he was advised to show it to Mark. A meeting was arranged. Late for his appointment, Burnand, hurrying along the Strand, 'caught sight of a very big man filling up a hansom, with the doors open, waving one very large hand' at him and ordering the driver to pull up to the kerb. Pushing aside all excuses, Mark told him to hop in. 'It was not easy to find the necessary space,' Burnand recounted later, 'but I continued to squeeze myself in, and he sat as triangularly as a very stout man could who hasn't an angle visible about him.' Mark then asked about the manuscript. 'Just *tell* me about it,' he suggested, dismissing Burnand's offer to read it to him. Dismayed by his bungling efforts to give its gist, the young author felt like stopping the cab, apologizing for wasting a busy editor's time, and hastily retreating. To his amazement, however, Mark beamed, slapped his companion's knee, and exclaimed, 'Bravo!' Never pausing, he continued exuberantly, 'We'll have it illustrated! I'll get the artists to

burlesque themselves! When shall I have a copy?' Burnand handed
over the manuscript, and again Mark exclaimed, 'Capital! we'll have
it set up at once.' In confidential undertones he outlined specific
ideas for its publication, at the same time urging secrecy. The secret
was well kept. On 21 February 1863 it burst upon *Punch* readers as
Mokeanna. A skit on cheap, sensational journalism, the melodramatic
story was aimed chiefly at the *London Journal*, whose front-page
make-up it imitated. Having been prevented by illness from coming
to the office the previous week, Bradbury, on opening the number,
was horrified at what he took to be a hideous mix-up, for he and
Evans printed the *London Journal*. He rushed to the office to stop the
issue.[19] Just then Mark arrived and explained the joke. Giving in
grudgingly, Bradbury complained that *Punch* had been lowered by
this stunt.[20] Only when the next number boosted the sales was he
convinced that Mark had again gauged public opinion accurately.

With illustrations, too, Mark had an eye for the sure hit. A case
in point was Tenniel's cartoon for 20 April 1867. Entitled 'They're
Saved! They're Saved!' it focused attention on the second Reform
Bill, then being debated in Parliament. The double-page drawing
shows Disraeli and Gladstone speeding away in a sledge marked
'Reform'. To the pack of pursuing wolves, two of them drawn with
heads of the opposition, Disraeli has already tossed a bundle labelled
'Dual Vote', while he protectively clutches his two infants, 'Personal
Rating' and 'Residence'. When the cartoon was first proposed Leigh
called it a 'mere commonplace record' and Keene rather snubbed the
whole idea. But Mark used it, convinced that it would be successful.
The response was overwhelmingly favourable. The artist Frith wrote
to congratulate Tenniel, the Prince of Wales sent for a proof, and
admiring letters poured in.[21]

Not always, however, did Mark's judgement yield such happy
results. It misfired when W. S. Gilbert, then writing for *Fun*, offered
him the first of the *Bab Ballads*, 'The Yarn of the Nancy Bell'. Mark
rejected it as being 'too cannibalistic' to suit the taste of his readers.
Though Gilbert had an occasional piece in *Punch* thereafter, he
never became a regular. This honour, Mark told him, would be
contingent on his severing all connexions with *Fun*. Gilbert refused,
and Mark lost the chance of adding a great humorist to his staff.

Mark's arrangements with his regulars virtually constituted a

[19] Burnand, *Records and Reminiscences*, I, pp. 417–21.   [20] Silver.
[21] Ibid.

closed corporation, for only occasionally would a contribution by an outsider appear in *Punch*. A poem by Coventry Patmore ('Vive la guerre!') in 1846, articles by Artemus Ward for a number of weeks in 1865, and Lewis Carroll's verses on 'Atalanta' in 1867 were among those that were accepted. For Ward there was only mild enthusiasm, the *Punch* staff agreeing that his bad spelling was a decided handicap.[22] Of the outside artists to appear occasionally, J. E. Millais was the most important. His mock-heroic drawing burlesquing his own style was used in Burnand's *Mokeanna*.

Now and then unsolicited pieces would obtain Mark's approval. One of these was a joke by a man from Edinburgh, who called at the *Punch* office to collect. Paid a guinea, more than the trifle was worth, he complained: 'Hoot, mon, what gude is that? I've taen a week's holiday and come all the way fro' Edinbro' on the faith o' the money I'd get fro' ye.'[23] Usually Mark had to reject manuscripts submitted to him from outside. That he found the time to do so with a personal note emphasizes his sympathetic nature: he was loath to inflict pain. 'I am very sorry to return the enclosed lines,' he wrote on one occasion, 'but I have read and reread them and cannot agree with you as to their fitness for *Punch*. Wishing you a prosperous and happy New Year.'[24] Remembering his own early attempts to break into print, he hated to discourage aspiring authors. 'Here I sit, like a great ogre, eating my people's little hopes,' he would say.[25]

Of his readers, too, Mark was ever considerate. He took care not to print anything painful, however humorous the author considered it. Once a young art student submitted a drawing showing a savage dustman beating his horse's head with the butt of a whip, while an onlooker objected: '*That* isn't the way to treat your horse! You should *poke it in his eye*, poke it in his eye, man!' Mark returned the picture with a note: 'The enclosed is rather too painful for *Punch*.'[26] Gruesome subjects to be humorous, he insisted, must never show actual details.

He was also determined not to violate Victorian propriety. Any joke the least bit suggestive he ruthlessly vetoed. Into the wastepaper-basket went poems with the slightest hints of seduction. Even such a harmless subject as midwifery on board ship did not escape his obliterating pencil. He objected strenuously to what he called

[22] Ibid.   [23] Hatton, *With a Show*, pp. 83–84.
[24] Nat. Lib. of Scot. MS., Lemon to Fraser, 4 May 1853.
[25] Spielmann, *History of Punch*, p. 256.   [26] Ibid., p. 518.

'Frenchy ideas of modesty'. During a discussion of a popular Parisian play he exploded, 'Filthy copulative beasts!' The nudities of the French stage disgusted him.[27] Thackeray once remarked in a public lecture that 'comic works of the past years are sealed to our wives and daughters', but assured his audience that it was not so with *Punch*: 'For where its editor is, there is decorous wit, and fun without the general attendant, coarseness.'[28] Mark's scrupulous regard for propriety once prompted his staff to play a prank on him. During one of his trips to Paris they sent him a cut of a man sitting on a water-closet, with a copy of *Punch* in his hands. 'Ha! Ha! cured in an instant!' read the caption.[29]

In addition to banning the sexually suggestive, Mark was on guard against slanderous or libellous statements. He knew how to make his butts look ridiculous, how to turn his readers' laughter on them, yet all with impunity. So expert was he at treading this dangerous territory that *Punch* was almost never threatened with a lawsuit. To be sure, now and then there were hints that an article was actionable, as when Brooks in his 'Essence of Parliament' (8 April 1865) took Cox to task for his bungling speech in the House against the flogging clause. 'When a man talks insufferable nonsense on the side of reform,' Brooks declared, 'he creates a number of anti-reformers, and when Mr. Cox said that if soldiers were flogged for absence from duty, members of Parliament ought to be flogged for not attending in their places, he excited contempt for himself, and for constituents who could elect such a Wind-bag.' Such nonsense, Brooks maintained, had only widened the margin by which the clause was carried. A few days later arrived a letter requesting the name of Bradbury and Evans's solicitor.[30] But nothing came of it, for Brooks's paragraph was innocent of libel.

Only in its anti-Semitic and anti-Catholic campaigns did *Punch* sometimes descend to the questionable. But even when it did point a finger at the Jews it concentrated on their behaviour, rather than their ethnology. Indeed, Leech, the most rabid of the anti-Semites, used to complain that 'we don't half pitch into the Jews'. He admitted that they were 'excessively polite to him, but with all their kindness there's something you don't like'. In spite of such prejudice, however, he was not above accepting a hunting invitation from a Jew.[31]

[27] Silver.
[28] Reported in *London Society*, XXVIII (Oct. 1875), pp. 354–6.
[29] Silver.   [30] Ibid.   [31] Ibid.

Jerrold, too, was known to be anti-Semitic. Generally, though, when the topic of the Jews came up, the staff would indulge in some good-natured banter, seldom in bigoted comment. Shirley Brooks, for instance, liked to address Horace Mayhew in Jewish accents at the *Punch* dinners with 'Horace, ma tear, will you 'ave shome pork?'[32] But when it came to racial persecution, Mark and his colleagues protested vigorously. In 'Crime Its Own Excuse: To Our Jewish Friends' (9 January 1864), Brooks rebuked Bayard Taylor, who, according to the American correspondent of the *Standard*, had condoned the Emperor of Russia's cruelties to the Poles (hanging the men, flogging the women, kicking the children) because 'out of every hundred Poles, ninety-nine are Jews'.

For its anti-Catholicism *Punch* concentrated on the campaign against 'Papal Aggression' in 1850, which, as already noted, led to Richard Doyle's sudden resignation. Tenniel's first cartoon showed Lord John Russell as David, a mischievous urchin who, having chalked 'No Popery' on the door of Dr. Wiseman, the Roman Goliath, was fleeing with the piece of chalk still in his hand. The cartoon carried the Legend 'This is the boy who chalked up "No Popery!"—and then ran away!' With the passing years *Punch* became more tolerant of Catholicism in England and waged its war chiefly against the ritualistic Puseyites.

In general, the paper relaxed its belligerence after it had left its early rampant liberalism behind. Repeatedly Mark reminded his men that its policy must alter with the times, that they 'must stand by and see how the stream runs' before taking a definite line. This was illustrated in the handling of Lincoln and the Civil War. When the President called for three hundred thousand troops and caused many Englishmen to condemn the conflict as a Northern effort to protect its capital rather than free the slaves, Brooks flung some scathing lines at him (*Punch*, 16 August 1862):

We're coming, Father Abraham, we're coming all along,
But don't you think you're coming it yourself a little strong?
Three hundred thousand might be called a pretty tidy figure,
We've nearly sent you white enough, why don't you take the nigger?

Mark also was cool to the Northern cause. Like Carlyle, who had deplored his nation's concern over the slaves in Jamaica when there were so many 'yellow slaves' in the factories of England, he insisted

[32] Ibid.

that there was much to be done at home. He wanted a cartoon with a miserable boy of the streets pointing a finger at a coddled Negro and asking, 'Am I not black enough to be cared for?'[33]

But when Lincoln was assassinated on 14 April 1865 and all England gave America her sympathy, there followed a dramatic recantation. 'This is terrible news!' the *Punch* writers agreed. So important an event must not be passed over. In the next number, accordingly, the principal cartoon showed Britannia comforting Columbia, with Negroes and white men united in their mourning. And in his poem 'Abraham Lincoln Foully Assassinated' (6 May 1865) Tom Taylor admitted the error of *Punch*'s earlier attitude: 'Yes, he had lived to shame me for my sneer, / To lame my pencil and confute my pen.' 'The avowal that we've been a bit mistaken', Mark explained, 'is manly and just.'[34]

Not always, though, did the staff accept Mark's editorial judgement. His policy of 'cutting out whatever is cutting' had made *Punch* 'too mealy mouthed by half'. It no longer hit hard. But Mark stood his ground. 'I don't agree that *Punch* should be all pitch and no praise,' he declared. Strong language having done its work, there was no need for it now. It could not be denied, however, that the paper had become thoroughly respectable. Mark admitted as much. '*Punch* keeps up by keeping to the gentlemanly view of things and its being known that Bohemians don't write for it,' he observed. Brooks took an even more lordly view. 'We don't write for the people in the cottages,' he insisted; 'our readers don't think of tea as a necessity of life.' A discerning comment had come from Douglas Jerrold some years earlier: '*Punch* sets its watch by the clock of *The Times*.' And Brooks agreed that the readers of *Punch* were also the readers of *The Times*.[35]

Commensurate with the growing respectability of his comic journal was Mark's own rise in the social scale. There were more invitations to important dinners, more tickets to fashionable entertainments, more nights on the town. Now a member of the Garrick Club—he had been proposed in 1854—he often lunched there, wrote letters and read, or just lounged and chatted. He also patronized Evans's, the well-known supper-rooms that combined features of a chop house, concert room, and night club. At one time a special table was reserved there for the *Punch* staff. Paddy Green, the short, florid, white-haired proprietor, always gave them a courtly greeting.

[33] Ibid.   [34] Ibid.   [35] Ibid.

In *Loved at Last*, his second novel, Mark paid tribute to Evans's as 'a sort of chapel-of-ease to the London clubs [where] may be found at times members of all the professions, who resort thither sure of the same immunity from annoyance as they would find in their own smoking-rooms'.

Occasionally Mark was invited to dinners presided over by Alexis Soyer, the famous chef of the Reform Club. 'The immortal Alexis Soyer can make more delicious soup for a halfpenny', wrote Thackeray, 'than an ignorant cook can concoct with pounds of vegetables and meat.'[36] For his Symposium during the Great Exhibition of 1851, Soyer had the walls of the staircase to his dining-saloon (across the road from the Crystal Palace) covered with paintings of celebrities, real and mythological. Mark Lemon was one of them.[37]

Known everywhere as the editor of England's leading comic journal, Mark received many letters with all manner of strange requests. Sometimes women sent descriptions of the dresses, ribbons, and bonnets worn by their enemies, with instructions to 'cut them up' in the pages of *Punch*. Social climbers who gave elaborate parties and never paid their debts were to have their knuckles rapped. There were also attempted bribes, one man promising to take twenty copies of *Punch* if Mark would publish his contribution. An hotel-keeper proposed a month's free lodging for any two *Punch* men in exchange for free publicity. But Mark would not be taken in.[38] Most of all, he hated puffing. Even his best friends were to be shown no partiality. Indeed, all who wrote for *Punch* were to forget personal considerations. As Brooks put it: 'Private arrangements must not interfere with public duties. Men who sit down at this table must not remember they have friends. "Leave friends behind, all ye who sit here" should be the inscription.' Not even for the thousandth number were there to be special literary fireworks. Such special notice would be 'claptrappy' and certain of exciting ridicule. Enemies would say, 'See how old *Punch* is getting.'[39]

With his reputation as editor established, Mark began to enjoy the financial rewards of his position. From a mere guinea a week he had risen to fifteen hundred pounds a year, the highest salary ever

[36] In *Vanity Fair*, ch. XIX.   [37] Dodds, *Age of Paradox*, p. 468.
[38] Brooks, 'Lecture on *Punch*', reported in the Durham *County Advertiser*, 2 Feb. 1863.
[39] Silver.

paid for such a position up to that time. Small wonder that he often bubbled over with optimism. The paper was indeed doing well: in politics, in art, in literature it was a force to be reckoned with. One salvo at the Government and Members of Parliament anxiously sounded out their constituents. A jeering review of a poem, novel, or play, and the author saw his hopes for a career dashed. Most important, the circulation of *Punch* had risen steadily, sometimes dramatically with special features. To this the annual *Almanac*, an extra number with the year's calendar and additional stories and illustrations, had contributed substantially, as had the *Pocket Book*, with its Diary and fund of useful knowledge. Beaming with goodwill as he annually commended his staff on the excellence of these supplementary numbers, Mark never failed to use his old formula: 'The best we've had in years!'[40]

Such exuberance was justified, for by the middle of its second decade *Punch* had fulfilled, if not surpassed, the hopeful expectations of its founders. Speaking for himself and his colleagues, Douglas Jerrold proudly assessed its accomplishments:

Punch was not intended to be a merely comic periodical. *Punch* was to be a grave philosopher, a tender romancer. He should have his political strength. He should bring his wit, and humour, and satire, to bear upon very great shams indeed. The rapid hold which . . . *Punch* took of the British public fairly astonished all the heavy wiseacres who had foretold the speedy discomfiture of the mountebank. The cap and bells were fitted on wise heads. The fooling was not purposeless, was even learned. The hunchback had been removed from the street corner to the drawing room and library, and might be seen in the palace of the sovereign and in the cabinet of the premier. Even reverend readers and lecturers, pacing quiet quadrangles of ancient colleges, found *Punch* a right welcome hour's laughter once a week.[41]

[40] Ibid.
[41] As reported by B. Jerrold in *The Best of All Good Company*, pp. 400–1.

5

PUNCH TABLE TALK

By what magic did Mark secure the outstanding talent that carried his journal far beyond its competitors? How did he manage to gauge public taste so accurately and lead his staff to exploit it? Above all, how was he able to generate in his colleagues a dedication and loyalty that ensured the continuing success of his paper? One institution, perhaps more than any other, was responsible for this achievement: the weekly dinner attended by editor, proprietors, and staff. Always referred to as the *Punch* Table, they gathered on Wednesday nights, usually at the office and in a room set aside for this purpose, to decide on the principal cartoon (the 'Large Cut') for the next issue. But these sessions often went beyond the bounds of business. They gave exuberant spirits a chance to relax over an excellent meal, to exchange points of view and match wits, to consider contemporary social, political, and intellectual issues. At the same time, such conversations furnished many of the topics that were later fed into *Punch* to keep it alive to the spirit of the time. Adroitly steering the discussions, quickly detecting the touchy areas of personal friction, frequently indulging in boisterous antics and off-the-record jokes, Mark built up an *esprit de corps* hitherto unequalled.

What went on at these dinners may be learned from the diary kept by Henry Silver from 4 August 1858 to 23 March 1870. Never published, this fascinating document consists of a single hand-written volume, today part of the *Punch* Office Library at 10 Bouverie Street. Surreptitiously taking notes under the table, trusting to an amazingly retentive memory to fill in the details, never missing any of the by-play, Silver assessed each meeting and, on his return home, recorded his impressions in closely written pages. A sampling of the week-to-week Table talk, reflecting as it does the prejudices and convictions of Victorian England, will illustrate how the lively ferment of opinion kept *Punch* strong.

The dinners always began promptly at six o'clock. Beaming at his men as they gathered around the large table with its curved ends— Thackeray had christened it the Mahogany Tree, though it was actually deal—Mark approached the evening with gusto: 'jolly and full of fun', Silver was to note repeatedly. Each diner sat in his special place, designated by his carved initials under the cloth. 'These things are great to little men', observed Silver.[1] Bradbury and Evans, who furnished the feast, thought nothing too good to put before their staff. Turtle soup, salmon cutlet, cold beef, pineapple fritters, cheese, strawberries and cream, cherries, pineapple punch, champagne, sherry and claret—such was a typical menu. ' "Man wants but little here below"—but wants that little good', wrote Silver as he savoured these items in retrospect. Another time, surfeited after trying too many tempting dishes, he addressed his conscience: 'And all this after reading of the Homes of the Poor in our to-day's Times!' But this was no occasion for scruples. 'Show what your young men *can* do, Mr. Evans,' said Leech. 'Life is short—let us be as miserable as we can—so Mark, my dear fellow, a glass of wine with you?' In the ensuing merriment authors and artists became a party of grown-up boys, roistering, buffooning, often bursting into song. Once, when the dessert was about to be served, the hilarity rose to such a pitch that Evans (nicknamed 'Pater') bowled a large pineapple at Bradbury, who had asked for a slice of it. To everyone's amazement, not a single wineglass was broken in transit. At another dinner 'Pater' achieved this feat with a melon.

Never did the evening pass without some amusement. Mark, for one, could always provoke laughter. Whether he gave one of his unforgettable impersonations of after-dinner speakers or told one of his earthy jokes, he could be counted on to relax tension. Time and again Silver was to refer to him as 'a glorious imitator', 'chatty and merry', 'full of anecdotes'. One of his stories was about a man who, on finding a copy of Shakespeare in a purchase of miscellaneous items, requested: 'When he writes some more, let me have it.' Another told of a worshipper sleeping in his pew. On dropping his prayer book with a thud, he started up and called out, 'Come in!'

At eight-thirty, the feasting over and everyone in an expansive mood, cigars were called for and the work of the evening began. An inkstand and a sheet of paper before him, Mark, surveying his staff,

[1] Unless otherwise designated, all references in this chapter are to the diary of Henry Silver, *Punch* Office Library.

asked, 'What is it to be?' Almost immediately he was jotting down notes for the Large Cut. Sometimes this business could be settled in a matter of minutes, but more often the deliberations continued well into the night. An idea would be bounced back and forth, battered, reshaped, polished, until it finally emerged so drastically changed as to bear little resemblance to the original suggestion—if indeed that had not already fallen into the discard.

Occasionally, when there was no significant national development or the *Punch* men felt dull and arid, one topic after another glanced off the anvil before something could finally be hammered into shape. Such laboured evenings Silver referred to crudely as 'hard stool'. Happily, at the last moment Shirley Brooks usually had an inspiration. At such times he would throw his knife on the table, exclaiming, 'There's your cut!'—leaning back the while and breathing hard. Struck by this eccentric behaviour, Burnand once yielded to a sudden impulse: he picked up a whole handful of knives and forks, threw them down with a jarring clatter, and gave a 'Shirleyan' sniff.

At one time or other nearly every current event, issue, or figure furnished topics for Table talk. The laying of the Atlantic Cable, the cattle disease (1865–7), the Fenian disturbances, the Jamaican revolt, the disestablishment of the Irish Church—such were the items scrutinized by Mark and his men. Proposed legislation got close attention from the start. The annual budget, the detested income tax, education reform, the Reform Bill of 1867—all were aired at the Wednesday-night dinners. So were the policies of leading statesmen: Russell, Gladstone, Palmerston, Disraeli, Bright, Lowe. Because of his opportunism and Jewish extraction, 'Dizzy' was a favourite butt in suggestions for cartoons. The staff proposed him for a clerical trapeze on the high ropes (after his speech on the Church in 1861), spoke of him as the blind leading the blind ('Dizzy' teaching the Bishops, following another windy oration in 1864), called him the Great Medicine Man after his 1867 Reform speech, and denounced him as Mephisto offering the Elixir Vitae of Reform to rejuvenate John Bull. All this, even though Disraeli had tried to ingratiate himself at a gathering of the Printers' Pension Society in 1845 by cleverly toasting Mr. Punch, 'towards whom, he protested, he felt no kind of malice on account of any strictures, pictorial or verbal'.[2]

Once its details had been agreed upon, the Large Cut was turned

[2] Vizetelly, *Glances Back*, I, p. 303.

over to the artist, Leech, Tenniel, Keene, and du Maurier contributing the most memorable drawings. Though the cartoon had to anticipate developments fully a week in advance, only rarely did it miss fire. More often it hit the target squarely. A case in point was the controversy over Governor Eyre, whose handling of the 1865 riots in Jamaica had been under investigation for over two years. On the very day that *The Times* announced the Grand Jury's verdict of 'no true bill' *Punch* portrayed Palmerston's ghost reproaching Disraeli for not defending Eyre: 'Benjamin! Benjamin! *I* wouldn't have left him in the lurch.' In contrast to its early humanitarianism, *Punch* had sided with Eyre from the first. After all, had he not met his responsibility by protecting the lives of English women and children?

Sometimes the artist was asked to withhold a significant detail until the last possible moment, as with the cartoon for 5 May 1866, after the Russell Government had been teetering precariously on the issue of the second Reform Bill. 'Leave out the corners of his [Russell's] mouth till Saturday,' suggested Taylor, 'and turn them up or down as the result indicates.' This was done. Following a vote of 318 to 313 for a second reading of the Bill, *Punch* entitled its Large Cut 'Rest and Be *Very* Thankful'. Pictured as a schoolboy, Russell sits at his desk and holds before him a sheet labelled '5 Majority'. At his side Britannia, his nurse, admonishes him: 'You've been so good a boy, Johnny, that I hope you won't get into another such muddle!' A wan smile flickers on his face.

An excerpt from Silver's diary for 14 January 1863, when attention was focused on the American Civil War and Lincoln's Emancipation Proclamation, will illustrate how suggestions were metamorphosed into the principal cartoon.

Man who won the fight. Abe Lincoln with black eye, etc. [Suggested by Leech.] Mark Lemon and Shirley Brooks agree that Lincoln's proclamation as to the slaves being free should be noticed—and saying, 'Massa, but you beat him first.' Southerner with pistol cocked: 'Wal, why don't you go?' Brooks suggests black as Othello: 'Were it my cue to fight I'd do it without your bidding'—also black Caliban: 'Beat him well and then I'll beat him too.' . . . Leech thinks Punch will stultify itself—always been for the North—but Shirley Brooks says two years hence we shall be sorry for espousing the side of the Cavaliers and Convicts. The Southerners have been in power for the last 20 years—and they it is who have insulted us—bought the New York Herald, etc. Joe Youngs, a rabid Northerner, says that Punch has surprised and offended the Americans more than anything else. Punch always as yet in favour of justice and now to pat rebels on the back. But what right had the States to secede from England? And Punch can't cry bravo to a bully or sympathize with an invader. South fighting for hearth and home and therefore successful.

As drawn by Leech, the Large Cut, 'Scene from the American *Tempest*' (24 January 1863), shows a crouching Negro (Caliban) receiving from Lincoln (pictured as a Northern officer) a scroll headed 'Emancipation Proclamation'. A scowling Southern officer, arms folded, looks on. '*You* beat him 'nough, Massa!' says Caliban as he points at the Southerner. 'Berry little time, I'll *beat him too*.' In parentheses this is identified as a 'Nigger translation' of Shakespeare.

Another entry in Silver's diary shows how the national excitement over Garibaldi's visit in April 1864 was reflected in the *Punch* Table deliberations. As usual, conflicting views clashed before the cartoon was agreed on.

Tom Taylor suggests Italy handing him [Garibaldi] to Britannia and saying, 'Take care of him.' Mark Lemon adds something about Garibaldi's lame foot: 'You'll soon be able to wear the (Italy) boot yet, if you keep quiet a bit.' Percival Leigh suggests Garibaldi presented by Punch with the freedom of his office, which Evans interprets to mean simply putting him on the free list. John Leech sneers at Garibaldi and Lemon thinks him the greatest man of his age—so unselfish and bravehearted. 'But weak in the head', says Brooks, who suggests Punch rowing him ashore—or receiving him on landing (à la William III)—a Roman triumph, Punch as a Roman welcoming him. Evans adds 'This is the noblest Roman of them all'—to which Leech would add 'Next to me.' Palmerston receiving him also suggested, but the other the best. Leigh suggested Garibaldi glad to breathe the British air, the air of freedom. 'Yes,' says Leech, 'make him landing in good English fog.'

Though Leech had been unsympathetic, his cartoon carried out the wishes of the Table: Mr. Punch welcoming Garibaldi with 'This is the noblest Roman of them all.'

*   *   *

Because the *Punch* staff often lingered at the table long after deciding on the Large Cut, sometimes until midnight, there was opportunity for serious talk, though interspersed with more clowning and light-hearted chatter. The topics brought out individual prejudices as well as typical Victorian points of view. With Mark usually initiating the spontaneous debates, it was to be expected that his liberal convictions should have a hearing. For he was a staunch Whig, especially in the early decades of *Punch*. Mrs. E. M. Ward has recorded how, when he visited her childhood home, he and her father, a conservative, would take hours to settle the affairs of state. At last Mark, 'thoroughly tired out with arguing', would rise to leave, only to be followed to the door by his host for another round. 'It was considered my duty on these occasions to remind my father that luncheon was on the table getting cold,' relates Mrs. Ward, 'and I used invariably to find that I was never heard; only the sound of Mr. Lemon's voice floated through the house, raised in anger or entreaty.'[3]

As already noted in the discussion of his own sketches and poems published in *Punch*, Mark had a strong social conscience. As long as underfed labourers had to live in pigsties, he declared, crime would persist among the lower classes. But give them decent cottages in wholesome surroundings, guarantee them work at fair wages, send their children to school, and they would become good citizens. But how was the Government to deal with those who had already been driven to lawlessness and violence? 'Castrate your ruffians after the second offence,' suggested Brooks. 'Eighty thousand thieves in thirty-five millions here. Logic says exterminate the nuisance.' Mark objected to such harsh measures. 'The State is to blame—no work for a man after prison,' he pointed out. 'Children of prisoners should be confiscated to the State and compulsorily educated.' Would hanging deter criminals? Brooks and Evans thought so. 'Without the dread of capital punishment,' added Bradbury, 'savage beastliness would be a constant threat.' And Mark admitted that he would rather be hanged than have to endure prolonged mental torture by life imprisonment. But he opposed speedy execution: there should be sufficient time for repentance.

Not infrequently he marched in the vanguard of *Punch* liberalism, as when he upheld the demands of labour. Though strikes had harassed industry by shutting down mills and putting hundreds of hands into idleness, as at Preston in 1853, he nevertheless argued for the right to combine. Buffeted by a 'savage recklessness of life', the poor working men must not be denied justice. But here Mark got little support from the Table: Silver reported a 'hot jaw' against him. 'Why', demanded Evans, 'champion a man not worth thirty-three shillings? A slow worker is always more expensive than a faster

[3] Ward, *Memories of Ninety Years*, p. 23.

man: he burns more gas while producing less. There must be free trade in labour before employer and employed will come together.'

With many poor workers unable to support their children, the subject of large families kept coming up. A full year before Matthew Arnold was to argue a similar view in *Culture and Anarchy*,[4] Shirley Brooks maintained that 'a man of moderate means should moderate his love: two children will be better cared for than twelve'. He admitted, however, that men do not reason in bed. 'Poor people have two pleasures,' he said, 'to get children and to get drunk. Since they are denied the luxuries of the rich, one cannot wonder at their having large families, though they have nothing to live on and know that half their sons must either steal or starve.' But Brooks's advanced views on planned families found no supporters. Evans, instancing his own brood of twelve, declared that man 'has no right to check nature. The thirteenth child may be our chief blessing. Love is not lust. Providence sends children.' For such Victorian rationalizing Brooks had nothing but scorn: 'Bah! Men have a fit of the Beast, and call it providence!' Mark sided with Evans. Denouncing Malthus and Mill for advocating curbs to population, he proudly referred to his own children as his 'chief comfort'. (By the spring of 1858 Nelly had borne him three sons and seven daughters.) What man dared to say that he could feed no more than four mouths? The four might all die and the fifth be a Shakespeare. But Brooks had the last word: 'The utmost that a man can do for his child's advantage in the world will hardly atone for the wrong of having brought him into it.'

Sometimes the ideas advanced by the Table would have been considered daring outside the *Punch* office. Such was the talk about eugenics, introduced by the speculation that idiots might have been begotten in a weak moment. 'Why not build up the breed as we do our beasts?' asked du Maurier. So, while Sir Charles Adderley, addressing the Warwickshire farmers, boasted that the Anglo-Saxon race was 'the best breed in the world',[5] du Maurier saw much room for improvement. He would 'select brides and grooms according to their physique'. At which Brooks facetiously pictured a spare fellow proposing to a thin girl and her father saying, 'Pauleana! No, Fatima is the girl you want.' And he also imagined a lover addressing his sweetheart, 'Dearest, I adore you—but tell me, is there scrofula in

[4] See especially 'Our Liberal Practitioners', ch. 6, sec. 4.
[5] As quoted by Matthew Arnold in *The Function of Criticism at the Present Time*.

ML–F

your family?' Once the men had warmed up to their subject, there was no limit to the preposterous proposals: for instance, the suggestion that the Army, if not allowed to marry, might be used as stallions. Why not 'utilize your immorality'? As for the necessity of woman, all agreed that she 'brightens the body and clarifies the wits'. Chanted Brooks: 'Who loves not wine, woman, and song / He lives a fool his whole life long.' 'The Professor' (Percival Leigh) held a more restrained view. Though accepting sex as a natural necessity, he argued that it could be combated with physic, as was done by the monks. 'That's unnatural!' retorted Thackeray. 'But it's one's duty to subdue the flesh and cultivate the mental over the sensual,' reasoned Leigh; 'you lose the taste for lust if you think of better things.' He was shouted down, however, as Brooks, Evans, and Thackeray chorused, 'But we don't want better things!'

Only occasionally was the current of serious Table talk checked by such frothy eddies. More often the stream flowed steadily in its deep channel, carrying its cargo of thoughtful comment. For here were some of the best-informed men of their time, conscious of their cultural heritage.

It was to be expected that the discussion of journalists should deal with language, especially the origin and appropriateness of words. Mark, for one, liked to tell the story of how *humbug* had come into being. According to him, someone had wagered that he could invent a word which would be in everybody's mouth within the week. So he chalked *humbug* all over the town and had everybody talking about it. As for the term *jolly*, this Mark considered a *euphemism* for *bloody*. 'The Professor' also had some linguistic theories. *Mormonism*, he joked, should be *Morewomanism*. In a more serious mood he decried *reliable* as a falsely constructed word. It should be *relyuponable*. '*Able* is an active termination, not a neuter', he insisted. Holding the conservative view of his time, he issued a warning: 'Literary men should prevent these Yankee word coinings; immorality springs from loose verbiage.'

Writing habits also furnished topics for Table talk, with authors comparing their techniques. Brooks composed rapidly, in a clear, quick hand, with numerous abbreviations. Thackeray, who envied him such a ready pen, said he generally spent two days thinking of a subject for one of his *Roundabout Papers*. He did his best work out of the house—anywhere except at home. As soon as he got his nose to the desk ideas began to flow, but he composed slowly, in a small hand with seldom a correction. For inspiration 'Professor' Leigh and Silver often needed to take a walk. They carried pencils and made jottings as they moved about. Jerrold could work at will, rapidly. From his early sprawling penmanship he had changed to a small hand, with no revisions. Taylor used a bold, splashy style, with numerous insertions, deletions, and references to 'back'.

Often the discussions would focus on literary trends and authors, past and present. There was, for instance, much talk about Shakespeare during the celebration of his tercentenary. Why did Englishmen quote nobody but him? Because he was so intensely quotable. But Brooks, in line with the accepted critical judgement of the period, felt that Shakespeare's low humour must detract from the sublimity of tragedy—for example, the scene of the grave-diggers. Tom Taylor, himself a recognized dramatist in his day, rebutted this thesis. 'If the grave-diggers spoke like witty gentlemen,' he said, 'it might. But their natural dullness serves as relief.' Considered, too, was the mystery of the *Sonnets*. Brooks argued that internal evidence hinted at abnormality. 'Could a man with a natural passion write on the reverse?' asked Silver. John Leech maintained that Shakespeare could feel and write about anything, for he was a universal genius.

'Burns was like Shakespeare,' said Taylor; 'he wrote for all men and for all time.' A heated argument ensued. 'He only wrote of three things which may be for all men,' insisted Brooks: 'to wit, lust, and drink, and blasphemy.' Taylor fired back: 'Either you've not read Burns or you've no soul and don't understand poetry, and as I cannot believe the latter of you, I am forced to think the former.' Brooks as usual had the last word: 'I've read more of him than most men, and I don't think such lines as those beginning "The fowls dung o'er your father's pate" have very much poetry or do credit to your pet, Tom.'

But what is poetry? Its aim, the Table decided, is the truthful representation of the beautiful. Since suggestiveness is its chief charm, horrors should not be described but hinted at, as in Scott's 'here an arm, there a leg'. This is more terrible in its directness, all admitted, than the cut-and-dried terrors of superior writers. Poetry suggests pictures to the mind: it is something more than music— the sound pleases and the thought remains. Finally, the poet must always be above art.

Of the contemporary poets, Tennyson was mentioned most often.

Judged by his readers to be the foremost Victorian author, he was 'cashing-in' on his popularity, according to the *Punch* men: his copyrights fetched unusual sums. From Bradbury and Evans, to whose *Once a Week* he contributed, he received two thousand pounds a year. And it was rumoured that in 1869 the publisher Strahan had agreed to pay him four thousand pounds annually. 'The greatest man of the age', Thackeray called him, maintaining that he had 'thrown the quoit the farthest'. But Brooks thought that *Vanity Fair* would always rank higher than anything of Tennyson's. 'Would you change your reputation for his?' he asked. Thackeray said he would. 'I don't believe you!' snapped Brooks. 'The Professor' felt that 'Tennyson is to Wordsworth what Mendelssohn is to Beethoven: graceful but not sublime'. He had been reading *In Memoriam* and found it 'smoky, gloomy, cloudy, with a torchlight glare breaking through now and then—but nothing hopeful or Christian'. For him, apparently, Tennyson had not resolved the uncertainties of religious belief that disturbed many earnest Victorians. Silver admired the Laureate, though, for such classic rhythms as his 'faultily faultless, icily regular, splendidly null' from *Maud*. A discerning comment, anticipating the judgement of Sir Harold Nicolson in the twentieth century, came from du Maurier. Tennyson, he believed, would live chiefly by his songs and minor lays, such as 'Ask me no more' and 'Break, Break, Break'.

To Browning, whose reputation was established later than Tennyson's, Silver gave only one brief diary entry. It is dated 31 August 1864, the year that Browning published *Dramatis Personae* and is thought to have written Book I of *The Ring and the Book* with its reference to the 'British Public, ye who like me not' (l. 410). Leigh, who had given his poems close study, praised *Caliban upon Setebos*, but deplored the 'little sentimentalisms and wife's squabbles' of other pieces. 'But life is made up of such trifles,' Brooks pointed out. 'We are not acting tragedies every day.' This comment set Silver wondering: 'What is *Othello* but a tragedy, founded upon a trivial event?'

For the most despicable of men among living poets the Table nominated Swinburne. Disgusted by his shocking behaviour and the flaunting paganism of his poems, they pronounced him a 'nasty, conceited, drunken, impotent beast, who recites his poetry with a St. Vitus dance'. When his *Poems and Ballads* appeared in 1866, Brooks proposed a versified dedication:

> This book of lust and foul desire
> A fitting dedication owns;
> One half I pitch into the fire,
> The other half to Mrs. Jones.

Swinburne's personal shortcomings notwithstanding, du Maurier still considered him a superior metrist, a 'weaver of words, the rhymer of rhymes, more musical than Tennyson'. Yet did he not sacrifice syntax for prosody? 'He's a Prosodomite,' punned du Maurier.

To contemporary non-fiction prose-writers the Table referred only occasionally. When the first volume of Carlyle's *Frederick the Great* appeared the general verdict was 'a waste of labour', even though it had sold ten thousand copies in Germany. Evans felt that he was neither better nor wiser for having read it. As for Ruskin, the consensus, influenced by the unsavoury publicity following the annulment of his marriage, was that he wrote 'like a eunuch: more brains than . . .' But Brooks and Thackeray, agreeing that it was a foul blow 'to hit a man in his privates', frowned upon a recent statement in *Blackwood's* that Ruskin would 'make a safe tutor in a ladies' school'. After all, a man deserved fair play. As an art critic, moreover, he was indeed formidable. Just let him write a slashing criticism of a picture, and all hopes for a sale would be blasted. This was to be the point of Brooks's clever lines in *Punch* (26 May 1856) under the heading 'Poem by a Perfectly Furious Academician':

> I takes and paints,
> Hears no complaints,
> And sells before I'm dry;
> Till savage RUSKIN
> He sticks his tusk in,
> Then nobody will buy.

N.B. Confound Ruskin; only that won't come into poetry—but it's true.

Scattered comments also dealt with the novelists of the day. For Dickens there was little enthusiasm when the first number of *Our Mutual Friend* appeared in 1864. It was said to be 'very weak, full of whirling absurdities'. Brooks repeated the old charge that Dickens, unlike Thackeray, could not draw a gentleman or a dinner party. Moreover, his names were 'simply comicality', whereas Thackeray's always had pith. Similarly negative were the estimates of other contemporaries: Bulwer-Lytton was 'a vain charlatan with no genius'; George Eliot's *Mill on the Floss* was 'dreary and immoral'; *Cometh Up as a Flower*, the double-decker by Rhoda Broughton, a minor novelist, was 'sensation stuff, a mixture of coarseness, scraps of Scripture, and dung'. How much better the earlier writers of fiction—Maria Edgeworth and Scott, for instance. Toward Trollope the attitude was charitable. Brooks found his power for work astonishing: 'Fancy getting up at five and sitting down in a cold room with grubby hands after lighting your own fire, and then writing about pretty girls and love matters.' Taylor praised him for making 'commonplace life and characters interesting', though his style was one of the worst.

Now and then the Table dwelt on the interrelations of literature and art. About the Pre-Raphaelites there were conflicting opinions, even after Ruskin had championed the group in 1851. Some believed that Rossetti and company were 'unhealthy mannerists, affected', charging a hundred pounds for a picture worth no more than thirty, and that primarily for its frame. Du Maurier, more knowledgeable about painting, defended them, placing Millais in the first rank, with Rossetti and Burne-Jones immediately after. At the same time he noted their eccentricities, to be delightfully exaggerated in his five-part parody, with illustrations, 'A Legend of Camelot' (*Punch*, March 1866). Braunighrindas, its main character, is an obvious take-off on the Pre-Raphaelite 'stunner' with her 'blazing hair [that] writhed and reached the floor', her long, blue-veined feet that 'glimmered like tombstones', and her chin that was 'thrust full many an inch beyond her head'. All these details distinguished the renderings of such Pre-Raphaelite models as Elizabeth Siddal, Jane Burden, and Fanny Cornforth.

In 1860 William Holman Hunt, the most dedicated of the Pre-Raphaelites, attracted considerable attention with his 'Christ in the Temple'. Though admitting that Christ's belt was painted to perfection, Tom Taylor argued that 'such perfection only leads to imperfection: the flesh and blood climax of the picture is the weakest part of it'. Silver agreed, commenting astutely: 'If you can't paint living flesh truly, it is an untruth to paint accessories so that they become the prominent features.' For 'The Eve of St. Agnes', a literary illustration by Millais, there was unstinted praise, however, especially for the 'mermaidish appearance' of the pretty girl with the 'seaweedy green dress' at her feet. Among the Old Masters, the landscapes and animals of Rubens won admiration, as did the unfinished marble *Pietà* of Michelangelo, with its dead Christ 'homely but pathetic'. It was agreed that Michelangelo 'rarely painted beauty, but always invested homeliness with grace', so that he made one *feel* the effect aimed at.

What might be said of an artist as a representative of his age? Here Brooks would place a caricaturist like Hogarth or Leech above all painters: 'Stamps the image of his time ineffaceably.' Though there were those who ranked Hogarth ahead of Leech, still the latter's work would live as long, some thought, mainly because it would always appeal to children, and 'whatever pleases children will live', as, for example, *Robinson Crusoe* and *The Arabian Nights*. The chief difference between Leech and other artists, Mark pointed out, was that his cuts could stand alone: they would amuse by themselves, even without the accompanying captions.

As for the Royal Academy, its policies were generally deplored at the *Punch* dinners, as indeed they were elsewhere. Why, after being helped by the Government for a hundred years and having become, in effect, a national institution, did it operate as a virtual monopoly? It rejected too many pictures. 'A man who has once exhibited should always have the right to show one picture,' Mark insisted: 'the Royal Academy is discourteous.' (Is it possible that he was smarting because the Academy had turned down a portrait of him by Fred Chester, the son of a lifelong friend?) After the Academy dinner in 1869 there was strenuous objection because the principal speakers (Gladstone, the Archbishop of Canterbury, and Disraeli) had maintained that literary men have no right to pass judgement on pictures. 'Why,' argued Silver, 'should not painting be criticized as well as stage playing or novelists or poets or other inventors? Beethoven is criticized and so is Joachim. Why not Millais? A man who can't play or sing a note can criticize a singer. Why need he practise painting in order to criticize?'

Though on the whole less well informed about music than art, the Table occasionally lauded their favourite composers. Beethoven's *Pastoral Symphony* they called a veritable sermon, the highest kind of poetry: 'Happy he who can truly relish it!' To lift the spirits and 'clear one's liver', there was nothing like Handel. Mark found him a 'compelling draught': after hearing a performance of *The Messiah*, he could attack his writing with renewed zest. Surprisingly, Brooks did not share this enthusiasm. 'Fiddlers are idiots,' he declared, 'and those who care for music can talk of nothing else.' Du Maurier accused him of being a musical eunuch: 'Can't enjoy music yourself and think no one else can.' Silver thought it odd that Brooks with his 'higher intellect' should be deaf to this great art. As for musical appreciation, the more developed one's taste, the higher the enjoyment. Handel would be better than Küchen—but 'one mustn't quarrel with one's custard because it's not roast beef'. The way to enjoy a concert, according to 'Professor' Leigh, was to precede it with a first-class dinner—then take a good seat, alone: 'If you have a chatterer next to you, all enjoyment ceases. In the middle of *The Requiem* you hear, "Gracious, what a frightful head-dress!"'

However considerable the interest of the Table in the fine arts, the theological discussions sparked livelier debate. At a time when scientific revelations threatened to undermine religious convictions— or even annihilate them—when many Victorians regarded Darwin's *Origin of Species* as a wanton attack on the word of God, when for Arnold and other troubled minds the 'Sea of Faith' had retreated 'down the vast edges drear and naked shingles of the world', Mark and his staff were also concerned over the jarring discords. They not only summed up prevailing attitudes, but often anticipated future liberal views. So, when J. W. Colenso, Bishop of Natal, shocked the ecclesiastical hierarchy with his *Pentateuch and the Book of Joshua Critically Examined*, he had his *Punch* champions. An attempt to have him deposed and excommunicated prompted Brooks to hurl some pungent banter at jockeying church dignitaries (*Punch*, 14 March 1863):

THE NATAL CORRESPONDENCE

I.

My Dear Colenso,

With regret,
We hierarchs, in conclave met,
Beg you, you most disturbing writer,
To take off your colonial mitre.
This course we press upon you strongly:
Believe me,

Yours most truly,
Lambeth.   Longley.

II.

My Dear Archbishop,

To resign
That Zulu diocese of mine,
And own myself a heathen dark,
Because I've doubts about Noah's Ark,
And feel it right to tell all men so,
Is *not* the course for

Kensington.

Yours,
Colenso

Why, asked Mark's colleagues, should Scripture be exempt from critical evaluation? Must intelligent men believe that the Creation had required only six days, that Jonah had survived being swallowed by a whale, that Moses had made the sun stand still? Such narratives ought to be viewed as fables, as should the Mosaic story of the Flood, a legend common also to the Chinese and others. The Church of England should have the courage to show that certain parts of the Bible must be read *cum grano*. But Mark took a more conservative stand. He argued that God could, by a miracle, have made the earth in six days with all the supposed geological proofs of greater antiquity complete in it. As for the idea of revising the Bible, that would be to castrate it. Evans and Bradbury thought otherwise. It needed retranslating, if only to expunge some of the coarse language offensive to the age. Revision would be justified, moreover, when inaccuracies required correction in the light of improved knowledge.

Opinion was also divided on the importance of conscience. Leech considered the inner voice a sufficient guide: 'If I do wrong I feel ashamed and sorry, and my conscience tells me that for my own happiness I had best do right.' But Silver felt that conscience might get blunted or warped—hence the need of prayer or something more. In any event, it would make a poor substitute for God, the final judge of good and evil. Taylor inveighed against the cruelty of sending a soul unprepared to God's judgement: 'As if God did not make allowance for human weakness and judge better than men.' Would He forgive suicide? 'Yes,' agreed Brooks and du Maurier, 'if one is a confirmed cripple and a bore to himself and everybody.' Such unorthodoxy the rest of the Table shouted down. A suicide is a murderer and a coward, they declared. A man must be an atheist and a fool to kill himself. Can one tell how much good he may do by keeping alive? What right has he to destroy the life which God alone should take? 'But God is too hospitable to turn away an uninvited guest,' quipped Brooks.

Church doctrine also got an overhauling. Why, when all men agreed on their belief in God and Christ, must dogma keep them at enmity? The Athanasian Creed, for instance, a subject of endless controversy, was written for a special time and purpose. Why should it be perpetuated? Sweep it and some other non-essentials away, and out would go Dissent and the Church would be greatly fortified. Too many parsons had been asserting opinions for facts. Though entitled to their beliefs, they had no right to say that apples are onions. Mark, who generally opposed creeds and doctrine, was able to dismiss the troublesome theological questions of the age by falling back on his simple faith. 'My religion consists of the Lord's Prayer and doing my duty to my neighbours', he told his men. He saw no need of churches. 'How can one man send another to heaven?' he asked.

On the subject of spiritualism, then enjoying the support of some prominent figures, Mark was outspoken in his opposition. 'It is blasphemy to say that man has power over spirits', he told the Table. 'Trading on the dearest affections of one's nature is detestable.' Deluded parents, made to believe that they were in communication with their dead children, lacked the necessary detachment for penetrating the deception. Mark disparaged Mrs. Milner Gibson, who told her boy to go and play with his dead brother. 'But why not let silly women have foolish amusements?' queried Brooks. Such practices would weaken children's minds, Mark argued. Further, if gipsies were to be prosecuted for telling fortunes, why 'suffer spirit rappers to get a living by pretended intercourse with the unseen world?' Miracles, he believed, could never be accomplished without some beneficial aid. Daniel D. Home, the medium, was nothing but a humbug. Jean-Eugene Robert-Houdin, the great magician, was far cleverer, in addition to performing his aerial suspension by daylight. So long as the spiritualists worked their tricks in the dark they did not deserve a moment's thought. Brooks and Silver remarked flippantly that they believed in only one class of spirits: 'little ones about a foot high, as high as gin bottles'.

There was some talk about enfranchising women. All took the conservative Victorian stand on this issue. They spoke derisively of Mill, declaring that if he had his will the dual vote would become the 'duel' vote. Brooks suggested as a slogan for the suffragettes: 'Mis-carriages provided for lady voters.' Mark, as usual, expressed his unshakeable views on male supremacy. 'Professor' Leigh was more moderate. 'Woman's intellect supplies the vacancies in man,' he held. 'She has quicker instincts, but no reasoning.' In general, the Table felt that the wife's place should be in the home.

From the topic of woman's responsibilities the discussion naturally drifted to the training of children and the behaviour of the younger generation. There was overall agreement that too many girls were lacking in becoming modesty. And they knew too little about household arts. Anyone who sneered at housewifery would not be fit to assume her chief aim in life. Among the boys, according to the Table, there was a distressing absence of respect for the older generation. To refer to one's father as 'Governor' or 'Old Cock' was deemed inexcusable.

A topic of unfailing interest was the Royal Family. When Prince Albert, sensitive about his unpopularity as a foreigner, tried to win favour as a sportsman and stock breeder, *Punch* did little to help him. Indeed, some of its cartoons having boldly twitted him, Queen Victoria let it be known privately that she was 'not amused'. But this did not end the joking at the Wednesday-night dinners. The Prince's shooting exploits, for instance, roused the Table to concoct with considerable relish a cartoon never to materialize on the drawing-board: 'Albert's taking his gun from a gentleman in waiting who takes it from his flunkey who takes it from his loader.' The mood of the Table changed abruptly, however, with the announcement of the Prince Consort's death. For the greater part of one evening, according to Silver, grave men weighed their country's loss.

General regret. People now feel how much he has had to do and bear. No easy thing to be a Queen's husband. And wherein can we find fault with him? Negative virtues are commendable in princes. 'Tis difficult in high places to abstain from committing oneself. Perched on a pinnacle, one's least fault is observable.—They say Lord Palmerston has felt the loss deeply. . . . They who had to do with him, all speak well of him. If he was proud of money, as some hint, surely his error was on the right side— seeing what precedents of extravagance he had before him. If the patronage of princes be a good thing for art, the nation should give them a purse adequate. It is a disgrace to a people that its rulers should be poor. The Queen is the first sovereign who has kept out of debt, and confined herself to her income.

At a later meeting Brooks read a letter telling of the Queen's first visit to Osborne after her husband's death. Seeing some alterations Albert had made to surprise her, she broke down. Everybody praised him as a 'respectable, well-informed man' and attributed much of the national prosperity to his good judgement. Forgotten, now, was the earlier light-hearted banter. But greatly as the loss would be felt, England should not be covered with Albert memorials, 'with obelisks—obelisk, a little spit, or lickspittle'. Leech was incensed on hearing that the poor were being bullied into contributing, and Thackeray considered 'sickening' a letter from Osborne begging him to subscribe.

Like many other Victorians, the *Punch* men eventually lost patience with the Queen for her long mourning and seclusion. The general dissatisfaction was clearly indicated, according to Mark, by the thousands of jokes sent him after smoking had been forbidden at Windsor: 'The only weeds the Queen allows there are widow's weeds.' At the wedding of the Prince of Wales and Alexandra in St. George's Chapel, Windsor, she was reported to have been the 'one black spot', highlighted by a burst of sun on the Royal pew, her eyes streaming with tears. According to rumour she had wanted the chapel hung in black, whereupon Edward had countered with 'Then I'd better bring my bride in a hearse.' Silver voiced the prevailing sentiment: 'Something selfish in such sorrow, surely.'

The official opening of a public sewer by the Prince of Wales set off a heated Table debate. In a note entitled 'A pretty Job for the Prince' (*Punch*, 8 April 1865) 'the Professor' poked fun at the ceremony. Admitting that the laying of a cornerstone might be considered worthy of Royalty, he maintained that 'a certain other function, of a needful, but also of an unsavoury nature', was beneath the dignity of a prince. 'There was something peculiarly British,' he declared, 'in the taste which invited the Prince of Wales to open the Southern Main Drainage works on Tuesday last, by starting the engine which was then, for the first time, to deliver their contents into the Thames.' Annoyed by such raillery, Tom Taylor pitched into his colleague. 'Sewers are the great moral as well as physical advances of the age,' he insisted, 'and no one but a fool will sneer at their being opened by a prince.' Remonstrating that he had meant no sneer, that he had merely hoped to show that opening a water-closet was hardly a suitable task for a prince, that he was really protesting against the emphasis on things material as the chief weakness of the age, 'Professor' Leigh still could not dent his critic. And du Maurier, objecting to Taylor's unfairness, was brushed off with 'Shut up—you're a minority of one, you melancholy Jakes.'

So it went on, week after week, as chronicled in the lively pages of Henry Silver's diary. The spontaneous debates often reflected the divergent opinions of the day; occasionally they anticipated advanced liberal views. Uninhibited because they were all men—only for special dinners were women invited—the fraternity discussed with the utmost frankness subjects ranging from the absurd to the profound, frequently in startling juxtaposition. Time and again the Rabelaisian humour was in sharp contrast to Mark's standard of purity for *Punch*. Whatever the shifting mood of the moment, the Table talk furnished ideas which might be translated into the cartoons and more equable comments that gave the paper its timeliness and vigour. The earnest give-and-take of the writers and artists, lit by laughter, inspired optimism. And such optimism bred success. In all seriousness did Charles Keene express the confidence of his colleagues when he prophesied, 'Mr. Punch will some day be drawn with a nimbus, ST. PUNCH.'

6

PUNCH 'JAUNTS AND JOLLITIES'

MARK and his colleagues did not confine their frolics to the sumptuous Wednesday-night dinners at the Mahogany Tree. Occasionally varying the pattern, they had their meetings elsewhere. Now and then they would reserve a table at a well-known inn or tavern for a purely social evening without the usual aftermath of *Punch* business.

The Bedford Hotel at 31 Bedford Street, Strand, was one of their favourite haunts. Kept by one Mrs. Warner, a Lemon family connexion, it stood on the site of a Renaissance tavern in which Shakespeare and his fellow wits were reputed to have lounged.[1] Mrs. Warner traded on this tradition by naming her private parlour the Shakespeare Room. Only a stone's throw from Covent Garden Market, the Bedford overlooked one of the busiest scenes in London. From six o'clock in the morning till noon the area was given over to costermongers, porters, flower girls, and buyers; carts and donkey barrows; mountains of fruit, vegetables, and flowers. To the very entrance of Covent Garden Theatre the cobblestones were permanently slimed and stained by trampled leaves.[2] Though business halted completely at noon, the moist air still held the mingled scent of onions and violets, cabbages and apples, turnips and oranges. Nor was the blend noticeable only in the market. It pervaded the whole area: it hung over Covent Garden Theatre, penetrated to the Garrick Club, and wafted in through the open windows of the Bedford, where it combined with the savoury smells of fish, poultry, and roast beef. As Mark and his friends took their places in the dining-room they could never trust their noses to identify the dishes on the menu, so persistent were the market odours. But the

[1] Layard, *Brooks*, p. 72.
[2] This description of the nineteenth-century Covent Garden Market is based on *Mayhew's London* ('Of Covent Garden Market').

Bedford's relaxed atmosphere and excellent cuisine more than offset this disadvantage.

Other places also catered for the astonishing appetites of the *Punch* staff. Often, on sheer impulse, the Table might decide to dine somewhere as a group, then seek entertainment afterwards. Thackeray once confided to his diary how they had gone to 'take port wine in the City' and dine on the 'admirable beefsteaks . . . served in a back parlour of a dirty little inn opposite the Excise Office'. Here the guests 'in various boxes were roaring with jokes and fun'. Overhead were piles of empty bottles. Repairing next to the wine cellars, Thackeray and his companions saw more bottles, five and six thousand in a bin. From here they went for punch at Tom's, 'a stifling and filthy place of resort', and gave themselves 'dandyfied West End airs . . ., Snobs all'. Not yet ready to go home, they watched the horse riders at Drury Lane and thrilled to the 'grace and perfection' of Mademoiselle Caroline's 'equitation'.[3]

Sometimes the inimitable Alexis Soyer would feast the group. 'It was a great deal too good,' declared Thackeray after one of these dinners, 'and wd have been better for the good things Mr. Soyer supplied in his anxiety to please Punch.'[4] Excellent meals could also be expected at the Star and Garter in Richmond. It was here that Henry Silver ate his first dinner with the Table. 'Covers drawn at six sharp—Morning Toggery', read Mark's brief note of invitation. 'We dined in a big room at the back of the hotel', Silver recorded. 'I had a good view of the river, which was really then worth looking at: for the Silver Thames was brightly shining beneath the golden sunset, and there were then no boat sheds or big chimneys to uglify the landscape.'

In the summer, when London became oppressive and activity at the *Punch* office slowed to a crawl, Mark and the proprietors planned river excursions to revive jaded spirits. Wives and lady friends sometimes accompanied the group. 'Champagne began the instant we got on board,' Thackeray noted in his diary after one of these expeditions, 'and the ladies sang songs one against the other.' From Mrs. Chambers, a Scotswoman, came 'especially sweet and simple ditties'. Mrs. à Beckett, trying 'to ecraser' her, rendered 'Charlie, Charlie' with the 'most approved shrieks and roulades', only to hear Thackeray remark impishly, 'What a sweet voice Mrs. Chambers has got!'

[3] B.M. MS., Thackeray Papers. 732. E. 46898.
[4] Ibid., 732. E. 46899.

For his part of the entertainment Jerrold 'chirped and laughed and made laugh with all his might' and Evans had his hat knocked off. After the water party, according to Thackeray, 'many instances of Bacchic fury occurred'. Already hilarious on champagne, some of the men made tavern stops on their way home. Such recklessness brought its aftermath of misery. Bradbury, 'rolling about on the box of the fly, helplessly bespattering himself"; Evans at his side, 'but only cheerfully drunk'; and Leigh, 'utterly stupid and speechless for some hours past'—it was an inglorious end to a day of merry-making.[5] Such spectacles were not uncommon, however, in an age when journalists and authors, whether assembled for business or pleasure, could not function without a few glasses. For the least robust, like Jerrold, it was too much, as is shown by the accounts of his frequent falls down the *Punch* office stairs. He even went so far as to carry identification and instructions for seeing him home, should he wander helplessly after a Bacchanalian escapade.[6]

Suggestions for staff outings were never lacking, especially after a few drinks. One night Mark made some punch of such potency that Tom Taylor got 'jolly thereon and talked like a dozen'. In his exuberance he proposed that they all go to the Derby in a hearse—or, even better, a van with a tombstone. Such a stunt should give *Punch* capital advertising, he thought.[7] No one took him seriously, of course.

One outing which did come off, however, brought Mark and his companions to the brink of disaster. Having decided on an excursion into the country, they set out one perfect summer day for Tunbridge Wells. In a four-horse coach, enticingly named 'The Exquisite', they raced along: Mark on the box, Tenniel, Brooks, du Maurier, and Silver behind him. There was some slight cause for uneasiness, though, because the driver bore down on all vehicles that would not clear his path, grazing them or even knocking against them. But the sun shone bright, the coach rolled smoothly, and before many hours they were within four miles of their destination. Then, without warning, the leader plunged and fell, 'dead as Julius Caesar'. Over him, before the driver could stop the coach, went the wheeler. 'Passengers all down!' cried the terrified coachman. In the mad scramble Fred Evans ('Pater's' son) landed on Brooks's head. Every-one was grateful that the accident had not happened as the coach was racing downhill or that the horse had not lived to kick after its fall.

[5] Ibid., 732. E. 46898.   [6] Spielmann, *History of Punch*, p. 75.   [7] Silver.

After considerable delay, the coach, drawn by a team of three, pulled ignominiously into Tunbridge Wells for dinner at the Sussex Hotel. Four of the party took the train back to London, but Mark, Brooks, and the others spent the night at the Sussex. They slept soundly, according to Brooks, whose final verdict was 'a very pleasant out, into the lovely country'.[8]

Of all the outside activities with his staff, none so delighted Mark as the theatrical ventures. The first of these, after the early *Punch* had been steered to the proprietorship of Bradbury and Evans, was a pantomime commissioned by the manager of Covent Garden for the 1842 Christmas entertainment. By now the journal was so generally recognized for its humour that its writers were expected to concoct a piece of unsurpassed wit. Written by Mark, with staff assistance, *Punch's Pantomime, or Harlequin King John* had for its climax the signing of the Magna Charta. But this historical event was lost in the welter of ludicrous by-play. Throughout the performance, tumbling and acrobatics titillated the spectators to raucous laughter and noisy stamping. The review in the *Athenaeum* (31 December 1842) damned the piece as 'the stupidest pantomime' and considered 'too tedious' any attempt 'to recount the absurdities that assail the risible faculties so unsuccessfully'. Such negative reaction was not unexpected, for Macready, asked to read the piece several months before its performance, had stated bluntly that he 'did not fancy it'.[9] When he saw the reviews and learned that W. H. Payne, then the chief pantomimist at Covent Garden, had caricatured his acting in the role of King John, he must have thought even less of it. But adverse comment notwithstanding, the *Punch* men had demonstrated their ability to work together and had the satisfaction of having brought down the house.

A more successful theatrical venture came twenty-five years later, 29 July 1867, when the staff, reinforced by a few professionals, gave a benefit performance at the Theatre Royal, Manchester, for the widow and children of C. H. Bennett. (Though with *Punch* only two years, Bennett had been one of Mark's best draughtsmen, having made a niche for himself with his Parliamentary drawings.) The evening opened with Burnand's *Cox and Box; or, The Long-Lost Brothers*, a lyrical version of John Maddison Morton's farce, with original music by Arthur Sullivan. After an address by Shirley Brooks came *A Sheep in Wolf's Clothing*, a one-act domestic drama

[8] B.D., 7 July 1869.   [9] Macready, *Diaries*, 3 Aug. 1842.

ML—G

which Tom Taylor had adapted from Madame de Giradi's *Une femme qui déteste son mari*. Shifting the action from the Reign of Terror to the Jacobite atrocities of 1685 and skilfully introducing incidents from English history, Taylor had successfully anglicized his adaptation. Mark impersonated Colonel Percy Kirke, whose Lambs had been notorious for terrorizing the country by tracking down Monmouth's men for torture and execution. John Tenniel, as Colonel Lord Churchill of the Life Guards, was the hit of the evening, the entire audience rising as he entered. But Taylor, though author of the play, made little impression in the leading part as Master Jasper Carew, whose wife Anne (Kate Terry) eluded a searching party of Jacobites. The youthful Ellen Terry was cast as Anne's servant. *Les deux aveugles*, a bouffonnerie musical by J. Offenbach, and *A Family Failing*, a one-act farce by John Oxenford, concluded the evening's entertainment, with Mark, Taylor, and Ellen Terry in the principal roles.

None of the staff diversions brought more whole-hearted response than the observance of members' birthdays. Brooks, who carefully recorded these dates, once threatened to publish them in the *Punch Almanac*. So great was his enjoyment of these occasions that he wondered why the Table could not have daily birthday parties. 'If, as the Apostle Paul says, "I die daily",' he argued, 'must it not follow that one is born daily?'

A memorable celebration honoured Horace Mayhew in 1868. Invitations went out to the staff: 'The pleasure of your Company is most earnestly requested on Saturday, July 11th, at the Albion Tavern, Aldersgate Street, to meet Horace Mayhew, and wish him joy on his 50th birthday. Dinner at 6 o'clock sharp. Ponny pays.' At opposite ends of the table, facing each other over a centrepiece of Japanese lilies, sat Mark (as toast-master) and the honoured guest. With a quiver in his voice Mark proposed 'Ponny's' health: 'I'm your oldest friend at the Table—we've grown old together in years and iniquity—that is, I've done the years and you the iniquities. You are, next to me, the oldest worker on *Punch*, and so we accept your invitation.' The reference to Horace Mayhew's iniquity evoked hearty guffawing, for his amatory exploits had become a legend. 'All my female models', du Maurier once jokingly reported, 'exclaim when they see Ponny, "C'est mon père." '[10]

Replying to Mark's toast, 'Ponny' thanked the staff for the 'large

[10] Silver.

compliment' paid him by coming to drink his 'poor health'. Then du Maurier sang a song written especially for the guest of honour, Keene warbled 'The Three Ravens', and Brooks did humorous sketches of the Table, not omitting himself: 'Here's to the writer of horrible books, / I hardly need mention his name, Shirley Brooks.' He climaxed the evening by toasting Mark as 'one who appreciates a good suggestion and does not snub his writers'.[11]

Mark was always inventing some prank to amuse the *Punch* men. On one occasion, as much in earnest as in jest, he suggested that 'Pater' Evans should give them a children's party, all to come dressed in jackets.[12] Whether anything ever came of it is not known. But there is a story that the staff once levelled the score with Mark for all his fooling. For this they chose a time when he was at the sea- side for a few days' rest. Copies of *Punch* were to be sent him there. All too soon his freedom from editorial worries ended; for, as he read the number printed in his absence, he grew pale and began to tremble. A vulgar cartoon had been substituted for the Large Cut; one paragraph was printed upside down; libellous material stared at him from every page. 'This comes of my being away!' groaned Mark as he rushed to catch the next train to London. Having hastily bought up all available copies of the offending issue, he took the bundle with him into the railway carriage. Only after he was seated did he find time to look at another copy. All was as it should be: his own paper had been made up especially for his benefit. Then he realized that he had been 'sold'. (Another version has it that just before he boarded the train a telegram informed him that it was all a joke.)[13] This prank may have suggested to Thackeray the episode in *Henry Esmond* (Bk. III, Ch. III) in which Henry, assisted by Richard Steele, publishes a dummy *Spectator* to pique the coquettish Miss Beatrix.

The *Punch* merrymakers once joined in a great national celebra- tion, the reception of Princess Alexandra of Denmark on her arrival in London, 7 March 1863. As the procession of open carriages bearing her party moved into Fleet Street after a brief ceremony in St. Paul's Churchyard, the bells of St. Bride's and St. Dunstan's began to peal joyously. In his diary Silver captured the excitement of the spectacle. 'What a sea of waving handkerchiefs,' he reminisced a few days later. 'They seemed almost to lift the carriage from its wheels and some of the handkerchiefs must have flapped in her

[11] Ibid.   [12] Ibid.   [13] Spielmann, *History of Punch*, p. 266.

[Alexandra's] face. Wondrous to see the mass that filled all Fleet Street jammed against the houses, when divided by the troopers, coming six abreast at last, and how the tide came flap together again when the wedge had passed.'

At No. 85 Fleet Street, the headquarters of *Punch* at the time, rows of seats ran along the entire front to accommodate the staff, their families, and special guests. Occupying the place of honour in the front row, a small statue of Mr. Punch bowed greetings. In keeping with the occasion, he bore a crown of bridal roses and carried the white ribbon of the Order of the Wedding Ring—'somewhat of a cross between a beadle and a ballet girl', observed Silver. The work of the German sculptor Adolph Fleischmann, the figure had the colouring and features of Doyle's cover design and was so ingeniously constructed with springs that its head, eyes, arms, and legs could be put in motion by pulling a string. 'Funny to see that fat old Alderman and the stiff military swells all gradually burst into a broad grin as they passed,' Silver recalled. 'And touched by her mother's elbow, how smilingly the Princess herself looked up at *Punch* and what a good view of her the Punchites obtained.' Mark and his colleagues agreed that Alexandra's beauty was 'not merely in her features', but in her 'good and amiable' appearance and her desire to please, 'as if she had brains and used them'. She charmed the crowds with 'the glimpse of that fair face, bowing so incessantly that nearly every one believed himself personally bowed to'.[14]

In a special *Punch* article (21 March) Silver called Alexandra's beauty such as no photographer could capture. Better even than features or complexion were 'the loveliness and cleverness and goodness in her face'. At this point Silver became lyrical: 'Well may the young Prince be proud of his fair Bride, and well may his future subjects feel a pride in his heart's choice!' There was also special commendation for the national happiness and goodwill engendered by this contact between the sovereigns and their people:

Such days serve to unite a nation with its rulers, and do more for Law and Order than many Acts of Parliament are able to effect. Affection is the bond whereon loyalty is based, and if a people is to love its rulers it must be brought in contact with them, and not be held aloof. It is quite impossible, men tell you, to please everybody: but that the Princess in her

[14] Silver.

prettiness pleased every one she bowed to (and to whom did she bow not?) Mr. Punch feels quite as certain as he is that she pleased him.

* * *

Some two years later, in November 1865, Mr. Punch saw a change in his firm: Bradbury and Evans retired as proprietors and were succeeded by their sons: and in 1866 the Agnews, art dealers, joined the partnership. At a special dinner honouring the retiring heads, Mark feelingly proposed the health of his old friends, who had 'weathered so many storms and brought their ship into harbour successfully at last'. In reply Bradbury spoke of the 'brotherly affection' between Mark and his proprietors. Next to take the floor, 'Pater' Evans recalled how he and Bradbury had begun by 'making mistakes—went on making mistakes—and ended making mistakes'. Despite their shortcomings, however, the 'acorn of their business' was now 'a goodly oak'. He hoped the new firm would profit by the errors of the old. Then Bradbury proposed the health of Mark, who thanked his men with tears in his eyes. Some lusty singing followed, Mark rendering 'Cupid's Garden' and Silver 'Beautiful Kitty'. 'So we pass a jolly evening and bear in mind Pater's remark that sociability is the seat of the success of *Punch*,' wrote Silver in his diary that night.

A notable occasion was *Punch*'s Silver Wedding (27 June 1866), on the completion of its fiftieth volume. 'It would please dear old Mark, I am certain, if we, the writers and artists, gave him some trifle (pin, ring, or something) on the Silver Wedding', Brooks had written in advance to each of his colleagues. 'Let us subscribe a pound apiece. If you like, I will see to the very small trouble.'[15] The celebration took the form of a day's excursion to Burnham Beeches. Setting out in the morning, the men stopped *en route* at Stoke Poges and visited Gray's churchyard. At Burnham Beeches they had a picnic lunch of lamb, lobster, veal and ham pie, salad, and champagne—all laid out on a cloth spread on the ground. After they had eaten, Brooks handed over the gift from the staff, a gold watch and chain with eleven links, one for each member of the *Punch* Table. Sitting at the head of the cloth, flanked on the right by 'Pater' and on the left by Brooks, Mark covered his eyes and remained speechless for a few moments. 'It needeth not this, my friends, to assure me of your esteem for me,' he said at last in a trembling voice. 'But I

[15] P.O. MS., Brooks to Leigh, 7 Sept. 1866.

shall ever wear it next to my heart.' Struggling to check his emotions, he commended his colleagues. 'You have lightened my labour by your readiness at all times to help me all you can,' he assured them. 'The Punch Brotherhood has been one of the most extraordinary literary brotherhoods the world has ever seen. We have never had a serious dispute. . . . Our brotherhood shows that, irritable as authors may be called, they can yet work together, if joined by real friendship and working for a good end.' Breaking down at this point, Mark continued apologetically: 'Forgive my mother's weakness—I feel more than I can say. I know I have done my duty—but I did not expect this kind acknowledgement from you.' He went on to tell his staff that he had been made a hundred guineas richer that morning, the gift of his old proprietors. As much as the money he valued the letter accompanying the cheque. 'This is Punch's Silver Wedding,' he concluded. 'I cannot hope to live to see the Golden one. But Punch must always prosper if confidence prevails.'[16]

Another presentation followed these remarks: a neatly bound volume containing all the replies to the request for contributions to the fund for Mark's gift. Heading the volume was an introductory note by Brooks:

My dear Mark, It will, perhaps, give entire completeness to our little testimonial presented to you to-day, if I offer you, with the assent of the writers, the notes in which they signify their gladness to join in this demonstration of regard. Accept, these, this *fasciculus* of 'Verdicts' in your favour. You will not, I know, value them the less that they have been gathered by your old and affectionate Friend, Shirley Brooks.

The shortest of the replies was Keene's: 'All right.' Tenniel offered '2 lbs if necessary' and called the gesture 'a great and good thought!' Du Maurier hoped that whatever form the 'trifle' might take, Mark would 'wear it, or drink it, or smoke through it for many years to come, while exercising his mild though benignly despotic sway over his very devoted and stick-to-him-through-thick-&-thin kind of a sort of crew—no—ship's company'. This was accompanied by a skilfully executed sketch 'Man at the Wheel (Mark)' with the legend 'Mind how you speak to the Man at the Wheel'. 'Ponny's' note referred to Mark as 'my dear Guide, Philosopher, and Friend'; and Taylor's emphatic 'With all my heart' was interlined and corrected

[16] Silver.

much like his usual copy for *Punch*. 'The Professor' and Silver simply expressed their happiness to contribute.[17]

After lunch Burnand and Tenniel had a mock sparring match, while Keene and 'Professor' Leigh hunted for mushrooms. Others went rowing and got drenched in a thundershower. So the time passed until dinner, served at Skindles in Maidenhead. At the table Bradbury proposed Mark's health and presented him with a 'noble' silver cup. Again Mark buried his face in his hands while his colleagues rose and gave him rousing musical honours. Recovering, he spoke of the key to the success of *Punch*: the mutual understanding and confidence of all associated with it. Then he drank to the two men who had 'made *Punch* what it is—who had confidence in it and its editor from the first'. Once more Bradbury and Evans declared that their best friends had always been Punchites. Thomas Agnew, the new-comer to the firm, next proposed the contributors. 'Professor' Leigh, expected as senior member to respond, began to wander hopelessly, leaving Brooks to round off the remarks. 'We are, there's no denying it, a remarkable lot,' he boasted. 'There's no mock modesty in me, or real modesty either. But look at us. All come from different spheres of society and bring our experiences thence to be fused in *Punch* fire.' And he continued with clever thumbnail sketches of the whole Table. After this all drank his health and Mark testified warmly to his worth. A few more songs, and all returned to London on the eleven-o'clock train. 'A most pleasurable and memorable day', commented Silver.

Reflecting on the affection and esteem of his staff, Mark could congratulate himself on having brought together one of the most closely knit coteries in the history of journalism. Though often poles apart in their fundamental convictions, sensibilities, and tastes, they were a cohesive brotherhood, solidly behind their paper and their editor. 'The key to the success of *Punch* is sociability,' 'Pater' Evans had declared. Mark agreed.

[17] This bound volume of letters is among the holdings of Miss Winifred A. Myers (Autographs) Ltd., 80 New Bond Street, London. I am indebted to her for permission to quote.

7

FRIENDS AND ENEMIES

THOUGH Mark thought of his colleagues as his best friends, his intimates also included a few men not connected with *Punch*. Because of his interests in politics and the theatre, he had occasional contacts with prominent persons outside his immediate sphere. Of these Herbert Ingram was typical.

Two years younger than Mark, Ingram had grown up in Boston, had been educated at the free school there, and at fourteen had been apprenticed to a printer in the market place. In this Lincolnshire river town the two boys approached manhood together. From 1832 to 1834, a few years before Mark found employment in John Verey's brewery, Ingram worked in London as a journeyman printer. He went next to Nottingham, where, in partnership with his brother-in-law, he set up business as printer, bookseller, and newsagent. From a Manchester chemist he bought the secret formula for an aperient pill, to whose powers legend attributed the longevity of Old Parr—152 years. Set on promoting the patent medicine, beguilingly named Parr's Life Pill, Ingram moved back to London. Here his next venture brought him into direct contact with Mark.

Having noticed in Nottingham how engravings greatly increased the demand for a paper, he decided to found an illustrated weekly combining art and news. Its name, the *Illustrated London News*, grew out of his recollection that his Nottingham customers had always called for 'London news' whenever word of important developments in the metropolis reached the provinces. With Mark as his chief adviser, he issued the first number on 14 May 1842, nearly ten months after the birth of *Punch*. A week later he announced his editorial policies. 'We shall be less deeply political than earnestly domestic', he promised. The concern of his paper would be 'with the English poor; with the comforts, the enjoyments, the affections, and the liberties, that form the link of that beautiful chain which should be fashioned at one end of the cottage, at the other of the palace. . . .' Strongly underlining a spirit of liberalism, doubtless with Mark's endorsement, Ingram announced that 'three essential elements of discussion with us will be the poor laws, the factory laws, and the working of the mining system in those districts of our soil which nature has covered with her treasures, and cruelty disfigured with its crime.'

Profits from advertising and a growing circulation soon ensured the success of the paper. And Mark, though still occupied with the early struggles of *Punch*, found time to give Ingram editorial assistance, getting him first of all to drop the promotion of Parr's Life Pill as a safeguard to his professional dignity and the welfare of his publication. For his own part, however, Mark saw in the legend of Old Parr a subject of interest to theatre-goers, and wove it into a play for the Haymarket (9 October 1853). Under the title *Old Parr*, this two-act drama credits the legendary hero with foiling an attempted swindle despite his growing senility. The *Illustrated London News* hailed the production as 'most eminently and deservedly successful'. But *The Times* condemned it as 'deficient in action' and lacking in 'dramatic interest'. (Its editor being under no obligation to Mark, the reviewer could be candid.)

In 1842 Mark launched the first Christmas supplement to the *Illustrated London News*, a special holiday feature he had charge of annually thereafter during Ingram's lifetime. His *Punch* colleagues were frequent contributors. For each number he was paid a hundred pounds. Further earnings came from his poems and Christmas stories in these supplements.

In 1856, during a hotly contested Parliamentary election, Mark and his staff actively supported Ingram as the Liberal candidate for Boston. At first the prospects of Ingram's winning a seat in the House of Commons looked dim: a split in his own party greatly jeopardized his chances against his Conservative opponent. No time was to be lost, therefore, in educating the public to the advantages of a Liberal victory. With Mark acting as his personal secretary, Ingram prepared statements for the county papers. To his prospective constituents he gave assurances that he would support civil and religious liberty and that he stood for 'rational progress and social, moral, and political advancement of the people'. He advocated popular education, considering it 'not only cheaper, but more just and merciful, to spend the public money upon schools . . . than upon prisons and penitentiaries'. (Here he echoed a conviction that Mark had aired repeatedly at the *Punch* dinners.) Underscoring the Victorian desire for peace, he declared himself an enemy of war, especially those conflicts 'waged by despots against the liberties and independence of other nations'. Finally, he promised unequivocally to 'oppose any attempt to interfere with the inherent privileges of Englishmen;—the right of local self-government;—a right which is the very foundation of our liberties'.[1]

On the day that Ingram's statement reached the voters an editorial expressed suspicion of lofty idealism and insisted on practical measures. 'Let us send a man of business to Parliament to watch over the business of the country', it urged. 'We must have a representative who is at once the product and the embodiment of the progressive spirit of his age . . . a man who will really represent our business energy and act upon our business maxims.'[2]

It remained for Mark to convince the Bostonians that their Liberal candidate could indeed be practical. For this he, Jerrold, and Brooks, with several other *Punch* men, accompanied Ingram to Boston in early March for some last-minute campaigning. Called on to address a political rally of Liberal supporters at the Lord Nelson Inn, Mark told his listeners, amid cheers, that he was no stranger among them, though the town itself had undergone great changes since his time. The few flickering oil lamps had given way to brilliant street lighting by the new gas company, and the pump in the Square, once the sole source of water, had been replaced by an extensive system of pipes. These improvements, he pointed out, were 'mainly owing to the energy and liberality of Mr. Ingram', who had urged the necessary legislation. At this there was a burst of applause. Next Mark outlined the national prominence won by Ingram through his paper. 'They in London know how largely [his] support has influenced many national undertakings,' he declared, 'and I have come to the country to see how such a man would be received by his old friends at home.' Waxing eloquent, he asked his listeners to remember how their candidate, the printer's boy, had gone to seek his fortune. Having attained it by 'industry, honour, and integrity', he now wished to represent his townsmen in Parliament. Would they not elect him as an example to their sons? 'Tom, go to work,' a father could then demand with pride; 'Mr. Ingram was a boy like you. He made his way in this world by strict honour

[1] The Boston and Louth *Guardian*, 27 Feb. 1856.   [2] Ibid.

and industry, and we sent him to Parliament, to show how much we admired and respected him.' After an interruption of spontaneous cheers Mark concluded with a strong endorsement of Ingram 'as an honest, earnest, and energetic man', who, if elected, would serve Boston well and 'never look at any other interest than that of his constituents and his country'.[3]

Whether Ingram, when he took the floor, could match such eloquence appears doubtful: a disturbing mannerism was said to weaken his performance. One of his listeners went so far as to ask Mark to beg Ingram not to scratch his seat so much as he talked.[4] Despite this distraction, however, the election soon promised to go well for the Liberal candidate. 'The townsmen and agriculturists receive their old school-fellow with the warmth of friendship', reported an editorial several days after Mark's speech. 'It is beyond all doubt that he is the man of their choice, their free, generous, decided choice. Every one who has watched the progress of the canvass now confesses that the full tide of popularity flows in favour of Mr. Ingram, and that on its buoyant waters he will be carried into the political haven of the House of Commons.'[5]

This forecast proved accurate. On 7 March the voters gave Ingram an overwhelming victory. Immediately after the announcement of his success, the bells of St. Botolph began to peal. But Ingram had disappeared. An hour later he was found at the home of his aged mother, the widow who had been his sole support during his boyhood and to whom he had hastened now with the good news.

At the victory celebration Mark again addressed the Bostonians, answering the toast to the ladies. 'Your honourable member told you a short time since . . . that one of the proudest moments of his life was that which decided his election as your representative', he began. 'What must be my feelings when I find myself suddenly elected the representative of the ladies?' It is interesting that Mark in his reply should use the term 'House of Ladies', but with an intent more bland than in his one-act burletta by that name (1845), which ridiculed the idea of women in politics. Any such emphasis he now tactfully suppressed. 'I am not only a member, but also the Speaker of the House of Ladies,' he announced. And he hastened to explain: 'The proceedings of the House of Commons, gentlemen, affect your business generally, but the proceedings of the House of Ladies affect

[3] Ibid., 5 Mar. 1856.   [4] Silver.
[5] The Boston and Louth *Guardian*, 27 Feb. 1856.

not only your business, but your bosoms.' Loud laughter greeted this remark. Further elaboration followed: 'In the House of Commons you take into consideration the ways and means—in the House of Ladies, I think, gentlemen, you know pretty well the same thing is done.' After more laughter Mark concluded with a tribute to the ladies, to whom the 'English nation is indebted for having produced such a fine collection of voters as I now have the honour to thank for the kindness with which they have listened to my remarks.' Vigorously applauded as he returned to his seat, Mark joined in the glee 'Here's Health to All Good Lasses'.

Not without repercussions were Ingram's campaigners allowed to enjoy their triumph. Almost immediately, with all the scurrility characterizing the worst in nineteenth-century journalism, several papers accused the *Punch* men of making a cheap bid for publicity by staging political rallies. Jerrold, seriously ill after the election, complained in a letter to John Forster that 'Boston made it no better', for he had since been 'nicely abused' by the papers.[6] Coming to the defence of Ingram's promoters, the Boston and Louth *Guardian* (12 March) called the 'onslaught as unworthy as it is unjust'. Jerrold, Brooks, and Lemon could, of course, 'despise the calumnious charge', their names being 'household words' from the 'hours of pure enjoyment they had given'. Still, why should members of an 'honourable profession treat one another with special unfairness'? On another page an editorial struck a more positive note. Referring to the 'war of principles' that had dignified the election as something 'to be proud of', it concluded optimistically, 'We have inaugurated a new era in political life.'

That Ingram's constituents had no cause to regret their choice was shown by his re-election in 1859. Stories of his Parliamentary competence occasionally found their way to the *Punch* dinners, as also did a report that he had gone into the wrong lobby to vote for the repeal of the Paper Duty. Instead of checking at the desk, he had sneaked past, only to find himself with the opposition. 'Ingram looks more like a detective than a Parliamentarian', joked Mark.[7]

In 1857 Ingram bought the *London Journal*, an illustrated weekly featuring tales and romances, and turned the editorial work over to Mark, who tried to improve the quality of the paper by reissuing the Waverley novels in its pages.[8] In spite of the boast (after the con-

[6] V. and A. MS., Jerrold to Forster, 13 Mar. 1856.
[7] Silver.   [8] Ibid.

clusion of *Kenilworth* in 1858) that 'we have made a literary experiment . . . crowned with the most signal success', the circulation declined so alarmingly that the serialization of *Ivanhoe* had to be stopped abruptly after seven months. The promise that it would be 'continued in our next' was never fulfilled. To avert further blunders, Mark gave up the editorship. For years thereafter, whenever his colleagues wanted to embarrass him, they would refer to his debacle with the *London Journal*.

In 1860 Mark, along with the entire nation, mourned the death of Ingram, who, with his son, had gone to America to gather illustrations covering the Prince of Wales's tour. Father and son were both drowned on 8 September when their excursion vessel, boarded at Chicago, collided with another ship on Lake Michigan. Though Mark continued to send poems and stories to the *Illustrated London News* thereafter, he no longer edited the Christmas supplements. According to Silver, the management 'became jealous of his influence when Ingram died, and so have declined his service—and he's too proud to resent it'.

Another of Mark's intimates, Joseph Paxton, was such a favourite of the Table that he was one of the few privileged outsiders invited to the Wednesday-night dinners. The superintendent of the Duke of Devonshire's gardens at Chatsworth, he reciprocated by occasionally bringing the *Punch* men to the ducal estate for an afternoon of relaxation. Because he had a controlling interest in most of the railways, he usually provided transport by means of a special carriage of the Great Northern.[9]

His rise had been phenomenal. Once earning only eighteen shillings a week, he had attracted the attention of the Duke of Devonshire while working on the Chiswick gardens, and had ultimately been appointed to the important post at Chatsworth. Over the years he had built up his capital through shrewd investments and lucky speculations. On 10 April 1848, for example, after witnessing on Kennington Common the dispersal of the defeated Chartists, he had gone to his broker and bought stocks. The transaction had brought him a profit of five hundred pounds.[10]

After his election to Parliament in 1854 as the Liberal Member for Coventry, he became increasingly interested in *Punch* as a means of serving the public and improving popular taste. He heartily approved its shift towards respectability and urged Mark to keep

[9] Ibid.   [10] Ibid.

raising the level of its readers. 'Write over their heads a bit,' he advised during one of the Wednesday-night discussions; 'the circulation keeps up—so keep up the tone.'[11]

Mark welcomed Paxton's suggestions and frank criticism. In turn he may have offered useful advice to his friend. Because Bradbury and Evans had an interest in the *Gardener's Chronicle*, of which Paxton was one of the founders, Mark was the logical person to consult about the make-up of that paper. Support also came from the *Punch* staff in 1850, when Paxton decided at the last moment to submit a design for the Great Exhibition building. After 245 plans by others had proved unsatisfactory, he set to work in his garden office and drew his sketch on a sheet of note-paper. It was an adaptation of the three-hundred-foot-long conservatory (entirely of glass and steel) at Chatsworth. 'But surely you're too late', protested one of his friends on being shown the drawing. (After rejecting all the plans sent in, the committee had engaged an architect to proceed with a design of its own.) 'I don't mind that', replied Paxton; 'they must have this. Look at the economy of it, and consider how short a time will be required to erect the building.'[12]

His drawing carefully folded in his pocket-book, he hurried to London. Here he met Mark and explained the purpose of his trip. 'But you're too late,' he was told again; 'the architect's plans have already been decided upon.' With a confident 'I shall take my chance', Paxton left to call on the committee. Prince Albert gave him a warm reception and enthusiastically approved the design. Urged to develop it further, Paxton added the final details and published an engraving of it in the *Illustrated London News*—probably at Mark's suggestion. His plan won the approval of the Royal Commissioners, who paid and dismissed the architect previously negotiated with.[13]

As the structure took form, for want of a better name it was usually referred to as the Great Exhibition Building in Hyde Park. Then a *Punch* man made his contribution. Viewing the vast canopy of glass, Douglas Jerrold christened it 'The Crystal Palace'. And by this name it was henceforth known.[14]

Of all his friends, Benjamin Webster was perhaps the one from whom Mark benefited most materially. Lessee of the Haymarket from 1837 to 1853 and of the Adelphi from the middle of the century,

[11] Ibid.   [12] Hodder, *Memories of My Time*, pp. 130–1.
[13] Beale, *The Light of Other Days*, I, pp. 192–3.
[14] Mackay, *Forty Years' Recollections*, II, p. 293.

he was able to encourage and advise an aspiring playwright. An actor himself (on occasion in Mark's own plays, as noted earlier), Webster could readily suggest revisions in Mark's pieces, some of which he produced at the Haymarket. The best of these included a comedy adapted from the French, *Grandfather Whitehead* (31 August 1842—constructed around an indulgent and misguided old man as the central character); and two dramas, *Old Parr* (9 October 1843—inspired, as already suggested, by Ingram's patent medicine) and *The Sempstress* (25 May 1844—based on the theme used so successfully by Thomas Hood in 'The Song of the Shirt'). When Webster took over the Adelphi, Mark's pieces appeared there also. The most popular of these were *The School for Tigers* (28 October 1850—a farce set in the back of a cigar shop), *Sea and Land* (17 May 1852—a three-act drama portraying social oppression), and *Slave Life* (29 November 1852—an adaptation of *Uncle Tom's Cabin* in collaboration with Tom Taylor).

Not always, however, could Mark persuade Webster to produce his plays. 'Will you give 20 or 25£ on account?' he pleaded in one of his letters. 'As for my disturbances at home I am very hard up. I wish you could produce some of my pieces and relieve me from the load of obligations I feel to be under to you.'[15] Another time he inquired about a manuscript submitted so long ago as to be quite forgotten. 'I am only reminded that on this day *nine years* ago I gave you a drama called The King's Rogues', he wrote. 'The family in anticipation of the coming glories offered up a Goose to Minerva and a similar burnt offering is now sending up its savour from the kitchen. I am vain enough to think that there is some English bone and muscle about those said rogues if you would undertake them—always provided that you see benefit to your treasury. If you *do* really doubt the result let me have the MS.—I may not think yr. opinion a correct one but I shall be certain that it is an honest and friendly one.'[16] (The piece, never staged, was finally adapted as a prose tale.) When another play, *Twice an Emperor*, was rejected, Mark wrote, 'I am heart-broken. . . . I thought I had written a first rate "starring" piece for you.' He suggested some revisions, but these did not change Webster's decision.

Such disappointments were interspersed, though, with happier results, as when Mark's Christmas entertainment *Mother Shipton's*

[15] U. of T. MS., Lemon to Webster, 8 Mar. 1851.
[16] Pa.H.S. MS., Lemon to Webster, 30 Sept. 1855.

Wages; or, Harlequin's Knight of Love scored a triumph at the Adelphi in 1856. Constructed on the theme of devoted love that can ensure a man's constancy against numerous pitfalls, it appealed to its Victorian audience. There were times during rehearsals, however, when Mark experienced anxious moments because Miss Wyndham, cast in the leading part, felt that she was not appreciated. In his habitual role of mediator Mark tried to mend matters. 'If you could say a civil word,' he suggested in a note to Webster, 'I don't think it would be thrown away as she is very uneasy under the impression that you dislike her.'[17] Following the performance he wrote again, to acknowledge the receipt of fifty pounds, his share of the proceeds: 'I am glad you are satisfied with what I did as it was for *you* that I did it.'[18]

As one of Webster's special friends he had a key to the Adelphi office and could often be found there, reminiscing about the past glories of the theatre. In return he always watched for an opportunity to serve his friend. Such was his championing of Madame Celeste, the French pantomime artist who, after triumphant appearances in America and important engagements in England, starred with Webster in *Louison* (1843) and later became with him the joint lessee of the Adelphi. They were soon acclaimed one of the brilliant teams of the day. In 1855, however, Madame Celeste was subjected to some harsh criticism by the Press. 'I am so disgusted with the cowardly attack on Madame', Mark told Webster, 'that I want to give a short article upon her merits as an actress and her remarkable energy of character in the Illus. London News.' His remarks were to be accompanied by a good engraving of her. From Webster he requested specific information: 'the number of times she has been in America, the probable number of miles she has travelled, her residence with the Indians'. He would also publicize her unusual role as Harlequin in his forthcoming Christmas entertainment: *Jack and the Bean-Stalk; or, Harlequin and Mother Goose at Home Again.*[19]

The article appeared on 23 February 1856, complete with an attractive miniature of Madame Celeste. After reviewing her triumphs in America, where her popularity had 'exceeded anything that in England we can form any idea of' (she had earned forty thousand pounds in three years), Mark assessed her achievements at

[17] U. of T. MS., Lemon to Webster, n.d.
[18] Harvard MS., Lemon to Webster, 21 Jan. 1857.
[19] Haverford MS., Lemon to Webster, n.d.

home, where she had 'assumed her just position on the theatrical boards, notwithstanding all rivalry from older and more experienced performers'. Over everything she played 'her simple and fascinating manners' cast a charm. Her role as Harlequin deserved special mention. 'Yes, *Harlequin*!' Mark emphasized. 'She is the first actress that ever impersonated that motley gentleman upon the English stage.' A performance 'more delicate or graceful' could not be conceived, he declared. Taking a sly dig at Madame Celeste's detractors, he referred to her 'generous motives (by some misunderstood)' and averred 'that one more amiable, kind, considerate, and generous, does not adorn any class of society'.

In 1862, when Dion Boucicault, the Irish dramatist and actor, brought charges against Webster in Chancery, Mark had another opportunity to demonstrate his loyalty. According to the written injunction, Boucicault had undertaken in 1861 a three-year joint management of the Adelphi with Webster. The formal agreement made him responsible for the choice of plays and the publicity, and assigned the finances to Webster. Profits were to be shared equally. After a half year friction developed, Boucicault alleging that Webster, without consulting his partner, had advertised plays which could not possibly be staged as scheduled. His written protests having gone unanswered, Boucicault gave notice that the plays would not be produced. Whereupon Webster uttered a warning that his joint lessee would be responsible for the consequences. After reviewing the case, the Court temporarily restrained Webster from issuing playbills, with the understanding that Boucicault would make up any losses from this order.[20]

During this litigation Mark rallied to support his friend. Setting aside for the moment his no-puffing policy, he applauded Webster and ridiculed Boucicault in *Punch* (21 June 1862). Under the heading 'Extraordinary Benevolence' appeared his first statement:

MR. BENJAMIN WEBSTER (whose name is synonymous with kindness and liberality) has contrived to get at odds with the tremendous DION BOUCICAULT, and it appears from Chancery Reports, that MR. WEBSTER, so far from resenting the ingratitude of his protégé, has actually taken proceedings to prevent the GROUPER becoming the Lessee of the Drury Lane Theatre! If that is not returning good for evil, we should be glad to be privately informed what constitutes that commendable operation.

20 Public Record Office: 'Dion Boucicault *v.* Benjamin Webster'.

ML–H

Two weeks later, in a paragraph entitled 'Sensation Advertising', Mark renewed his jabs at Boucicault, ridiculing him for acclaiming his own achievements while in charge of publicity at the Adelphi: 'So, it appears from the report of the proceedings in *Webster v. Boucicault*, that all those astounding puffs in the Adelphi advertisement were inserted by BOUCICAULT himself!' And he cited glaring examples: 'Another musical success achieved by the Author of the Colleen Bawn'; 'On every occasion experienced a rapturous reception'; 'It is on the character of GRIMALDI, and its thorough elaboration by MR. BOUCICAULT, that the attraction of the piece depends.' The braggart was advised to 'apply for the next presentation to the office of City Trumpeter with the privilege of blowing his own trumpet'.

Even if he had not felt himself heavily in Webster's debt, Mark would still have considered Boucicault's 'blackguardism' and moral laxity sufficient excuse for public rebuke. The *Punch* men detested his impudence. And for his *Octoroon* Thackeray substituted the *Expectoroon*.[21]

It is quite possible that Mark showed his gratitude to Webster in yet another way: by interesting him in the *Field*, a gentleman's sporting magazine launched by Bradbury and Evans in 1853. It began with Mark as editor and Robert Surtees as principal hunting correspondent and general adviser. 'I hope you will like No. 1', wrote Evans as plans for the paper developed. 'It seems to promise well and Lemon is entering heartily into it.' In spite of such optimism, however, Bradbury and Evans abandoned the venture after eleven months of publication; and Webster, probably at Mark's suggestion, took over. The two men were closely associated at the time, for Mark's *Mr. Webster at Home* was then playing at the Adelphi, with Webster in the leading role introducing the actors who had migrated with him from the Haymarket. It is doubtful whether Mark had ever given his full energy to editing the *Field*, his contributions consisting largely of overflow items from *Punch* and the *Illustrated London News*, all lumped together in a 'Miscellaneous' section.[22]

As Mark's crowded career introduced him to friends in journalism, politics, and the theatre, so it also subjected him to occasional abuse from occasional outsiders. The most publicized of his clashes was with Alfred Bunn, a third-rate poet whose management of Drury

[21] Silver.   [22] Rose, *The Field*, pp. 18, 46.

Lane involved him in frequent literary feuds. In 1833 he had blocked the passage of a Bill, already voted by the House of Commons, for the abolition of the patent theatres. Thereafter he was repeatedly under attack. When *Punch* came along it was one of his most out-spoken tormentors in the forties. It ridiculed his operatic produc-tions and absurd librettos, taunted him for turning to foreign quarters for talent, jeered at his versifying. On 29 November 1845, under the heading 'The New Opera at Drury Lane', it accused him of introducing one of his own ballads in the second act. 'This is such a jumble', it concluded in mock-frustration after quoting sample lines, 'that we give it up at once, and offer one pound (of ginger-bread) reward to any charity-boy . . . who will produce a more complicated piece of nonsense than this, which . . . the Poet Bunn has perpetrated.' He was called 'The Poet Bunn' when the occasion demanded playful irony and 'Hot Cross Bunn' when he had to be admonished for showing annoyance. One time he was referred to as 'His Dramatic Majesty Alfred—surnamed the Poet', in an invented account of how he had opened the theatrical season with a speech delivered from the orchestra pit. 'I have to congratulate my people on the increased demand for capers which will give perpetual enjoyment, at fifteen shillings a week. . . . With reference to taxation, I have only to observe that I shall continue to tax the patience of the public as heavily as heretofore.' *Punch* could even exploit matters of national interest to twit him. When the proposal for a statue of Cromwell at the Palace of Westminster was under discussion, Mark published a column of letters headed 'Should the Poet Bunn Have a Statue?'

After six years of persistent sneering by *Punch*, Bunn finally decided to strike back. His retaliation, a pamphlet entitled *A Word with Punch* (1846), cleverly copied the format of *Punch* itself. The frontispiece, a parody of Doyle's cover design, shows the old hunch-back in the pillory, Toby in his master's gallows, and the puppets scattered in confusion. Included, too, are caricatures of the *Punch* staff: Thackeray propped up against the broken *Punch* drum; Tom Taylor standing beside him; Horace Mayhew sprawling in his box; Gilbert à Beckett lying face down, his barrister's wig on his 'block-head'; Douglas Jerrold, scrutinizing his baton, pictured as a wasp; and Mark, in potboy attire, reaching for his pewter pot. The colo-phon features a box of pills and a bottle of medicine inscribed: 'This dose to be repeated should the patients require it.' Shown on a page of mock advertisements, Mark contemplates a polished boot. Extravagant claims puff his 'Patent Blacking': 'You have only to look in your boot, when the varnish is dry, and you will instantly see a

RECENT FAILURES IN THE CITY.

IN consequence of the late numbers of *Punch*, of the *Comic History of England*, of Jerrold's *Shilling Magazine*, of the five-penny, two-penny-half-penny, three-penny *Daily Newspaper*, and of other publications issuing from the same press, being pronounced dead failures, they will be sold in any quantity, and at any price, on the premises.

TO BUTCHERS AND CATTLE DEALERS.

WANTED, by a set of Bullies, who will provide their own "sheeps' heads," a corresponding quantity of "pluck." For further particulars, apply at St. Bride's, Fleet Street.

☞ WEEKLY DINNER?

THE Proprietors of "Punch" announce that they have a table d'hote once a week, where all, who can supply a humourous article upon anything, can have a dinner for nothing.

PATENT BLACKING.

THE Proprietor of this valuable commodity, whose work on "French polish" had already obtained for him a very high reputation, has now invented the most remarkable Blacking ever yet put on leather; you have only to look in your boot, when the varnish is dry, and you will instantly see as perfect a resemblance of yourself, as if you were before a looking glass.

To be procured of all Druggists and Oilmen in town and country.

N.B. Neither beer, nor spirit of any description, is used in the preparation of this blacking.

From *A Word with Punch*

perfect resemblance of yourself, as if you were before a looking glass.' Mark's reflection shows a braying ass.

In the next box, headed 'LEMON, Tailor, Removed from Wych Street to Fleet Street', appears this versified taunt:

Oh, come to Mark Lemon,
Who'll fit any gem 'on,
With new patent Trowsers,
Made—no one knows how, Sirs,
For rowing, or steering,
Or taking our beer in—
'Loose habits' per hundred,
At which all have wondered!
The registered jackets,
For playing at rackets—
And *over-alls*, cooling,
All kinds of *measure*-ing
Lemon takes pleasure in.—
And one thing he knows, is,
He's mostly like Moses!

Only look, PUNCH!

Thickhead, - - - Mr. MARK LEMON.

It will be perceived that this remarkably fine likeness is taken in his celebrated character of THE LITERARY POT-BOY, as best calculated to convey an idea of the extraordinary individual who can purvey poetry and porter with equal ability, and edit *Punch*, and mix it, at one and the same time.

From *A Word with Punch*

The greater part of the pamphlet is devoted to 'the respective merits' of *Punch's* three 'puppets', Wronghead (Jerrold), Sleekhead (à Beckett), and Thickhead (Mark). Having been reminded by his *Punch* detractors that he must expect ridicule because of his public character, Bunn asks whether Jerrold, hissed off the stage, and à Beckett, damned for his dramatic pieces, have not laboured for the public. As for Mark, is he not a public character by virtue of his having kept a '*Public House*'? For the 'most ill-conditioned, spiteful, vindictive, and venomous of writers in existence' Bunn nominates Jerrold. For the 'slabberings' of à Beckett he has only contempt. But it is chiefly at Mark that he aims his darts, the 'literary pot-boy, who can purvey poetry and porter with equal ability'. He quotes Mark as having replied, when asked about the costume of a theatrical character, 'Dress it in your own conceit.' And with this quip the editor of *Punch* was so delighted that he 'tried on the dress himself, and *has worn it ever since*! ! !' Mark is also accused of appropriating others' jokes: 'Dullness is pardonable, plagiarism is not; and I do hold it to be imperative on any man, who elects himself to the office of Editor, to publish his own writings, or sayings, however stupid they may be; or at all events *not* to give publicity to those of other people, without their sanction.' The entire pamphlet is much of a piece, a vicious diatribe meant to silence Bunn's detractors. It accomplished its purpose, for Mark and his staff did not retaliate. This proved to be Bunn's final word with *Punch*.

So witty and trenchant is this production, however, that it hardly accords with his generally recognized dullness. The explanation is that it was planned and largely executed by George Augustus Henry Sala, the journalist whose versatility also included competence as a draughtsman. That he had reason for wishing to embarrass Mark is clear from his own admission. At the age of fifteen, having already demonstrated proficiency in art, he had sought unsuccessfully to become a *Punch* contributor. Armed with drawings and accompanied by his mother, an operatic soprano and singing teacher, he had called on Mark. 'The genial editor of *Punch* greeted us with effusive, I may say with unctuous kindness and a whole cascade of smiles', he recalled much later. 'He smiled at my mother; he smiled at me; he smiled at my drawings, and promised to look them over with a view to their favourable consideration; and then he smiled us down a very rickety flight of stairs to Bouverie Street.' In a week Sala's portfolio had come back with a note from Mark professing to be 'unfeignedly sorry' not to be able to use any of the 'very amusing but, as yet, immature productions'.[23]

It was a disappointment never to be forgotten. When, therefore, Bunn needed help with his counter-attack on *Punch*, he found a willing accomplice in Sala, who had already designed masques for some of the Christmas pantomimes at Drury Lane. 'I drew on wood a series of caricatures, which were certainly of a nature not very complimentary to the editor of *Punch* and his staff', Sala confessed. And he admitted 'having further co-operated by writing a considerable quantity of the letterpress'.[24] In 1848 he went even further by lampooning *Punch* and its editor in the *Man in the Moon*. Small wonder that Mark always referred to him thereafter as that 'graceless young whelp'.[25] And whenever anyone remarked that Sala aspired to write for *Punch*, Mark emphatically vetoed the suggestion with 'Wouldn't suit us!'[26]

Mark reserved his strongest resentment for anyone launching a rival comic paper, for he bristled at any threat to the continued pre-eminence of *Punch*. Nor would he countenance any slurs on its performance. One of his first adversaries in this area was Albert Smith, an early contributor to *Punch* who, as stated earlier, had been reprimanded for passing proofs around at the Cheshire Cheese and submitting adaptations from the French as his original compositions. After leaving *Punch* early in 1844, he started the *Man in the Moon* in collaboration with Angus B. Reach, with the express purpose of needling his former editor. As already mentioned, it was for this paper that Brooks, while briefly one of the contributors, wrote 'Our Flight with Punch', which led to the decision to win him over to the Lemon camp.

Smith frequently accused *Punch* of stealing jokes from the *Man in the Moon*. 'Why, *Punch*—you, who are always the first to cry out about picking and stealing—what are you about?' he demanded. 'For goodness sake, turn over a new leaf, or we shall have you so reduced in circumstances as to be found haunting our office, begging bits of superfluous manuscript, and crying—"Any Jo'; any old Jo'?"' Accompanying this admonition was a malicious cartoon of Mr. Punch as a miserable beggar with Toby dragging along behind. Another drawing showed a disconsolate Mr. Punch bearing a placard reading, 'I have not made a joke for many weeks!' while

[23] Sala, *Things I Have Seen*, I, pp. 62–63.
[24] Ibid., I, pp. 87–89.   [25] Layard, *Brooks*, p. 40.   [26] Silver.

Toby held out a can for coppers. Under the caption 'What to Eat, Drink, and Avoid', a later sketch showed a loaf of bread, a pot of ale, and a copy of *Punch*.

For such effrontery Mark and his staff always held Smith in contempt. They liked to quote the lines which Jerrold had composed to damn him and his uncle, an ironmonger in Fleet Street:

> My uncle Water Closets makes
> He is odorous of vapour,
> And I who scribble books for Bogue
> Of course supply the paper.[27]

When Smith died in 1860 it was conjectured that he had killed himself with 'guttling' and guzzling. The Table greeted with indignation a report that he had left more money to his mistress than to his wife.[28]

In his relentless campaign against Mark, James Hannay was even more insolent than Smith. The founder of the *Puppet Show*, he used his paper to fire away at Mark's alleged dullness, his pointless jokes, his early tavern connexions. 'Is Mark Lemon one of the most eminent writers of the day?' he asked facetiously. 'Yes, he is,' came the answer, 'and he writes the Index to *Punch*.' Under 'Births' appeared this item: 'On the 26th ultimo, at Whitefriars, Mr. Mark Lemon of a joke, still-born.' In 'Literary Derby', a section of derogatory titles, Mark was credited with *Dullness*, by Himself, out of *His Own Head*. In the department of 'Remarkable Dreams' there was an announcement that 'Mark Lemon dreamed last week that he would shortly make a joke'.

Though Hannay, like Brooks, later contributed to the paper he had once disparaged, his connexion with *Punch* was brief. Apparently he could never respect the editorial capacities of one whom he considered his cultural and intellectual inferior.

Another journal on Mark's black list because of its slavish imitation of *Punch* was *Fun*, begun in 1861. Indeed, its format and cartoons made it look much like a copy. So striking was the resemblance that Thackeray suggested calling it *Funch*. Mark used to tell the Table that he ought to sell his rejected jokes and letters to *Fun*— 'quite up to their Mark'. He had no fear that this new competitor would steal his market. '*Punch* was never so prosperous as now,' he announced in October 1862, 'spite of the plagiary of *Funch*.' In time

[27] Ibid.   [28] Ibid.

MARK LEMON
First Editor of Punch

JOHN LEECH

DOUGLAS JERROLD

JOHN TENNIEL

GEORGE DU MAURIER

SHIRLEY BROOKS

LEMON'S CARVED INITIALS ON THE
'MAHOGANY TREE'
From M. H. Spielmann's History of Punch

the declining level of the taste in the jokes of *Fun* disgusted the *Punch* staff: 'Coarser and worse than usual' they called a particularly offensive number.[29] After 1865, however, when Thomas Hood the younger took over the editorship, the Table no longer condemned it. After all, Mark and his colleagues could not forget how the elder Hood had given a tremendous boost to the circulation of *Punch* with 'The Song of the Shirt'. And their loyalty to an old friend, now dead, embraced also his son, even though he edited a rival paper.

Not so cordial, however, was the relationship with Arthur William à Beckett. Though his father had collaborated with Mark on several plays and helped to keep the early *Punch* going, the close association seems not to have continued into the next generation. Learning that the position of dramatic critic for the *Sunday Times* was open, the young à Beckett asked Mark for help in getting the post. 'No,' Mark told him, 'I cannot help you. I want all my influence, if I have any, for my own family.' And he looked at the door. The caller then asked about his chance of writing for *Punch*. 'Well, we always consider anything that's sent us,' he was told, 'but you, with your knowledge of *Punch*, for I suppose you are old enough to have heard your father speak of his connexion with *Punch*, will know that the staff is a very close one, and there is not much chance for outsiders.' After a pause Mark bowed the applicant out with: 'To be frank with you, I don't think you have a chance.'[30]

Thus rebuffed, Arthur William à Beckett decided to launch his own journal. With the help of an Anglo-Indian who had befriended his father and now furnished the paper, office, and printer, he started the *Tomahawk*. In one of his characteristic sallies Brooks suggested that a fitting motto for the new magazine would be 'We'll axe our way'. Actually, it did axe its way, but with something less than vigour. 'Our innocuous old friend *Punch*, whose garrulous egoism sometimes does succeed in making one smile, talks with that dry affectation of waggish juvenility which so well becomes him', it quipped. Annoyed by this brash upstart, the Table did some head-shaking when the *Tomahawk* published an unflattering cartoon of the Queen (10 August 1867). To attract attention, the drawing appeared in full colour, on a sheet so large that it had to be folded. The fawning lion looking up at the protective John Brown and the inscription on the throne (*Honi soit qui mal y pense*) struck Mark as 'disgustingly disrespectful'. Though *Punch* itself had joked about

[29] Ibid.   [30] à Beckett, *The à Becketts of 'Punch'*, pp. 154-5.

Queen Victoria's John Brown at one time, there was now only out-raged condemnation. 'Is loyalty dead?' asked Silver. 'Are there no boots to kick a scoundrelly libeller who flings mud at the Queen? A little dirty scandal is a small fillip of excitement to a blasé brute.' Du Maurier wanted to see Arthur à Beckett turned out of the Arts Club for editing the *Tomahawk*.[31]

No competitors so elicited Mark's cunning as those bent on harassing *Punch*. Such was the *Comic Times*, launched by Ingram to needle Bradbury and Evans because of a disagreement. With Edmund Yates as editor, this paper never enjoyed a large circulation, never even covered its expenses, but Ingram was willing to subsidize it in order to rival 'old Poonch'. When it brought out a first-rate almanac in 1855, Mark decided to crush this journal before it encroached too far on his territory. Ingram's secretary at the time, in preparation for the Parliamentary election campaign, he adroitly manoeuvred himself into position at the Ship Inn, Brighton, where Yates had arranged to call on his publisher one Sunday morning for breakfast, to present some new ideas for publicity. When Yates arrived he was amazed to find Mark opening the door. 'He smiled expansively, rubbed his hands, and seized mine', Yates recalled later. 'Over his broad shoulders I could see the room, the table laid for an excellent meal, Ingram . . . in Sunday clothes, and the ladies in whom I recognized Mrs. Ingram and Mrs. Lemon.' Yates worked his way over to Ingram, only to have Mark pounce upon his hand once more. 'He shook it as we progressed all around the room,' Yates recalled; 'he never left off shaking it, and gently propelled me, until he had shaken me out to the landing and shut the door between us.'[32] Not long afterwards the *Comic Times* ceased publication.

Foiled in his ambition to hold an editorial post, Yates always resented Mark's toughness, bolstered by unctuous flattery and an eye to the main chance. This will explain why, as pointed out earlier, he called Mark a Jew on such slender evidence as his *prénom* and surname. And it doubtless explains why, in his reminiscences, he insisted that the *Punch* Prospectus 'was not Lemon's sole work, but rather a composite effort'. Mark, he declared, was the amanuensis only.[33] An exact analysis, he believed, would apportion the contributions thus:

[31] Silver.
[32] Yates, *Fifty Years of London Life*, pp. 211–13.
[33] *London Society*, XXVIII (Sept. 1875), p. 237.

Henry Mayhew	.	.	.	95
Stirling Coyne	.	.	.	3
W. H. Wills		.	.	$1\frac{1}{2}$
Mark Lemon		.	.	$\frac{1}{2}$

100

That Mark and his staff regarded Yates as a contemptible trouble-maker not worth their serious attention is clear from Silver's diary. They noted with amusement that his wife dyed her hair, and commented on the muddled state of his finances leading to his bankruptcy. As for his supposed cleverness, all evidence pointed to the contrary. Addressing the Artists' Benevolent Association, he had borrowed a gag used by Sala many years earlier. 'And there are your young wits!' exclaimed Mark in disgust.

*   *   *

Whatever his contacts outside the *Punch* office, whether with friends or enemies, Mark followed a pattern. With his intimates he could always find time for a leisurely lunch, an occasional evening at the theatre, a week-end at the sea-shore. Completely relaxed, fortified with an inexhaustible supply of stories, he kept his companions guffawing. He could embroider the most trivial detail and make it memorable. If he had financial and family worries at the time, as all too frequently in later years, those who enjoyed his good company never suspected his burdens. In dealing with adversaries, he was calculating, resourceful. Sometimes he would disarm an antagonist with a broad smile, or a pat on the back, or a joke followed by prolonged laughter. Should such strategy fail, Mark could always assume an air of unruffled aplomb. In spite of his apparent aloofness, however, he never relaxed his tenacity. He was ever on the alert, either to foil his opponent or effect a reconciliation. It was the latter that he wanted most, for, though often insulted, he harboured no lasting ill will and preferred to be on amicable terms with everyone. He was, above all, an outgoing and peace-loving man.

8

'OUTS' WITH 'SPARKLER'

OF all the men in his circle, at one time none was closer to Mark than Charles Dickens. They were drawn to each other by common traits. Both were persons of astonishing energy, both sparkling conversationalists, both bon-vivants. They never tired of the ludicrous— of incongruous situations, practical jokes, endless buffoonery. Yet for all their clowning they were unabashedly sentimental. A poignant scene in a play or a newspaper account of human misery could move them to tears. Sympathetic with the poor and openly hostile to nineteenth-century oppression, they both had a strong social conscience.

Exactly when the two began their friendship is uncertain. As already pointed out, it is doubtful whether Mark's few sketches in *Bentley's Miscellany* in 1837 and 1838 led to any personal contact at the time, even though Dickens as editor assumed the sole responsiblity for approving all contributions. On 17 July 1841, in Dickens's *Master Humphrey's Clock*, appeared a prospectus announcing the first number of a new paper, *Punch*. Sometime thereafter the two men met, probably through one of their friends: Jerrold, Webster, or Leech. By 6 April 1843 their social intercourse had begun, for a letter of that date from Dickens with the formal salutation 'My dear Sir' invited Mark to dinner.[1] Fourteen months later both Mark and Nelly were guests of the Dickenses, together with the Bradburys, the Evanses, and Leech.[2] Earlier that year, 19 February 1844, a dramatization of Dickens's *Chimes*, the joint effort of Mark and à Beckett, had appeared at the Adelphi. Though the novelist generally disapproved of such adaptations, rather than have the pirates mangle his works, he authorized reputable persons to stage them, so that he could exercise some control over the

[1] Ports. MS., Dickens to Lemon, 6 Apr. 1843.
[2] Nonesuch, I, p. 605, T. Chapman, 3 June 1844.

production. Mark and à Beckett rendered *The Chimes* admirably: they adhered closely to the dialogue, handled some of the descriptive passages through the speeches of minor characters, and omitted nothing essential. Mark was to dramatize yet another of Dickens's Christmas books, *The Haunted Man*, whose presentation at the Adelphi in 1848 was acclaimed an outstanding success.

The founding of the *Daily News* in 1846 forged another link in the Dickens-Lemon friendship. Heavily underwritten by Bradbury and Evans (Dickens's publishers since 1843), Joseph Paxton, and a few others, the paper was formally established by agreement on 17 November, publicly announced in *Punch* on 27 December, and introduced to the readers on 21 January. Dickens accepted the editorship at a salary of two hundred guineas a year. Among his sub-editors were Mark and Jerrold, whose liberalism as demonstrated in *Punch* accorded fully with the announced policies of this new and independent organ: the repeal of the corn laws, social improvement, and civil and religious liberty.

In spite of these worthy aims it got off to a bad start. In the first place, the sales hovered around four thousand, too few to make the venture profitable, for salaries alone were a considerable drain on its capital. To its reporters, for example, it paid seven guineas a week, well above the scale of other papers. In an effort to increase circulation, the proprietors reduced the price from fivepence to twopence-halfpenny per copy. Disastrous losses followed. Thirteen years later, at one of the *Punch* dinners, Evans, Bradbury, and Paxton still shook their heads sadly as they reflected on this move in retrospect. It had been the day of W. H. Wills's marriage, they recalled, that they had decided to lower the price. 'We ought to have gone to the wedding and then the fatal error would have been avoided', they observed with rueful hindsight.[3] In time they had been forced to go back to fivepence, the charge for other papers.

Added to the monetary losses was the growing friction between the editor and the proprietors, who tended to favour Paxton's vested interest in the railroads. Dickens considered this a threat to both independence and liberalism. He was increasingly annoyed, moreover, because Bradbury and Evans did not hesitate to challenge, or even override, his editorial decisions. Finally, considering the gap between himself and his proprietors unbridgeable, he resigned his post on 9 February after having seen only seventeen numbers

[3] Silver.

through the press. He was succeeded by his friend John Forster.

This paper was to prove Bradbury and Evans's unluckiest investment. For the first dozen years the losses were nearly two thousand pounds. Nor did passing decades dull the smarting memories of this debacle. A reference to it was even injected into the toast at the dinner (1 November 1865) honouring the reorganization of the firm of Bradbury and Evans. There were hopes, soberly expressed, that the new management would profit from the errors of the old and avoid 'Daily Newses'.[4]

Dickens's resignation left undisturbed his deepening friendship with Mark. Tacit understanding and mutual trust easily withstood the shifting fortunes of business. Even before the paper had actually been launched, when Dickens had almost decided to pull out of the venture because the failure of a brokerage firm had threatened to affect the backers, he had asked Bradbury and Evans to let Jerrold and Mark know: 'I have a sincere regard for them both, and should be deeply hurt if they misunderstood the part I take, in any degree.'[5]

As their tastes and interests brought Mark and Dickens into closer intimacy, the relationship embraced their families also. Both men were strongly home-centred, having fulfilled their obligations under the Old Testament mandate 'Be ye fruitful and multiply.' By 1852 Dickens had his quiver full with the arrival of his tenth child. Having married several years later than his friend, Mark was blessed with number ten in 1858.

For Mark and Nelly the rising fortunes of *Punch* had been accompanied by a succession of moves to accommodate their growing family. From lodgings in Newcastle Street, Strand, where little Mark had arrived in 1840, they went to King's Road, Chelsea. Here Alice, familiarly known as Lally, was born on 1 May 1842. Shortly thereafter they moved to Hammersmith, 'The Lodge', No. 12 Brook Green, a house whose distinguishing feature was a small turret with a weather vane.[6] But they soon outgrew this home, as three more children swelled their brood in rapid succession: Betty on 9 January 1844; Harry on 18 June 1845; and Helen on 18 October 1847. On 16 July 1849, while they were living at 3 St. Anne's Villas, Royal Crescent, Notting Hill, then an attractive residential area, Annie was

---

[4] Ibid.   [5] Nonesuch, I, p. 717, Bradbury and Evans, 6 Nov. 1845.
[6] The weather vane was later presented to the Central (Carnegie) Library, Hammersmith. (Information supplied by Mr. K. G. Hunt, chief librarian.)

A LETTER WRITTEN BY MARK LEMON
while living at 'The Lodge'
No. 12 Brook Green, Hammersmith
(1843–1844)

born.[7] Hard pressed to keep an ample larder for his growing family,
Mark made certain that there would at least be enough fresh milk:
he pastured some cows in Westbourne Grove. In the London
Directory he was listed, accordingly, as cow-keeper. The remaining
Lemon children were born at 11 Gordon Street, St. Pancras: Mary
Kate on 8 March 1853; Frank on 20 January 1855; Kate on 26 July
1856; and Florence on 10 March 1858. With this final addition Mark
must have felt, as had Dickens repeatedly, that he had done his
duty by his country and posterity. That paternity by now had lost
its lustre may be gathered from his matter-of-fact note to Mrs.
Ingram: 'Nelly has added a daughter to our stock this morning.'
But he could not resist a humorous touch: 'Estimated weight of
Baby, 10 lbs. Complexion (supposed to be blonde) at present Rose-
pink.'[8]

When the Lemons came to Gordon Street early in 1851 their
house, a large one with basement and three stories above the ground
floor, had just been completed.[9] Next door lived Dr. James Mar-
tineau, Harriet's brother, who later held the chair of mental and
moral philosophy and logic at University College. Two doors away
stood All Saints' Church, consecrated in 1842. Farther up the street,
facing Gordon Square, the Catholic Apostolic Church, an imposing
Gothic structure, was nearing completion. Its worshippers were
known as the 'Irvingites', followers of Carlyle's one-time friend,
Edward Irving, who in later years heard 'voices' and practised
'speaking in tongues'. Beyond stretched Torrington Square. The
whole area had once been called Long Fields, a famous duelling
ground, 'the field of the forty footsteps'.

Everything considered, it was a highly respectable neighbourhood, and Mark's residence there was tangible evidence of his rising
social status. But all too soon came reminders that living on this new
scale carried certain financial responsibilities. These Mark occasionally had difficulty in meeting. Only after some delay, for instance, did
he clear up his arrears on the poor rates and sewer tax.[10] Never one
to pinch pennies, he spent his money freely on dinners, the theatre,

[7] The house is still standing.
[8] Adrian MS., Lemon to Mrs. Ingram [10 Feb. 1858].
[9] The house was destroyed by bombs in the last war. For much of the
information in this paragraph I am indebted to Mr. Eric Jeffcott of
Highgate Library.
[10] Information based on the St. Pancras rate-books.

and travel, even as he tried to shoulder the burden of maintaining a large home and feeding, clothing, and educating an expanding family. Sometimes, when the situation became critical and bill-collectors hounded him, he would, as a last resort, apply to Bradbury and Evans for a loan or an advance on his salary. 'Young ravens must be fed', he explained. 'Marriages may be made in heaven, but expenses have to be paid here on earth.'[11]

It may have been because he wanted to be near Mark that Dickens moved in November 1851 from Devonshire Terrace to Tavistock House, only a short distance from 11 Gordon Street. In any event, the move brought their families closer together. Hardly a day passed without an exchange of visits between the two house-holds. Mark taking leave of Dickens at the corner of Tavistock Square after a brisk ramble; Nelly and Catherine calling on each other to exchange recipes or the latest theatre gossip, both of them keeping up with the new plays; the Lemon and Dickens children racing back and forth for romps in the garden or games in the nursery—such activity became routine. Often, when their own home had to be kept quiet because their father was hard at work on another novel, Mary (Mamie) and Katie Dickens would skip over to Gordon Street and spend the day with Lally and Betty Lemon. 'Aunt Nelly' always seemed happy to see them, and 'Uncle Mark' made them feel that they belonged there. He had a way with the young, as Edgar Browne, son of Dickens's illustrator, was to recall from his own boyhood contacts: 'He made himself most agreeable to us children, [whereas Dickens] appeared to us overwhelming, very splendid as to clothing, and rather unapproachable.'[12] That Mark's little friends did not stand in awe of him is borne out by testimony from yet another source, Mrs. E. M. Ward's recollection of a girlhood experience. Mark had 'good-naturedly' offered to take her and a companion to hear a lecture by an explorer. On the way the two girls 'arranged a little entertainment', to see who 'could butt against our portly friend the more often'. With a child on each side, 'he trundled along all unconscious of the fun we were deriving from our strenuous exer-cise'.[13]

Nothing so delighted Mamie and Katie Dickens as one of 'Uncle Mark's' funny stories. His pudgy hands folded over his ample stomach, a twinkle in his eye, he was often so carried away by his

[11] P.O. MS.   [12] Browne, *Phiz and Dickens*, pp. 45–46.
[13] Ward, *Memories*, p. 24.

anecdotes that he would throw back his head and shake with laughter, tears rolling down his fat cheeks and collecting in the creases of his triple chin. 'Uncle Porpoise' the girls called him affectionately. No wonder Dickens referred to him as a 'mountain of child-pleasing fun'.

His love of children and his eagerness to please them would explain why he occasionally wrote fairy tales. One of these, *The Enchanted Doll*, was completed in 1849 and dedicated to Mamie and Katie Dickens, then ten and nine respectively. Published by Bradbury and Evans and illustrated by Richard Doyle, it had a format attractive to young readers. The events of this story revolve around an ill-tempered and envious doll-maker, Jacob Pout, who finds love and contentment only after renouncing his selfishness and working for the happiness of others. The narrative is freely interspersed with Victorian moralizing. There are pointed references to 'good little girls at school', to the 'ridicule and imposition' awaiting those who 'pretend to be other than they really are', to the cruelty practised on animals in the so-called 'good old times'. But Mark made such moralizing palatable by spicing his story with details that would fascinate little girls, like his description of the wooden dolls:

They had such red cheeks, such curly hempen wigs, and legs as good as any wooden doll could wish for! And you might leave them on the window sill, in the broad glaring sunshine, without their noses melting away; or you might drop them out of the nursery window without damaging more than a leg or an arm, or perhaps only chipping off a little of the paint.

Mark also introduced realistic touches, a prominent feature of all his writing. Typical is the description of the Black Fairy, who brings the enchanted doll to Jacob Pout. Her voice is 'sharp and small' and sounds 'like the voice produced by blowing in the barrel of a watch-key'. And Pout dons breeches 'so puffed out about the hips with buckram and wadding' that his body seems 'to rest on two drum sticks'. Finally there is a long account of a Christmas Eve celebration, strongly reminiscent of the Fezziwigs' party in Dickens's *Christmas Carol*. Taking part in the festivities are the Dickens children themselves, all introduced by name, together with their dog Timber. Another echo of the *Carol* is Jacob's reformation. As the reviewer in the *Athenaeum* (30 June 1849) observed, this legend 'would hardly have been imagined had Mr. Dickens's *Scrooge* never existed'.

Acknowledging Mark's intention to dedicate this tale to Mamie and Katie, Dickens replied that it would be 'a real delight to me, and to all of us'. And he declared further: 'I know well that you propose it in "affectionate regard", and value and esteem it, therefore, in a way not easy of expression.'[14]

The following year Dickens also contributed to juvenile literature by writing an adaptation of the New Testament: sixteen short chapters based largely on St. Luke's Gospel. Designed exclusively for his children, it was not intended for publication.[15] 'I am very anxious that you should know something about the History of Jesus Christ,' the foreword explained, 'for everybody ought to know about Him. No one ever lived, who was so good, so kind, so gentle, and so sorry for all people who did wrong, or were in any way ill or miserable. . . .' This moving narrative with its simple and direct style was to be read aloud to the youngsters, usually by Catherine's sister, Georgina Hogarth, who had lived with the family from the age of fifteen. Perhaps it was as a token of gratitude to Mark for his dedication of *The Enchanted Doll* that Dickens asked her to copy the manuscript of his New Testament narrative for the Lemon children.

When Alice and Lally were guests at Tavistock House they often begged Catherine Dickens to tell them another of her favourite jokes. Her thick Scots burr fascinated them. They also admired her expert needlework, especially the cross-stitching of her chair covers and cushions. Later she taught Lally the difficult art of tatting. So much a part of the family circle were the two oldest Lemon girls that they were invited to spend the summer of 1854 with the Dickenses in Boulogne. Charles and Catherine preceded them, to prepare the living-quarters, and were followed a few days later by the children, all 'in every style and aspect of sea-sickness'. To ensure warm, dry feet for their daughters, Mark and Nelly had 'discreetly packed two dozen pairs of bran new stockings in their luggage'. Reported Dickens tersely: 'Duty on said stockings, 8 francs.'[16]

Even before the two families lived in the same neighbourhood, the fathers had already seen much of each other. Often restless after a hard day of writing, Dickens would lure Mark away from the *Punch* office for an evening on the town. 'I have been at work all day, and should greatly like a small—very trifling—"out" in the streets or

[14] Nonesuch, II, pp. 132–3, Lemon, 28 Nov. 1848.
[15] It was not published until 1934.
[16] Nonesuch, II, p. 565, Wills, 22 June 1854.

elsewhere, tonight', he explained in a characteristic note one afternoon in early spring. 'As you say you are "wanted" until 7, I will
come down to that attic in Whitefriars, *not later than 8*—maybe
sooner—on the chance of your being available.' The message was
signed 'Sparkler', a name Dickens used with a few of his intimates.[17]
Frequently together at the theatre, the circus, or other places of
amusement, Mark and 'Sparkler' liked to study humanity and pigeon-
hole for future reference any oddities or amusing incidents. The
trivial often struck them as comical. At an exhibition of art treasures,
for instance, they were intrigued by the billowing crinoline of a
stylishly attired woman gliding along just ahead of them. 'Classical,
eh, Mark?' whispered Dickens. 'No,' came the quick reply, 'false
quantity.'[18] Two evenings a week were usually devoted to a London
ramble, often in some of the most sordid districts. Such 'outs' provided Dickens with first-hand information about gambling and
opium dens, fever houses, and prison cells, all later to be woven into
the fabric of his novels.

One nocturnal stroll proved to be more than usually exciting.
As the two men were walking along Edgware Road, Mark felt a
motion in his pocket. Turning round quickly, he saw a rough-
looking man withdrawing his hand. He raised his stick and sharply
rapped the culprit, who, in taking off, hurled back insults. Joined by
a constable who had noticed the disturbance, Mark and Dickens
pursued the thief and soon overtook him. In the ensuing scuffle Mark
got some hard kicks on his knee. Arraigned at Bow Street Police
Court the following day, the prisoner was found to have a record of
convictions for attempted robberies. Despite overwhelming evidence,
however, he brazenly denied the current charge against him. 'I was
walking along quietly,' he insisted, 'when the gentlemen suddenly
stopped, and I came against one of them. They turned round and
struck me, and I said, "What do you do that for?" When they laid
into me again, I got away and they called, "Stop, thief." ' After
Dickens had testified to seeing him in a house of correction, the
prisoner broke in vehemently: 'Now, your worship, he must have
been in quod himself, or he couldn't have seen me. I know these
gentlemen well; they're nothing better than swell mobmen, and get
their living by buying stolen goods.' Encouraged by guffaws from
the courtroom, the thief pointed at Dickens and, without flinching,

[17] Adrian MS., Dickens to Lemon, 18 Mar. 1849.
[18] Glover, *Reminiscences*, p. 184.

continued: 'That one keeps a "fence", and I recollect him in prison, where he was put in for six months, while I was only there for two.' Covering the trial, *The Times* (21 March 1849) reported that 'both literary gentlemen seemed to enjoy amazingly the honour which the prisoner had with such unblushing effrontery conferred upon them'. The judge sentenced the thief to three months' hard labour.

Whenever Dickens wanted to get out of London he liked nothing better than taking his fat friend in tow. 'I'm all agony for an outing', he would write. Could Mark manage 'a day down by the sea—Dover for instance . . . for a stroll and a breeze'? Or what would he say to a trip in the country? Another time Dickens planned to celebrate his birthday at Gravesend. Would Mark change his *Punch* meeting and come down for five-o'clock dinner?[19] One day they went to Rochester to inspect Watts' Charity before Dickens wrote *The Seven Poor Travellers*. Some of their out-of-town expeditions were more ambitious, like their tour of Salisbury Plain in 1848. Joined by Leech and John Forster, they visited Stonehenge and inspected Hazlitt's 'hut' at Winterslow. Later that year they went to Norwich, then on to Yarmouth, which so impressed Dickens that he made it the home of his 'little Em'ly'.[20] For an excursion in 1849 Mark was to hire the carriage and horses. 'Damn it—,' urged Dickens, 'let's have four horses, and do you engage the best carriage at once.'[21] 'Sparkler' himself would see after the six bottles of champagne, with a 'japanned footbath' as the 'most brilliant thing for ice', and a hamper from Fortnum and Mason.

Whatever the frolic, Mark was never deterred by prospects of strenuous exercise. At Jerrold's home, for instance, when Dickens, Maclise, Macready, and Forster, in a burst of exuberance, tried turning somersaults on the hay cocks in the orchard, he joined them. Landing on his head, he kept his fat legs oscillating wildly for several minutes before he could regain his upright position.[22] Once, while visiting the Dickenses at Bonchurch in the Isle of Wight, he ran a race with Dr. Edwin Lankester, an equally stout competitor, with Macready acting as referee.[23]

[19] Nonesuch, II, pp. 543, 559, 620, Lemon, 1 Mar. 1854; 13 May 1854; 13 Jan. 1855.
[20] Forster, *Life of Dickens*, p. 523.
[21] Nonesuch, II, p. 153, Lemon, 19 May 1849.
[22] B. Jerrold, *Douglas Jerrold*, p. 276.
[23] Ley, *Dickens Circle*, p. 239.

So much did Mark contribute to the general holiday merriment that the Dickens family missed him sorely if he did not accompany them. This was especially true once when they were spending the summer in Brighton. Finally Dickens drafted an appeal to the tune of 'Lesbia hath a beaming eye':

> Oh, my Lemon, round and fat,
> Oh, my bright, my right, my tight 'un,
> Think a little what you're at—
> Don't stay at home, but come to Brighton!

The lines bore the signature 'T. Sparkler', followed by the names of Catherine, Mamie, and Katie Dickens, Georgina Hogarth, and John and Annie Leech.[24]

Volatile, ever ready with quips, Mark was one of the friends Dickens turned to as the combined strain of writing and domestic unhappiness brought increasing restlessness. In such company it was impossible to harbour tensions. As Hans Christian Andersen observed during a lengthy visit to the Dickenses, 'Mr. Lemon is most excellent full of comic.'[25]

Certainly Mark gained similar benefits from his association with 'Sparkler'. For under his surface optimism and flamboyant spirits lurked always the gnawing consciousness of imminent financial crisis. 'I have rescued Mark from a state of the deepest depression', Dickens once reported to Georgina Hogarth.[26] The two friends also consoled each other when personal sorrow struck. In 1851, when Mark and Nelly lost their two-year-old Annie, Dickens immediately sent a sympathetic note: 'You will have found comfort in the blessed belief, for which the sacred figure with the child upon His knee is, in all stages of our lives, inseparable, for such is the kingdom of God!'[27] A few months later, when Dickens himself experienced the loss of his little Dora, Mark stayed with him for a night and a day while John Forster went to get Catherine, who had been sent to Great Malvern to try the water cure for her periods of depression. In 1855 Dickens again wrote a feeling note after the death of Mark's

[24] Nonesuch, II, p. 158, Lemon, 25 June 1849.
[25] Yates, *Fifty Years*, p. 317. According to Yates, Andersen said this to him after seeing Lemon go through some amusing tomfoolery at a garden party.
[26] Nonesuch, II, p. 741, Georgina Hogarth, 8 Feb. 1856.
[27] Ibid., p. 267, Lemon, 31 Jan. 1851.

infant son, Frank. 'I have no need to tell you, my dear fellow, that my thoughts have been constantly with you, and that I have not forgotten (and never shall forget) who sat up with me one night when a little place in my house was left empty', he assured Mark. 'It is hard to lose a child, but there are many blessed sources of consolation in the loss of a baby. There is a beautiful thought in Fielding's "Journey from this world to the next", where the baby he lost many years before was found by him all radiant and happy, building him a bower in the Elysian Fields where they were to live together when he came.'[28]

*   *   *

None of their joint undertakings so excited Mark and Dickens, none brought out such bursts of energy and so challenged their ingenuity as the amateur theatricals. Begun in 1845, after Dickens's return from a year's residence in Italy, these entertainments were to continue at intervals for more than a decade. Already a prolific writer of comedies, farces, and melodramas, in some of which he had actually played, Mark was a natural for these undertakings. 'A most excellent actor', Dickens pronounced him. In rehearsing a piece 'with a rugged pathos in it', he had been 'extraordinarily good'. Above all, he was endowed with 'instinctive discrimination', which kept his impersonation 'from being too droll at the outset', while at the same time permitting penetrating glimpses into human depths.[29]

The opening production, Ben Jonson's *Every Man in His Humour*, was presented at the Royalty, a small private theatre in Dean Street, where Frances Kelly, the 'Fanny' once cherished by Charles Lamb, gave instruction in dramatics. Besides Mark as Brainworm and Dickens as Bobadil, the cast included other *Punch* men: Jerrold, Leech, Leigh, and à Beckett. To the performance (20 September) were admitted only guests holding cards of invitation. Crowding the little place was a brilliant assemblage that included the Carlyles, Macready, the Duke of Devonshire, Lady Holland, and Alfred Tennyson, who had made a special trip of several hundred miles to be present. Jane Carlyle's astringent comments on the audience notwithstanding, the play was a success, with Macready praising in particular the impersonations of Brainworm and Bobadil.[30]

[28] *Unpublished Letters of Charles Dickens to Mark Lemon*, p. 118.
[29] Nonesuch, II, p. 42, Ireland, 11 July 1847; p. 288, Lytton, 25 Mar. 1851.
[30] Macready, *Diaries*, 20 Sept. 1845.

Jubilant over this triumph, Mark and Dickens readily yielded to
the clamour for a repeat performance. The proceeds were to go to
Dr. Southwood Smith's nursing home. To meet the demand for
more seats, they engaged the St. James's Theatre. Again the list of
guests included prominent names: the Duke of Wellington, Lord
Melbourne, Mrs. Norton, Lady Duff Gordon, Baron de Rothschild.
And in a special box, accompanied by his retinue, sat Prince Albert,
at whose request the presentation had been arranged for 15 November to make possible his attendance. Though the acting even
surpassed that of the previous performance, the audience was un-
enthusiastic. 'I knew this play would be dull,' grumbled Melbourne
between acts, 'but that it would be so damnably dull I did not
suppose.'[31] On 3 January the troupe appeared again at Miss Kelly's
theatre in a benefit for her of Massinger and Fletcher's *Elder
Brother*.

In the summer of 1847 *Every Man in His Humour* was planned
for Manchester and Liverpool. Proceeds were to go to Leigh Hunt,
struggling under a mountain of debt, and to John Poole, an im-
poverished dramatist. As the day of production approached and final
arrangements were still far from settled, Dickens, on holiday in
Broadstairs, appealed to Mark. Would he find professional actresses
for the women's parts yet unassigned, see to the ordering of wigs, and
give his opinion about casting the after-piece? 'I confess I have a
fear of a farce without either you or me in it', he confided. Frenzied
notes followed. Manchester and Liverpool were 'persecuting' him
for the full bill. Would Mark, 'for the love of mental repose in
general', fill up the blanks in the dramatis personae and return
'with all speed'? Perhaps he could even 'run down' to Broadstairs
by rail? But 'of course not', Dickens added apologetically, though he
could provide a bed—'but—well—do something to help me out . . .'
The cast and farces at last decided upon, rehearsals were fixed
nightly for an entire week at Miss Kelly's theatre. 'Rehearsals, my
dear fellow, I cannot reasonably postpone: having made such an
immense point of it with all the people concerned—and the time
will be so very short', Dickens reminded Mark, who demurred about
missing the Wednesday-night *Punch* dinner. Could he not come later
or change his *Punch* day to Friday?[32]

[31] Greville, *Diaries*, I, p. 566.
[32] Nonesuch, II, pp. 33, 38, 41, Lemon, June 1847, 4 July 1847, 9 Sept.
    1847.

In spite of the hectic last days of preparation, the engagements came off as announced. At Manchester (26 July) the farces were *A Good Night's Rest* and *Turning the Tables*. At Liverpool two days later the after-piece was *Comfortable Lodgings*. Though the gross receipts in both places were large, the expenses left a balance of only four hundred guineas, not enough to pay all Hunt's debts or give Poole permanent security.

Having lived in a world of fantasy and acknowledged tumultuous applause, Mark and Dickens were not long in finding an excuse to continue their theatricals. Since Dickens was a member of the London committee to set up a permanent curatorship for the Shakespeare House, he saw fund-raising possibilities in a revival of *Every Man in His Humour*, to be fittingly alternated with *The Merry Wives of Windsor*. Rehearsals were soon under way at Miss Kelly's theatre. Among the professional actresses was Nelly's cousin, the petite Ann Romer, billed as Ann Page in *The Merry Wives*. The only amateur actress in the cast was Mary Cowden Clarke, who had volunteered to play Dame Quickly. As the compiler of the Shakespeare *Concordance* she would add lustre to the company. Since most of her stage appearances would be in the company of Falstaff, played by Mark, Dickens accepted her offer with a note of warning. 'Falstaff (who depends very much on Mrs. Quickly) may have, in his modesty, some timidity about acting with an amateur actress,' he explained, 'but I have no question, as you have studied the part, and long wished to play it, that you will put him completely at his ease on the first night of your rehearsal.' But Dickens's precautions proved quite unnecessary. 'Lemon's fine open countenance, sweet-tempered look, and frank shake of the hand, at once placed Falstaff and Mistress Quickly "at ease" with each other', reported Mrs. Clarke. There was, however, a possibility that her bulky companion would block her from the view of the spectators. 'Mind you stand well forward on the stage while you speak to Sir John,' Miss Kelly advised her, 'and don't let that great burly man hide you from the audience; you generally place yourself too near him, and rather in the rear of his elbow.'[33]

At the Haymarket, chosen for the London engagements, a good house saw *The Merry Wives* and the farce *Animal Magnetism* on 15 May 1848. 'A fine embodiment of rich, unctuous, enjoying raciness', Mrs. Clarke called Mark's Falstaff. His was 'no caricatured, rolling greasiness and grossness, no exaggerated vulgarization of

[33] Clarke, *Recollections*, pp. 298–9, 301.

Shakespeare's immortal "fat knight"; but a florid, rotund, self-contented, self-indulgent voluptuary—thoroughly at his ease, thoroughly prepared to take advantage of all gratification that might come his way; and throughout preserving the manners of a gentleman, accustomed to the companionship of a prince.' Two days later the play was *Every Man in His Humour*. In the farce (*Love, Law, and Physic*) Mark gave a hilarious performance as the loutish, conceited Lubin Log. His 'lumpish approaches', his kisses thrown at the stage diamonds with which a sham Spanish heiress had fastened her veil, his loud asides—all kept the audience in an uproar. Throughout, he and Dickens took liberties with the dialogue, introducing ludicrous scraps of their own invention. 'Eh? All real, I suppose, eh?' Mark would ask in a stage whisper as he pointed at the diamonds worn by the Spanish lady. And when she spoke of her proficiency in music, he turned to Dickens with 'What?—so?' and went through the motions of playing a violoncello. At the mention of 'poonah-painting' he queried in a loud aside, 'What? Pony-painting? Does she draw horses?' So infectious was the laughter of the audience that even the cast lost control and guffawed in the wings.[34]

The London performances were to be followed by another provincial tour, again to the North: Manchester, 3 June; Liverpool, 5 June; Birmingham, 6 June, with a return engagement on the 27th; Edinburgh, 17 July; Glasgow, 18 July. A new after-piece, *Past Two O'Clock in the Morning*, was added to the repertoire, but only after Mark, cast as Stranger, and Dickens, as Snobbington, had spent an entire evening condensing it. In the two weeks between Birmingham and Edinburgh they rehearsed another farce, *Used Up*.

The provincial engagements were not without irritating complications. First, John Leech, whose slowness in memorizing his lines had caused concern earlier, spoke of dropping out because one of his children was ill. Since this would necessitate some reshuffling of parts in *The Merry Wives of Windsor*, he was urged to make up his mind at once. But he kept stalling. Exasperated, Dickens turned to Mark. 'And now we cannot drivel about Leech, but must either have him in, or leave him out,' he demanded.[35] Never enthusiastic about the theatricals—he always regretted that Dickens and Lemon had 'set the stage for amateur acting'[36]—Leech found his child's illness a convenient excuse to leave the tour after Birmingham.

[34] Ibid., pp. 306, 312.
[35] Nonesuch, II, p. 98, Lemon, 12 June 1848.   [36] Silver.

Further annoyances resulted when George Cruikshank, who was to play the blacksmith in *Used Up*, gave up his part because of his wife's illness. On her recovery he wanted it back. Then Mark, who would have acted the blacksmith in Cruikshank's absence, voiced dissatisfaction with his own role, Adonis Leech. By this time Dickens had exhausted his patience. 'The parts are distributed,' he reminded Mark, 'and I am fully convinced that your not playing Leech *or* the Blacksmith would sacrifice the piece.' And he added chidingly, 'Pray remember that Leech was your idea originally, and don't make a Jackass of yourself by coming out with such preposterous suggestions.' He even threatened to do something drastic himself if Mark intended to 'go on with such monstrous imaginings'. His note was signed '*In*flexible' (in *Love, Law, and Physic* he had played the part of Flexible).[37]

All these carking uncertainties finally disposed of, the provincial tour got under way again. New theatres, new audiences, even a new farce—it was a succession of memorable engagements. Equally memorable was the hilarity following each performance. Usually a collation awaited the players on their return to the hotel, climaxed by Dickens's famous punch, for which Mark squeezed the lemons. Then, though the hour was late, came further frolics. One night, when *Lemon* was the word decided upon for the guessing game 'How when, and where', all allusions to punch and *Punch* got no results. Finally someone asked, 'How do you like it?' At which Dickens exclaimed, 'With a white choker on!' All eyes turned quickly to the only person wearing a white neckcloth, Mark, who, with characteristic clowning, thrust a spread hand under his chin and affected an expression of deepest pain.[38]

Another evening, after he had gone to bed and the merrymaking flagged without him, he yielded to Dickens's urging to return to the drawing-room. The door opened. There, in flannel dressing-gown, each hand raising a lighted candle to frame his head, stood Mark. His face ludicrously grave and drawn, he looked around in mock-seriousness, as if to suggest that, in spite of illness, he had come down to please his 'Implacable Manager'. A dour Scot who witnessed such antics one night shook his head in disbelief. 'I never saw anything like those clever men; they're just for all the world like a parcel of boys!' he exclaimed.[39]

[37] Nonesuch, II, p. 98, Lemon, 12 June 1848.
[38] Clarke, *Recollections*, pp. 318–19.   [39] Ibid., p. 323.

The hit of the tour was Mark's laugh, invented especially for his small part as one of Sir Charles Coldstream's fop-friends in *Used Up*. Initiated during rehearsal, it became the chief attraction in his appearances. It was 'so original, so exquisitely insane, so ludicrously disproportioned in its high falsetto pipe, to the immensely broad chest from which it issued', Mrs. Clarke recalled, that Dickens made him repeat it over and over again. 'A kind of squeaking hysterical giggle closing in a suddenly checked gasp', it was unique.[40]

Proceeds from the next theatrical venture were to endow the Guild of Literature and Art, founded to provide needy authors and artists of established reputation with rent-free cottages and annual grants. For the site of these dwellings Bulwer-Lytton, one of the principal backers, had generously set aside a portion of his land at Stevenage. Though the houses would be unfurnished, Dickens wondered whether the floors should not be carpeted to keep out the cold. 'What do you say, Lemon? Carpet, my boy?' he asked playfully, turning automatically to Mark as to one whose appearance suggested softness and comfort.

On 18, 19, and 20 November 1850 Mark and Dickens, with most of the original cast, presented *Every Man in His Humour* in the great hall of Lytton's Knebworth. An impressive assemblage of country gentry from miles around filled every seat. Nelly Lemon made her début as Tib, having at the last moment volunteered to replace Catherine Dickens, who had sprained her ankle during rehearsal by falling through a stage trapdoor. In the dialogue between Knowell and Wellbred the epilogue alluded to this accident:

> Knowell: A word on her sad accident; but, quite
> Impromptu, not intended for to-night.
> Oh, may she soon recover from her sprain,
> To tread with us, her friends, these boards again.
>
> Wellbred: That fall sank all our spirits; but in need,
> 'Tis said, a friend is found a friend indeed.
> Successful friendship has one's cares allayed.—
>
> Knowell: Ay, and the case relieved by Lemon-aid.[41]

Again Mark was a sensation as Brainworm. Accomplished with amazing dexterity, the various disguises required of his part were so convincing, according to reports, as to elude the most astute detective. Not so successful, though, was his scheme for supplement-

---

[40] Ibid., pp. 322–3.   [41] *Dick.*, X, p. 202.

ing Lytton's light refreshments of cake, biscuits, and wine, served after each performance. Always ravenous after acting, Mark needed heartier fare and made the players buy food in the village, to be smuggled up to Jerrold's tower room for a midnight snack. When word of this surreptitious feasting reached Lytton, he responded by serving a substantial supper the following night.[42]

Fund-raising for the Guild of Literature and Art was resumed in 1851 with Lytton's *Not So Bad as We Seem, or Many Sides to a Character*, written expressly for the occasion. For this production the Duke of Devonshire generously offered his town house in Piccadilly. 'I knew only one duke,' Mark used to say of him, 'and he was the noblest and best man in the world.'[43] Under the expert supervision of Paxton as architect and machinist, the spacious picture gallery was fitted with seats and the adjoining library converted into a stage. Lighting was by lamps burning special oil guaranteed not to smoke or give off offensive odours. Tickets sold at five guineas each. Queen Victoria and Prince Albert, present on the opening night (16 May), sent a hundred guineas for their box.

At this performance Mark, cast as the gentlemanly Sir Geoffrey Thornside, came uncomfortably close to missing his cue. In one of the upstairs bedrooms set aside as a dressing-room he had been struggling to get into his stiffly embroidered waistcoat. Excited after the call boy had twice summoned him to be ready for his stage entrance, he took the wrong stairway and soon found himself near the kitchen. Puffing back up the steep steps, he plunged into a gallery, only to discover that this opened into a still longer gallery, lighted but empty. Just as he was about to dash in the opposite direction, he noticed a tall man. 'Where—where's the stage?' gasped Mark, perspiration dripping from under the edges of his powdered wig. Only after he had been set right did he realize that it had been the Duke himself who had directed him.[44]

So delighted was the Duke with the play that he begged for a second performance. This was quickly arranged for 27 May. An after-piece, *Mr. Nightingale's Diary*, was added, it having been omitted on the opening night as a precaution against tiring the Queen. Co-authors of this farce, Mark and Dickens also impersonated all the characters.

In the opening scene Mark, masquerading as a German student—he

---

[42] Ibid., VII, p. 188.   [43] *London Society*, XIX (Feb. 1871), p. 98.
[44] *Gentleman's Magazine*, VI, N.S. (Feb. and May 1871), pp. 247–62, 660–72.

looked more like an overgrown schoolboy—took the part of a rogue living by his wits. This was followed by a succession of transformations, Dickens at one point becoming a Sam Wellerish waiter. The principal action of the piece dealt with an abortive attempt to deceive Mr. Nightingale about a son allegedly borne by his wife during his absence. The dialogue, freely extemporized, became increasingly absurd as the audience roared approval.[45]

After further London appearances at the Queen's Concert Rooms, Hanover Square, the troupe toured the provinces in late autumn. The itinerary included the Duke's Chatsworth estate, Bristol, and Reading. In 1852 another tour took in Manchester, Liverpool, Shrewsbury, Birmingham, Nottingham, Newcastle, Sunderland, and Sheffield. Once more the nightly exertions were followed by feasting and hilarity. For recreation there was leap-frog, played round the supper-table. Whenever Mark offered his back few could hoist themselves over so wide a hurdle. Usually they landed in the middle and stayed there. When in turn he threw his bulk into action, the strongest backs collapsed under the burden.[46]

Marring the succession of stage triumphs and midnight merriment, however, was one incident which, had it not been for some quick thinking, might have ended tragically. During a performance of *Not So Bad as We Seem* a player, rushing on to the stage from the wrong side because he was late for his cue, knocked over a lamp that had been flickering behind a painted glass transparency to simulate a blaze in the fireplace. Almost immediately flames shot up around the tinder-dry scenery. On the stage in seconds, Mark and Dickens threw a heavy overcoat on the fire and stamped it out, glass crashing underfoot. Soon all was under control, even before the audience had thought of stampeding toward the exits. It was thought best not to let the public know exactly what had happened. Those who had witnessed the incident were led to believe that someone had carelessly tossed aside a lighted cigar.[47]

Having revelled in the thrills of creating a new world in the glare of the footlights, Mark and Dickens could not rest from acting, even though their engagements were temporarily concluded. Why not produce plays with their own families as actors? The Twelfth Night festivities, annually honouring the birthday of Dickens's oldest son, Charley, would provide the occasion. So, in the schoolroom at Tavistock House, in what Dickens called the 'smallest theatre in the world', the two fathers and their children presented *Tom Thumb* on 4 January 1854 before a select audience of invited guests. Betty (Princess Huncamunca), Lally (Frizaletta), Mark, Jr. (Doodle), and Harry Lemon (a Grenadier Guard) assisted the elder Mark, who, as the Infant Phenomenon, played the Giantess Glumdalea. Dickens was billed as the Ghost of Gaffer Thumb. The hit of the evening was his son Henry Fielding, not yet five, in the title role. So amusing was the production that Thackeray, sitting in the audience, lost his balance in a fit of laughter and landed on the floor. Equally entertaining was the next year's Twelfth Night presentation, Planché's *Fortunio, and His Seven Gifted Servants*. Again appearing in the leading part, Henry Fielding Dickens was to slay the dragon, played by the portly Mark under the name 'Mudperiod'. 'Such an inviting dragon, with its enormous paunch extended on the stage, almost asking to be pierced!' Henry reminisced later. 'When the cue did come I rushed and gave him such a triumphant dig that I fear Uncle Mark must have felt the effects of it for some time after.'[48]

The next few years saw 'Uncle Mark' considerably involved in the theatricals at Tavistock House. Encouraged by the success of the Twelfth Night performances, Dickens decided to use the children's theatre for more ambitious productions, full-scale dramas with adult casts. The first of these was *The Lighthouse*, a melodrama written especially for the occasion by Wilkie Collins, now one of Dickens's intimates. Against an elaborate seascape backdrop by Clarkson Stanfield, the piece was presented nightly from 15 June to 19 June 1855. The curtain rose on a set representing the interior of Eddystone Lighthouse. At a round table, his wind-swept hair looking as if he had just been out in a storm, his ample figure covered with a wet oilskin wrapper, sat Mark. Stretched beside him on the floor, Wilkie Collins appeared to be just awaking from a deep sleep. The story of a crime and a shipwreck, the play had moments of emotional intensity and demonstrated again Mark's talents as an actor.[49] The after-piece was *Mr. Nightingale's Diary*. 'Lemon and I did every conceivable absurdity, I think, in the farce,' reported Dickens; 'they never left off laughing.'[50]

The next major production, timed for the Twelfth Night festivities on 8, 12, and 14 January 1857, featured another melodrama by Collins, *The Frozen Deep*. A story of suspense, revolving round an

[48] H. F. Dickens, *Recollections*, pp. 5–6.   [49] Clark, *Recollections*, p. 277.
[50] Nonesuch, II, p. 673, Stanfield, 20 June 1855.

Arctic expedition, it had many of the guests sobbing as the climax showed magnanimity triumphing over the baser passions of a disappointed lover set on murdering his rival. The piece was felt to be almost 'too real, too painful'. And Mark, who as Lieutenant Crayford had rehearsed it many times, finished each performance with a tear-stained face. 'The softest hearted of men', Dickens called him.[51] In July the play was presented at the Gallery of Illustration in Regent Street, the opening performance on the 4th being a private one for the Queen and her party. In August the cast, reinforced by professional actresses, appeared in Manchester. Again Mark played and wept.

Grateful for Mark's substantial part in the success of the amateur theatricals, Dickens now and then reciprocated by suggesting improvements in his friend's plays. A sense of the dramatic and an eye for detail distinguished his critical judgement. 'I would take out the baby—or take it straight into the house as it comes from christening,' he advised after seeing Mark's *Mind Your Own Business*. There were further recommendations: to curtain a long window in the second act so as to suggest the arrival of night, to introduce more emotion in another scene, to tighten up the third act.[52] On the whole, though, aside from these minor matters, it was an excellent production, Dickens thought. He was less complimentary, however, to another piece (not identified), of early composition. Mark was urged not to produce the play. Though it had some 'telling' points of dramatic interest, it showed too many traces of having been written by a 'young and unpractised hand'. Young Lemon had been guilty of infelicities which would not redound to the credit of the 'sixteen stone four' older Lemon in his editorial capacity.[53]

On at least one occasion Mark used a plot supplied by his friend. 'The enclosed is a paper by Dickens', he explained in a note to Webster. 'I propose (with his consent) to write a farce . . . upon the subject should you approve.'[54] Webster did approve, and the finished product, which Mark entitled *A London Fog*, had its première at the Adelphi on 10 April 1851. That Dickens was not parting with a masterpiece in permitting this adaptation is obvious. Its incredible situation, involving a Mr. Simple, who is made to

[51] Ibid., p. 877, Coutts, 5 Sept. 1857.
[52] Ibid., p. 390, Lemon, 25 Apr. 1852.
[53] Trinity MS., Dickens to Lemon, 11 June 1854.
[54] U. of Tex. MS., Lemon to Webster, 8 Mar. 1851. I have not been able to identify the Dickens piece on which this farce is based.

believe that the fog has caused him to wander into the wrong house (actually his own, but altered by an intruder's rearrangement of the furniture and pictures), amused an undiscriminating audience.

Even in his editorial position Mark sometimes turned to Dickens for help, a notable instance occurring in 1853. Beset by worries over unpaid bills, expenses far in excess of income, uncertainties about the children's future, he confided all during an evening at Tavistock House. Why could he not share in the rising prosperity of *Punch*? Dickens promptly drafted a letter to Bradbury and Evans, which was then copied over Mark's signature. Carefully worded, it opened with an avowal of Mark's gratitude to his proprietors for their past generosity. At the same time, it pointed out that nothing had ever been allowed to interfere with his editorial duties. These preliminaries concluded, a bold proposal followed:

My time of life, my family, and my close and long connexion with you, all taken into account, decide me, after much anxious consideration, to ask you whether you think you can give me some share in Punch. I do not seek a large one—my expectations are modest, I hope—but if I could have some little proprietorship in Punch that could be made an Editorial one, so that the share and the Editorship should be inseparable and my present position thus rendered superior to any chances and changes that may lie beyond ourselves, it would be a relief, a comfort and an encouragement to me that I cannot possibly express.[55]

Of course, the letter continued, Bradbury and Evans should not be swayed by Mark's private circumstances. But perhaps, 'a little influenced' by their 'unvarying friendship and consideration' for him—which he gratefully acknowledged—they might feel that his 'faithful services' would lend his application 'some color of reason'. Just what effect this letter had on the proprietors is not known. Though Mark was never to own shares in *Punch*, it is significant that at his death he was the highest-salaried editor in the country.

Because of his friendship with Mark and his cordial business association with Bradbury and Evans, his own publishers and part owners of his weekly *Household Words*, Dickens was a frequent guest at the *Punch* dinners. And when Princess Alexandra of Denmark arrived in England on 7 March 1863 he made one of that select group assembled at the *Punch* office to watch the procession as it forced its way through the throngs in Fleet Street. Yet for all his

[55] Nonesuch, II, p. 456, Lemon, 1 Apr. 1853.

intimacies with its editor and proprietors, Dickens never appeared in *Punch*. His sole offering, an attack on the deplorable conditions of the suburban water supply in 1849, was not published. This piece set forth with characteristic Dickensian exaggeration the threats to public health: the only water available was 'an intermittent and irregular leakage of liquid filth', which swarmed with 'marine monsters, loathsome to the sight, odious to the taste, offensive to the smell'. Added to all this were the quarterly appearances of 'a savage of a hostile tribe', the 'War-Taw-Rate-Col-Lec-Taw', who 'derided' all complaints and 'cruelly tomahawked' some of the victims.[56] Found among Mark's papers after his death, the manuscript bore a notation in his hand: 'Dickens' only contribution to *Punch*.' It may have been rejected because the suburban water system was then under attack in the illustrated papers, whose cartoons may have struck the editor as a more effective means of protest.

* * *

On 7 February 1858 Mark, as was his custom, sent Dickens a congratulatory birthday message. This was acknowledged a few days later with sincere thanks. It was to be among the last cordial notes from one who had been Mark's closest friend for fifteen years. Within a few months Dickens's domestic rift introduced an unhappy sequence of events that doomed further intimacies.

When the Dickenses, after years of marital unhappiness, decided in the spring of 1858 on a legal separation, Mark agreed to act for Catherine during the negotiations. With John Forster, Dickens's representative, he carried on a time-consuming correspondence as the painful details evolved. His heavy editorial responsibilities and his own financial worries notwithstanding, he did not begrudge the hours spent in working out a satisfactory settlement. Keeping in close touch with Catherine, he relayed her wishes in frank, carefully worded, unbiased notes. At the same time he tried not to annoy Dickens with her letters. 'This morning I have received the enclosed (the second to the same purpose) and shall decline to forward it to Dickens unless you think he ought to have it at once', Mark notified Forster on one occasion. 'Of course I shall never refuse to see Mrs. Dickens,' he added, 'but whatever she may do for the future must be without my interference.'[57] To emphasize his position, he once

[56] Spielmann, *History of Punch*, p. 350.
[57] *Mr. and Mrs.*, Ap. III, p. 278.

more addressed Forster on this subject: 'You will of course do as you please with Mrs. Dickens's letter but be kind enough to say that I declined to forward the letter to Dickens except with your concurrence.' Since he could proceed no further in the matter, the letter was not to be returned to him.[58]

After reporting to Forster that 'Mrs. Dickens thankfully accepts the proposal—as made by you on May 7th',[59] Mark concluded his part in the settlement by naming a trustee for her. Asked to serve, 'Pater' Evans at first refused, then consented when Dickens insisted he would like no one better.[60] But at the last moment the choice was vetoed. 'From your remark in last night's note,' Mark told Forster, 'I shall not ask Evans to act as trustee, and it seems to imply some hostility to Dickens. I thought otherwise and selected him as the person least likely to be objectionable.'[61]

Why had Dickens suddenly turned against Evans? Had he perhaps suspected his publisher of sympathizing with Catherine? Or had Evans, whose daughter Bessie was engaged to Dickens's son Charley, expressed private fears that a domestic rupture might jeopardize the happiness of the young couple? Whatever the reason, the final break came when Bradbury and Evans failed to publish in *Punch* Dickens's public proclamation setting forth his reasons for his separation from Catherine. It had already appeared elsewhere: in *The Times* on 7 June, on the front page of *Household Words* on the 12th, and simultaneously in various papers throughout the country. But it never occurred to Bradbury and Evans, they declared later, to insert 'statements on a domestic and painful subject in the columns of a comic miscellany'. Nor had they or Lemon ever been asked to do so. Dickens's only grievance, then, was that they had not taken 'upon themselves, unsolicited, to gratify an eccentric wish by a preposterous action'.[62]

Determined that those he took to be his enemies should not profit by his pen, Dickens severed all connexions with Bradbury and Evans. He forced them to sell out to him their one-fourth share in *Household Words*, then dissolved the journal and founded *All the Year Round*. Henceforth Chapman and Hall, his old friends, would be his publishers. 'I have had stern occasion to impress upon my children that their father's name is their best possession,' he wrote to Evans, 'and

[58] Ibid.   [59] Ibid., p. 277.   [60] Silver.
[61] *Mr. and Mrs.*, Ap. III, p. 279.
[62] *Unpublished Letters of Charles Dickens to Mark Lemon*, p. 157.

that it would indeed be trifled with and wasted by him, if, either through himself or through them, he held any terms with those who have been false to it, in the only great need and under the only great wrong it has ever known.' And he concluded testily: 'You know very well, why . . . I have been forced to include you in this class. I have no more to say.'[63]

As editor of a paper that had not published the separation proclamation, Mark was likewise branded an enemy. Perhaps he was also suspected of siding with Catherine, though he had done his best to avoid personal involvement. In any event, the old friendship was dead. There were to be no more letters to 'My dear Mark', to 'My dear old Boy'; no more 'outs' with 'Sparkler'; no more amateur theatricals climaxed by hilarity. Nor were there condolences from the master of Tavistock House that year when Mark and Nelly followed little Florence, their last baby, to the churchyard. Never again did Dickens set foot in the *Punch* office for a chat with the editor or a Wednesday-night dinner; never again did he tease Mark into spending an afternoon in the country. All was over between them.

But at the *Punch* office the rumblings set off by this broken friendship were to reverberate for years. At the weekly dinners some chance reference to Dickens would inevitably dredge up bitter memories, old insults, angry recriminations. There were stories of how Dickens had publicly cut Bradbury and Evans, how he had passed Mark without recognizing him. Evans insisted that he had never been able to find out how he had offended Dickens. And Thackeray recalled how Dickens, questioned at the Athenaeum about the quarrel, had broken down and wept. But this, the Table declared, merely proved that Dickens was always acting. It was probably the applause at the amateur theatricals that had first turned his head, Mark thought, and brought on his unforgivable conduct to Catherine. Professor Richard Owen, the eminent anatomist, had anticipated a catastrophe several years earlier when he remarked, 'Dickens has grown so arrogant.' So arrogant, said Leigh, that it would not surprise him if Dickens should proclaim himself to be God Almighty. Commented Shirley Brooks with his usual pungency: 'Thinks himself God now. If he is we are atheists, for I don't believe in him.'[64]

Also aired by the *Punch* staff was the story of how Dickens and

[63] Nonesuch, III, p. 33, Evans, 22 July 1858. [64] Silver.

Thackeray had got themselves embroiled in the much-publicized Garrick Club affair. Touched off when Edmund Yates had written an unflattering piece on Thackeray for *Town Talk*, a minor weekly, the bitter quarrel kept tempers simmering for months. Thackeray, stung by Yates's references to his opportunism ('cutting his coat according to his cloth'), by the charge that all he wrote showed a 'want of heat', by the surmise that his reputation was 'on the wane', by the tactless comments about his appearance (especially his nose), had demanded an apology. This had been refused in an insolent letter, sent with the full knowledge of Dickens, who felt indebted to Yates for his published denial of unsavoury gossip following the domestic rupture. Believing that the offensive letter had been the work of Dickens himself, Thackeray turned against him, at the same time getting Yates expelled from the Garrick Club. So ended another friendship.

In discussing the affair, Mark and his men naturally upheld Thackeray. Brooks insisted that Yates was merely acting for Dickens, who had never spoken well of Thackeray or anyone else. Mark concurred. Thackeray wondered why Dickens had written the offending letter. And he told how, at the Lord Mayor's dinner, Dickens's daughter Mary had ignored him. 'Let fathers hate like hell,' he had called after her, 'but why should children quarrel?' As for Yates, he was no gentleman—wanted kicking. Why should one handle a Bohemian with kid gloves? Base, ungentlemanly, mean, he had the low manners of the canaille.[65]

The Garrick Club affair was to rankle in Thackeray's memory for a long time. When 'Ponny' Mayhew mischievously referred to Yates at one of the *Punch* dinners in August 1863, Thackeray exploded: 'Damn it, your fellows still seem to think it was because of my nose that I fell foul of him. But he imputed dishonourable conduct to me—and for that I got him kicked out of the Garrick.' 'Ponny' only fanned the flame by retorting, 'With your strength you might have been more generous.' A terse note in Silver's diary records the conclusion of this scene: 'And Thackeray blazes up, and finally bolts.'

The Table spoke with contemptuous amusement of yet another Dickens friend, John Forster, who in 1852 had resented Thackeray's reference to him as Addison's man in *Henry Esmond*, Addison being Dickens. Brooks reported how, at the opening of the Lyceum Theatre, he had taken a seat next to Forster, who had immediately

[65] Ibid.

got up and ostentatiously moved away 'because the great Dickens was with him'. Another titbit came from Leech, who, staying in the Midlands on the night of an earth tremor, had awakened, run to the door, and cried, 'Who's there?' To Dickens the earthquake had felt like a great beast under the bed. The beast, commented the *Punch* staff, must have been Forster.[66]

When Dickens galvanized England by giving public readings from his books, the *Punch* Table did not swell the chorus of adulation. After hearing him in *Pickwick* at St. James's Hall, Burnand maintained that Dickens was the only man there who did not understand its humour. Sam Weller fell flat. Brooks reported that his wife had come away quite unimpressed from a presentation of the Nancy and Sikes scene in *Oliver Twist*.[67]

Not until the spring of 1867, nearly nine years after their estrangement, did Mark and Dickens meet again on friendly terms. For their reconciliation Clarkson Stanfield, who had joined them on holiday excursions and painted backdrops for their amateur theatricals, was responsible. On his death-bed he appealed to Dickens to make it up with Mark. A few days later, on a chilly March afternoon, the two clasped hands beside Stanfield's open grave. Though deeply moved by this meeting, Mark seldom referred to it.[68] Nearly seven months later, when a farewell banquet was planned in Dickens's honour before his American reading tour, Mark was one of the sponsors. 'It will give me much pleasure to have my name announced with the list of stewards to the dinner to be given to Mr. Dickens', he wrote to Charles Kent, Secretary of the Banquet.[69] And the following year, while Mark himself was on tour with his Falstaff impersonations, Dickens sent him congratulations, adding, 'If Dolby [his reading manager] and I can do anything for you in the country or give you any little result of practical experience by way of information we shall at all times be glad to do so.'[70] After reading this note, Mark paced back and forth in silence. 'Falstaff has reminded Dickens of old times,' he volunteered at last as he showed the communication to a friend. '[This is] more like himself than when his actions are controlled by others.'[71]

But in spite of such overtures, Mark and Dickens could never

[66] Ibid.   [67] Ibid.   [68] *London Society*, XXVIII (Nov. 1875), p. 410.
[69] Hunt MS., Lemon to Kent, 26 Oct. 1867.
[70] Nonesuch, III, p. 670, Lemon, 6 Oct. 1868.
[71] *London Society*, XXVIII (Nov. 1875), p. 411.

recapture the intimate and light-hearted companionship of the old days. Once sparkling with wit and gossip, often begging for some new excitement or ramble, Dickens's letters now were little more than notes, restrained in tone. And for his part, Mark, though he had fully forgiven all, never quite forgot the old injuries. Invited in 1869 to attend a dinner to Dickens on 10 April in Liverpool, he made a slight railway accident an excuse for staying away. 'I am glad, for it was a muddle—very funny', Brooks wrote in his diary. Sympathetic because of his own experience in the 1865 Staplehurst railway accident, Dickens promptly sent a feeling note: 'I am heartily glad to know that you were but very lightly shaken by your "railway accident". The phrase has had a dreadful significance to me, ever since the Staplehurst occasion.'[72] But his formal conclusion, 'Faithfully yours', lacked the warmth of the 'Affectionately ever' that had usually ended the letters before the estrangement. Though 'Sparkler' and his 'Dear Old Boy' had indeed honoured Stanfield's death-bed appeal, the old 'outs' and the old *bonhomie* were beyond recall.

[72] Nonesuch, III, p. 720, Lemon, 16 Apr. 1869.

9

'FATHER OF CRAWLEY'

AT the end of May 1858, as if in anticipation of his break with Dickens, Mark gave up his London home in Gordon Street and took his family to Crawley, Sussex. According to the village correspondent, his 'fashionable arrival' preceded by two days the annual fête of the Friendly Society, where he 'graced the head of the table', which 'groaned under the savoury viands'. It was the first of many such local festivities at which he was to occupy the place of honour.

The move to Crawley had actually been pending many months, for Mark and Nelly had begun to realize that their children needed a change of environment. Already there had been disturbing evidence that young Mark, now seventeen, was cultivating some questionable friendships with the theatrical set. In one of the more serious discussions at the *Punch* dinners his father reported that the boy had recently confessed to sleeping with a girl 'sans kidding'.[1] As for Lally (sixteen) and Betty (fourteen), it was high time to remove them from the influences of the city, to ensure their growing up as proper young ladies. Mark was, above all, a puritan. Just as he had always insisted that no objectionable material should ever disfigure *Punch*, so he now safeguarded the innocence and good name of his daughters. Regardless, for instance, of the convenience of the railway to London or Brighton, he never allowed the girls this unprotected manner of travel. And despite his fondness for the theatre, he permitted them to attend no plays whose language or situations might be in the least offensive.[2] It was all very well for him to sprinkle his *Punch* Table talk with an assortment of *risqué* anecdotes, but his domestic hearth was a different matter. Like many another Victorian, he viewed his

[1] Silver.
[2] Information furnished by the late General Sir Cecil Romer, Lemon's grandson.

home as a sanctuary of refinement, a retreat from the bawdy and drunkenness of the outside masculine world.

So it was to Crawley that the Lemons decided to take their family. Thirty miles from London on the Brighton road, it had a station on the main railway line to Portsmouth: Mark would have no trouble in getting to the *Punch* office for his two or three days weekly. Should late engagements detain him there, he could always spend the night in a room reserved for him at the Bedford Hotel. Here also Nelly and the girls could stay whenever they came up for a day in the shops or an evening at the theatre.

Crawley was more than just a name to Mark. Though it was only a village then, a character it preserved for nearly another century before burgeoning into one of the sprawling New Towns, he had often heard of it, for John Leech had begun the study of surgery there under Dr. Thomas Smith. Only sixteen at the time, Leech had already shown his proclivity for drawing by sketching horses on the whitewashed walls of his bedroom. 'Oh, you wait and see,' he retorted when someone twitted him about his horses' tails, said to resemble banister brooms; 'I shall be a great artist one day.'[3]

Further first-hand information about Crawley came from John Verey, who had taken up farming at near-by Horsham after the failure of his brewery in Kentish Town. He may have spoken with pride about a local event of public note, the annual Crawley and Horsham hunt. Ever a lover of horses—one of his later lectures at Crawley was to be on horsemanship—Mark may well have been influenced by this feature in his final choice of a country home.

When the Lemons came to Crawley one wide street divided the village into separate parishes. All the territory to the east constituted the parish of Crawley. The west side, beyond the railway line, belonged to the parish of Ifield. Here, to the north of the level crossing, stood Vine Cottage, Mark's new home. In 1861 Crawley and Ifield had a combined population of just over a thousand.

New-comers to the village soon recognized its distinguishing landmarks. At the north end, on the London road, towered an ancient elm tree, reputed to be over six hundred years old. Still alive despite centuries of decay, its hollow trunk had the capacity of a small room and could easily hold a number of persons. Near it stood Dr. Smith's

---

[3] Information based on a note in a scrapbook of press cuttings and recollections related to Crawley; assembled by Miss Daisy Warren, Arundel, Sussex.

home, always referred to as 'The Tree'. Also famous was another tree, the 'County Oak', at the junction of Sussex and Surrey. Several public houses were equally renowned. The Old Punch Bowl, a fifteenth-century café, boasted an eight-foot fireplace. At the George Inn, a rendezvous for all sporting men, especially pugilists, theatrical people would drop in on Sundays for a hearty dinner.[4] At the Station Inn a large assembly-room accommodated sizeable groups for concerts and banquets. On three sides of Crawley lay the fertile acres that produced large yields of wheat, barley, and oats. Livestock breeding also flourished here. To the south stretched Tilgate Forest, today being nibbled away by the expanding New Town.

*   *   *

Vine Cottage, consisting of three separate stone buildings joined to form one continuous structure, had once been a farmhouse. After Mark's arrival it became a showplace. Having learned of it through an advertisement in the papers, the Lemons had gone there twice as lodgers to study its possibilities.[5] Delighted with its ingle-nook and bay windows, with the clean sweep of the fields at the back, with its easy access to the railway station, they decided to make it their home. Less than a mile distant, on the top of Hogg's Hill, a small farmhouse, picturesquely named 'The Malthouse', commanded a superb view of the countryside. Here Mark was to do much of his writing.

It must have been Vine Cottage that served as his model for Mr. Deering's home in *Golden Fetters*, his last published novel:

> The great parlour and the dining-room both had bay windows with latticed glazings, and looked out into a spacious garden, here and there intersected by thick yew hedges, which served as screens against the northerly and easterly winds. The ceilings of the rooms had oak traverses, with bosses and small pendants, and the wide fireplaces had been furnished with dogs, as wood—until the promotion of the adjoining railroad had made coal attainable—was the only fuel procurable. . . . The furniture was solid, old-fashioned, and faded by long usage, but carefully tended.

Whenever Mark showed a visitor around he pointed with pride to the 'velvety lawns and broad walks of the garden', the large arbour fitted up to be 'a chapel of ease', and the orchard that supplied the family with fresh fruit in season.

Spacious, airy, well designed, Vine Cottage was the perfect home

[4] Ibid.   [5] B.D., 8 Mar. 1871.

for the Lemon children. There was a room for each one, warmed on chilly days by a blazing fire in the grate. Partial to the old-fashioned features of the place, Mark and Nelly took pains to preserve them. Against this well-seasoned background their simple, sturdy furniture had a look of belonging. Because the house was large, some new pieces had to be added, like the dining-room chairs in Regency style and a dressing-table, all bought at an auction in near-by Staplefield after the dismantling of a home once occupied by a mistress of Lord Nelson.[6] A popular spot was the drawing-room, where the family spent many evenings round the piano. Hymns, ballads, arias—Mark would beat time to them all with his pipe, a look of rapture lighting his face as he listened to the clear voices of Nelly and their daughters. He had reason to be proud of the musical talent exhibited here, for it was indeed out of the ordinary. With more training Nelly could have qualified as a professional vocalist, like her sister Emma, the operatic soprano, for whom she sometimes sang offstage. And Lally was to win renown by her public recitals. (During practice, with only her family present, she had an amusing way of playing chords up and down the buttons of her basque.)[7]

In a small house next door Mark's mother and Aunt Betty came to live. Having given up their Oxford Street millinery shop, they had followed the Lemons to Crawley.[8] Mark always managed to spend part of every Sunday with his mother, now again a widow. Often he would read to her from the New Testament, for her eyesight had been failing steadily. Later she became totally blind. No matter how demanding his writing and editorial commitments, he always found time to look after her business interests. Together with her son-in-law, a Mr. Ritchie, who had married her daughter by Henry Verey, he administered her affairs.

Since Crawley was easily accessible by rail (approximately sixty-five minutes from London),[9] Mark and Nelly frequently entertained

[6] These pieces of furniture, still in excellent condition, are now in the home of Mrs. Sidney Matthews, a granddaughter of Lemon.

[7] Information supplied by Mrs. Sidney Matthews, Lally's daughter.

[8] The Verey and Lemon millinery shop is listed for the last time in the London Directory for 1858.

[9] According to the British Transport Historical Records of the Bradshaw Collection, one train left Crawley Station at 8 a.m. and arrived at the City Terminus, London Bridge Station, at 9.10 a.m. Another morning train left at 10 and arrived at 11.05. I am indebted to Mr. H. W. Hart of British Railways for this information.

their city friends at Vine Cottage. One of their first guests was Catherine Dickens. Having been taken by her mother to Brighton while the separation negotiations were being concluded—the final papers were delivered to her there on 4 June 1858—she spent a few days with the Lemons on her way back to London before moving into new quarters at 70 Gloucester Crescent, Regent's Park.[10] In the years to follow she would always be welcome at Vine Cottage. She had the special affection of the younger generation, to whom she had, in happier times, told Scots jokes at Tavistock House.

The most frequent visitor, so that he became almost a member of the family, was Shirley Brooks. Indeed, the girls called him 'Uncle Shirley'. Now Mark's closest friend, he often spent an entire week in Crawley. Here he worked on his first novel, *The Gordian Knot*, which he dedicated to Mark and Nelly. 'I have strong claims to the right of inscribing this book with your names', his dedication assured them, since he had composed 'the most agreeable portion' of the work in their 'quiet and delightful Sussex retreat'. He signed himself 'Your obliged and attached friend'.

The leisureliness of life in the country appealed to Brooks. He liked to play whist and visit well into the night, sleep and breakfast late, write his pieces for *Punch* after a morning stroll, and catch up on his reading. On Sunday he accompanied the Lemons to St. Margaret's Church in Ifield. (Even though the Church of St. John the Baptist in Crawley was much nearer, Mark and his family attended St. Margaret's because their home was just over the line in the parish of Ifield.) Though Brooks had no ear for music, he always joined the family as the girls gathered round the piano on a Sunday evening and sang glees and madrigals to Nelly's accompaniment. There were also guessing games and parlour tricks, interrupted by occasional mishaps. One night Harry, the younger son, splashed claret all over the wall and carpet while trying to demonstrate his wine-bottle wizardry. Brooks marvelled as Nelly remained 'perfectly equable' in the face of this accident. 'Capital thing, a sweet temper', he observed.[11]

[10] Her Crawley visit is mentioned in a letter written by her aunt, Mrs. Helen Thomson, to a Mrs. Stark. Once considered a forgery, this document has recently been upheld as genuine in a convincing article by Dr. K. J. Fielding: 'Charles Dickens and His Wife: Fact or Forgery?' *Études Anglaises*, VIII (July–Sept. 1955), pp. 212–22. Mrs. Dickens's Crawley visit is also mentioned in the *Sussex Advertiser*.
[11] B.D., 22 Mar. 1869.

Of the seven living children, Mary Kate (Polly) was his favourite. 'Large and handsome' as she grew up, she carried on a lively correspondence with him after each of his Crawley visits. 'She hath the brains', he noted in his diary after reading one of her delightful letters. At the same time he felt a tenderness for all the family, for he knew that an ominous shadow of debts hung over the household. 'Gave him [Mark] £50 to take up that bill', reads one of his diary entries. And he confessed to tipping the Lemon servants, for they 'do not get too much, I guess, of that'.[12]

Other *Punch* associates also visited Vine Cottage. Sometimes the whole Table would make an excursion to Crawley. Leaving London on an early train, they breakfasted at Mark's, then proceeded by chartered coach to Brighton. On their return they would have dinner at the George Inn, decide on the Large Cut for the next issue of *Punch*, and take a late train back to London. Among the occasional guests was one whose talents Mark had come to admire, George du Maurier, 'Kiki'. Cocky and often exasperating as a new-comer to the Table, he had settled down and in time won the editor's affectionate esteem. To Vine Cottage came also another *Punch* artist, John Tenniel. In 1864, casting about for a model after he had undertaken to illustrate Lewis Carroll's *Alice in Wonderland*, he chose the youngest Lemon daughter, Kate. Eight years old at the time, her golden hair falling to her shoulders, her sensitive face wearing an expression of childish wonder, she made a perfect Alice. Before long her likeness would delight children all over the world. But posing for her pictures was not an altogether happy experience, for she hated the striped stockings which Tenniel made her wear. Once the sittings were finished, they disappeared mysteriously through a crack in the staircase.[13]

* * *

The Lemons had hardly got settled in Vine Cottage before they were caught up in the whirl of village activity. As already mentioned,

---

[12] Ibid., 1 Apr. 1869, 11 Mar. 1869, 29 Mar. 1869.

[13] For these details I am indebted to Mrs. Norah Trevor, Kate Lemon's daughter. The claim advanced by Williams and Madan in *A Handbook of the Literature of the Rev. C. L. Dodgson (Lewis Carroll)* (1931, p. 22) for Canon Badcock's daughter as the model for Alice cannot be substantiated and does not appear in the revised version of the *Handbook* published in 1962. According to the authors, Tenniel's drawings were made from a photograph of the Badcock girl. It seems unlikely that Tenniel would have worked from a photograph when he could sketch

it was at the festivities of the Friendly Society that they made their début. The celebration began with a promenade headed by a brass band, after which all gathered at the church for a sermon by the Reverend Mr. Blaker. Using Matthew vi. 23 as his text, he 'elucidated the many benefits to be derived from social combinations', so long as the recreations were pursued 'in strict conformity to the laws of morality'. The evening concluded with a dinner and dancing. The local reporter commented on the record attendance, interest having been 'stimulated by the attraction of our literary guest and family'.[14]

A special event each autumn was the Harvest Home, held during Mark's first year in Crawley at Tilgate Forest Lodge, whose large barn, its floor temporarily lengthened, gave room for dining and dancing. Always a keen observer, Mark recorded his impressions in *Golden Fetters*:

The well-filled bags of the great barn were dressed out with green boughs and autumn flowers, whilst on the floor, which in good time would re-sound with the blows of the flail, were placed long tables covered with white cloths and huge joints, and the implements—horn-handled knives and two-pronged forks—needful for their consumption. Mugs and horn beakers were there also, some to be filled from the half-dozen kilderkins of harvest beer piled in the corner. The [host's] seat of honour was arched over with flowers and green leaves, and the places of his farmer guests were only distinguished from those of his work-people by having chairs instead of forms. Hanging like a chandelier from the centre beam of the barn was an empty twelve dozen wire hamper as a warning to the merry-makers about to assemble that no one was to be 'drunk on the premises', it having been the custom . . . to consign an offender to 'the cage', as it was called, and there leave him to be a spectator of the concluding festivities. . . . Just outside the barn was erected a large tent, formed of rick cloths, to be lighted up when the sun went down, for an hour or two's dancing, master always leading off the ball.

---

his Alice from a living model during his visits to Vine Cottage. Perhaps he made the drawings of Kate Lemon in 1864, told her he was using them for Alice, and then put them aside for later use in *Through the Looking-Glass*. It is only in this book that Alice wears striped stockings. For a discussion of the three models said by their descendants to have inspired Tenniel's original drawing of Alice, see 'Three Models in Wonderland' in the *Daily Telegraph*, 8 July 1965, and 'Alice: The Truth' in the *Sunday Times*, 11 July 1965.

14 Except where otherwise noted, all subsequent details concerning the Lemons' activities in Crawley will be based on items gathered from issues of the *Sussex Advertiser* for the years 1858 to 1870.

One of Crawley's most elaborate celebrations was a tribute to Princess Alexandra of Denmark. Having watched her triumphal procession through London on 7 March 1863, Mark returned to Vine Cottage in time to help the local planners with their elaborate programme for the Royal Marriage on the 10th. A charitable gesture, possibly at Mark's suggestion, opened the festivities with a dinner of roast beef and plum pudding for the poor: the George Inn, the White Hart, and the Station Inn each served fifty guests. At the Station Inn, Mark 'presided over the joints'. From all public buildings floated colourful banners. Even the steam engines were elaborately decorated, some like 'Jacks in the Green, embellished with yellow gorse'. After the feasting the band marched through the village and back to the square, where, with the church choir, the Lemons, and several other prominent families, they formed a central group encircled by the schoolchildren. It was, reported the local columnist, a 'holiday bedizened' spectacle such as the village had never seen before.

The merrymakers then withdrew to the meadows for field sports. There bushels of apples and gallons of almonds, brazils, and walnuts delighted the children, as did the antics of avuncular Mark, whose jokes and capers kept everyone amused. At seven came a brilliant display of fireworks, followed by dancing at the George Inn, with music by a 'very intellectual Negro' who had escaped from slavery in America and come to England with Mason and Slidell. He was accompanied by a violinist.

Since Crawley supported several musical organizations, there was no lack of entertainment. Nelly and her daughters had ample opportunity to display their talents here. During the winter months the combined church choirs of Crawley and Ifield gave benefit concerts whose programmes were surprisingly ambitious for so small a community. Selections ranged from popular ballads to classical pieces of considerable difficulty. 'Never since the time the celebrated American horse trainer gave his entertainment at Station Inn has there been such an assemblage of the *élite* as took place at the George Hotel', remarked the local reporter on one occasion. There was high praise for the duets, quartets, and choruses.

After another concert Harry Lemon, then just nineteen, broke into print with a flamboyant review. He opened with a flourish: 'Our picturesque village was awakened to intense activity last Tuesday from the heavy slumber in which it is usually found, by the announcement which had been made by the ladies and gentlemen of the

Crawley Choir, that their amateur concert would take place in the George Assembly Room, at eight o'clock that evening.' Confessing to little musical ability himself, the young journalist expressed a fondness for an occasional opera, but a strong dislike for the 'comic talent' of the London music-halls and an intense hatred of all organ-grinders. (Here he echoed his father, who often deplored the vulgarity of the music-hall and the disturbance caused by street musicians.) Most of all, he concluded, he enjoyed hearing 'the young fresh voices of our English girls, accompanied by the deep-toned bass and alto of the opposite sex, breathe forth the old English glees and madrigals, awakening in the hearts of young and old what nothing but sweet music can arouse'. Such a treat, he declared, had been the last concert.

For some of its appearances the choir had a visiting director, Frank Romer (Nelly's brother), who had collaborated with Mark on several operas. Referred to as the 'eminent composer' by the local columnist, he not only conducted the choral numbers but accompanied some of the solos. Among these was Lally's 'The Message', commended as a 'magnificent performance'.

Like the concerts, Mark's public readings from his own work helped to raise money to provide Christmas dinners for the poor. One of his earliest performances featured *The Enchanted Doll*, applauded as having 'a moral which comes home to all of us', in spite of its being 'especially written for the young'. During the Yuletide season he read some of the tales from his *Christmas Hamper*. The attention of 'the distinguished party assembled' was described as 'riveted on the mighty master', on his 'touching pathos and sentiment', set off by his 'rich vein of humour'. 'We almost wondered', mused the reporter, 'why some Oliver Twist did not astonish Mr. Lemon by asking for more.'

So popular were his appearances that Mark initiated the penny readings, at which he, his son Harry, and a few talented members of the community presented excerpts from well-known works. Though this was the period of his estrangement from Dickens, he was too broad-minded to let personal differences turn him against his former friend's masterpieces. Rising above pettiness, he added to his reading repertoire *A Christmas Carol*, the trial from *Pickwick*, and an impersonation of Sam Weller.

It was at these penny readings that Harry introduced what soon became a great favourite with his audiences, his original sketches of

a garrulous servant girl who recites all she has seen and heard.
Entitled 'Selina Worrits', these monologues were expanded as a series
and eventually found an imprint with a local publisher. 'I feel I
have taken a very bold step, in rushing into type,' wrote Harry in his
foreword, 'and the only excuse that I can offer for my boldness is
that I have done so at the request of my Crawley friends.' He hoped
that his readers would not judge him harshly, but, 'by accepting this
little trifle, give [him] encouragement to attempt something better'.
And he concluded with a quotation from *Henry VIII*:

> If I chance to talk a little wild, forgive me,
> I had it from my father.

That he did indeed have it from his father was demonstrated by
his respect for Victorian decorum, warmly commended by the
Crawley reviewer: 'The author has, while wishing to be mirthful,
studiously avoided vulgarity, too frequently infused into such writing.' He had succeeded in 'creating a smile, with no shade to mar
the feelings of the most sensitive reader'. Harry was also emulating
his father by writing for the stage. One of his early pieces, *Gertrude's
Money Box*, made its London début at Sadler's Wells. Shirley
Brooks noted in his diary that he and Mark had planned to be
present, 'only the young author called, and begged us not, as he was
uncertain of its success'.[15] An undisputed success, however, was
Harry's Christmas pantomime the following year, *Dick Whittington
and His Wonderful Cat*, presented at the Crystal Palace. Supposedly
based on an old manuscript buried for many years, the piece
advanced the thesis 'that Dick, the triple mayor, was evidently the
founder of the Society for the Prevention of Cruelty to Animals
because he befriended the cat throughout his dangers and difficulties'. For this he was rewarded 'at last by kindness and the
comforts of home'. The popularity of this pantomime, observed the
local chronicler, 'has afforded much satisfaction to the friends of
the author'.

To no one did it bring greater satisfaction than to Mark, who
followed with pride the realization of his own youthful dreams in this
son. Even as a child Harry had always been close to him. 'I have a
little boy home from school very ill I fear', the fond father had
written in distress during one of the early years at 11 Gordon Street
as he appealed to the eminent surgeon Erasmus Wilson. 'Mr. James

[15] B.D., 9 Jan. 1869.

ML–L

of Uxbridge who has been attending him will be here tomorrow at 5 o'clock and I should be greatly obliged if you would meet him at that hour.'[16] Having brought this boy safely through the trials of childhood, Mark and Nelly saw in the aspiring young author a worthy representative of his father.

How different from their other son, the young Mark! His removal to Crawley had come too late. Not inclined to the simple village life, he was to give his parents no end of trouble. He seldom showed any interest in the local activities. For him no plaudits from the village reporter, no speculations, even, as to his possible interest in any of the local beauties. Greatly discouraged, his father appealed to a few friends to use their influence in getting him a situation. But for such an unpromising youth the prospects were dim. 'I will do all in my power for the young man', wrote Alfred Crowquill, who had done drawings for *Punch*. But he added cautiously, 'He that expecteth nothing shall not be disappointed.'[17] Finally, in 1865 Mark got his older son an appointment in India. On top of an already burdensome debt he borrowed another two hundred pounds to pay for the boy's outfit and other expenses.[18] As the time for his departure approached Mark was often quiet and thoughtful. However difficult the last half-dozen years, he could not forget his cherished hopes for his first-born. 'Mark preparing his boy for India', Silver noted in his diary. 'So we drink to the father and wish his son success. "Mark will be crying all next week," says Pater. A tender heart he has.'

With the exception of Mark, jun., the Lemon children were a source of pride to their parents. Whatever the public entertainment—concerts, amateur theatricals, penny readings—Harry and his older sisters usually helped to initiate the project. They were particularly concerned that the proceeds should help the unfortunate. 'At no time have the poor of this district been so well cared for as at present', wrote the Crawley reporter after Mark and his family had lived in the village for several years. When Nelly and her daughters took over the soup distribution during the severe winter months there was a rush of people to fill their cans—'sufficient proof that this is a great boon to the hungering poor'. On Christmas Day everyone was looked after: in 'the taprooms, the open streets, and every nook

[16] Fales MS., Lemon to Wilson, Tuesday, n.d.
[17] Nat. Lib. Scot. MS., Crowquill to Lemon, n.d.
[18] P.O. MS., Lemon to Bradbury and Evans, n.d.

and corner where destitution would be likely to take refuge'. This was followed on New Year's Day by allotments of beef, bread, flour, and a quarter of a ton of coal for each indigent family. Having repeatedly voiced his humanitarian convictions at the Wednesday-night *Punch* dinners, Mark gave them practical application in Crawley. It was indeed fitting that, ten years after his death, his family should commemorate his charitable work with three lights in a memorial window in the Church of St. John the Baptist. The biblical inscriptions remain eloquent testimony to his sympathy for the suffering: 'Thirsty and ye gave me drink'; 'Naked and ye clothed me'; 'Stranger and ye took me in'.

The Lemons also initiated projects for the public good while on holiday. A case in point was their summer in the seaside village of Barmouth in Wales, where they were the guests in 1869 of Ellis Williams, a wealthy stockbroker. A lover of good music, Williams always invited talented friends to his home, the ivy-clad Bellevue, which overlooked the rocky headlands, the pounding surf, and the herds of black cattle on the sand.[19]

In gratitude to Barmouth for a carefree summer, the Lemons and their fellow holiday-makers sponsored a special concert to raise money for reseating the parish church. Preparations for the perform-ance generated great enthusiasm. For weeks rehearsals continued throughout the day at Bellevue, strains from Gounod's *Hand-maids of Irene* floating from the open windows. The Assembly Rooms were cleared of all sheep hurdles and firewood, a mound of sand was removed from the entrance, chairs were carted in, and branches of greens and garlands of flowers were strung from ceiling to wall. During the concert prolonged applause repeatedly called back the musicians for generous encores.

There were times, of course, when the Lemon family did not accompany their father on holiday excursions, especially when he went to the Continent. But no one begrudged him the few days' relaxation from the strain of editorial duties. Touring France with John Leech, then suffering from nervous fatigue, he watched a bull-fight in Biarritz, drank the burgundy of Dieppe, and enjoyed the provincial inns. (At one small inn, where he was accused of keeping the guests awake with his snoring, he tried to convince the chamber-maid that the disturbance had come from Leech, a somnambulist, who had been talking in his sleep.)[20] In Paris he visited the

[19] Beale, *Light of Other Days*, II, pp. 257–60.   [20] Silver.

theatres, but, as usual, railed at the nudities of the French stage.

During his travels Mark sent his family entertaining accounts of his experiences. Typical is his letter from Ireland, where he had gone to look into land speculation. (This scheme may have involved him in further financial difficulties.)[21] 'I am writing now with the beautiful Dublin Bay before me and the oddest of masters about me', he wrote one morning while waiting for breakfast in his Kingstown hotel. 'He is a sharp intelligent little boy of about twelve in a brown holland blouse with drab trowsers darned at the knees in the most wonderful manner. Yesterday he was the only person to receive us at an hotel twice as large as the Bedford.' The bizarre appearance of the chambermaid intrigued Mark: 'As the light at one end of the passage shone through her black stuff petticoat you saw a pair of very thick legs in very wrinkled stockings terminating in a pair of substantial boots fringed with fag ends of broken laces, her face smudged with black and her hands somewhat cleaner as she kept wiping them on her cotton bed-gown which formed the upper part of her dress—and this at an hotel where everything is served on silver!' He complained of a 'little stiffness' from riding in a low-backed jaunting car: he felt as if he had been 'out for a day's hunting', but thought it 'a most agreeable way of travelling when you get used to the machine and know how to sit'.[22] (Squeezing his bulk into the seat must have required some nice adjustments.)

As the Lemon children grew up it was inevitable that the family should begin to scatter. The first to marry was Lally. Her husband, Dr. Timothy Martin, had come from Wales to be a medical student and assistant to Dr. Smith at 'The Tree'. This match delighted Mark and Nelly, for their new son-in-law was a young man of promise; moreover, the couple would make their home in Crawley. Still, Mark experienced a father's mixed emotions after giving up his eldest daughter, even though Tim and Lally would be frequent visitors at Vine Cottage. What he felt during the wedding (29 April 1862) and how he escaped to the Malthouse afterwards for a cigar and reflections have been recorded in his second novel, *Loved at Last*, where his counterpart is an uncle who has just seen his favourite nephew married:

[21] In his diary Brooks records that he and Mark sat up at the Bedford until eleven one night and discussed Irish land.

[22] Dick. H. MS., Lemon to Family, Monday.

Then Jacob stole away to an old covert of a summer-house, until he was unearthed by two old cronies who discovered him by the wreaths of tobacco smoke which he was blowing forth to quiet his beating heart, and to hide the visions of other days, which rose before him full of tenderness and love. . . .

After a few weeks Mark, once more his old jocular self, turned from sentiment to practicalities. Why, he asked, should it be necessary to send out expensive cards before a wedding? He had spent between eight and nine pounds on these alone.[23] Something must be done to stop this wasteful practice. Nine months later, on 24 January 1863, there appeared an item in *Punch* entitled 'No Cards'. 'The sending out of wedding cards has long appeared to *Mr. Punch* a sadly stupid practice', it complained. 'Persons when they marry have quite enough to do in preparation for their union, without having time to spare for directing packs of envelopes, and putting wedding cards in them; and, moreover, *Punch* believes that a small squabble will be saved by the cessation of this quite useless custom.' A month later Silver, the author of these reflections, noted in his diary: 'M[ark] L[emon] thinks my touch about "No Cards" has had an effect—you see that postcript to half the nuptial notices now. Must be kept up.'

Whatever Mark may have felt about the 'useless' practice of sending cards, he had the assurance that his eldest daughter was happy in her marriage. On 15 April 1863 Silver recorded in his diary: 'Mark a grandfather at noon today. The Princess Alice of Crawley, as Shirley calls her, is therefore toasted and her infant heiress.' Three days later Mark sent Brooks a note, thanking him for his kind inquiries about 'my granddaughter Alice Martin and her mother'. Reporting that 'Mother and Child are both doing well', he could not resist boasting that the father 'gives it as his professional conviction—and he has had much experience in such cases—that my granddaughter is the finest, heaviest, handsomest baby that ever was seen—in which opinion all the cottage agree—except the grandmother who is not such a goose'.[24] There were to be seven more children in the Martin home, making a total of seven daughters and one son.[25] To her little ones Lally imparted her own love of

[23] Silver.

[24] Hunt. MS., Lemon to Brooks, 18 Apr. 1863.

[25] At the time of writing Beatrix (Mrs. Sidney Matthews) is the only surviving member of this family. Amazingly alert and active and, like her grandfather, quick to appreciate a good joke, she is youthful in her early nineties.

music. Seldom did an evening pass without nursery rhymes and glees around the piano.[26]

Over the marriage of Betty, their second daughter, Mark and Nelly were again elated. The bridegroom was a first cousin, Robert Romer, son of the composer. A senior wrangler at Trinity Hall, Cambridge, in 1862, he had been toasted at one of the *Punch* dinners, his Uncle Mark beaming with pride the while. He was to have a distinguished career, first as professor, later as judge. The wedding took place on 25 August 1864, at the Church of St. John the Baptist, where Lally had also been married. (Whenever the Lemons attended this church for regular service, they sat in a specially built pew in the gallery. Downstairs there was no seat large enough for Mark.)[27] According to the Crawley reporter, the chancel had been 'tastefully decorated with flowers and evergreens', and the six young brides-maids were 'conspicuous for beauty, grace, and elegance of attire'. After the impressive ceremony, attended by 'a large assemblage of neighbours and friends', a breakfast was served. Having examined their 'numerous and elegant presents, the happy pair departed *en route* to Paris, where they are likely to remain for some time'. As a footnote to Silver's 'No Cards' item in *Punch*, the reporter added that, 'in conformity with the sensible fashion of the present day, no cards were sent, to the great relief of the postmaster, who had no easy work on the occasion of Dr. Martin's marriage with the elder Miss Lemon about two years ago'.

* * *

Watching his children grow up and go on to homes of their own, Mark was convinced that Crawley had been good for his family. Where could they have found a more wholesome environment, ampler opportunity for identifying themselves with the community, truer friends? For their part the villagers felt heavily indebted to the Lemons for some significant improvements since their arrival. From the first Mark had been active in civic affairs. Appointed to an inspectorship by the Ifield Parish Vestry, he took his office seriously. One of the earliest improvements following his installation was the lighting of the high street. 'Lighted at last!' boasted the Crawley columnist in February 1859. Though not the 'most brilliant' at the start, in twenty-four hours the gas lamps were 'all that the most sanguine could hope for—and the quantity continues superb'. Like

[26] Information from notes in Miss Daisy Warren's scrapbook.   [27] Ibid.

a symbol of the humanitarian beam issuing from Vine Cottage, one solitary lamp glowed only eleven feet from the premises.

Further innovations were to transform Crawley from a sleepy village into a town of purposeful activity. The Cricket Club, the Rifle Club, the Volunteer Movement—for their organization Mark was largely responsible. To be sure, his participation in the regular activities of these groups was necessarily limited. 'I never could dress up properly', he explained with reference to the Volunteer Movement. 'If the dressing in front was good, I always put the company out behind. They allowed me to have a special tunic, a little longer than the rest, but I was obliged to give up drilling. And on the whole it was decided that I presented too much of a mark for the enemy to be of any practical good in the field.'[28]

Mark also stimulated the cultural life of the community by arranging two exhibitions. All should have the opportunity, he felt, to see paintings by well-known artists, *objets d'art*, and sundry curios. Proceeds from the small admission charge would go to charity. To the first exhibition (February 1866) prominent artists like Maclise, Frith, and E. M. Ward sent their pictures. 'Your kindness has been the "shoeing horn" to draw on a great number of contributions', Mark told Maclise. He was happy to report seven hundred entries, 'some of great value'.[29] A specially printed catalogue identified these as an inkstand given by George IV to Mrs. Fitzherbert, a spyglass used by Napoleon at Waterloo, and chairs surviving the Smithfield fire. So successful was this venture that a second exhibition followed two years later. Again a catalogue listed the treasures: paintings by Royal Academicians ('some of the finest examples of art in modern times'), together with 'armour, antiquities, curiosities, mechanics, models, and miscellanies'.

Because of his interest in the past and his great love of horses, Mark used his influence to bring coaching back to Crawley. Where once fifty coaches had passed through in a single day before the middle of the century, with the coming of the railroads not one remained. The colourful travel of an earlier period had ended. But not for Mark. 'What was our gratification', observed the Crawley correspondent, 'when a well-appointed coach in the best style of the older time came rolling along, crowded with passengers, drawn by four spanking horses.' Christened 'Ye Old Time Coach', it made the

[28] Hatton, *With a Show*, p. 69.
[29] Adrian MS., Lemon to Maclise, 17 Feb. 1866.

run from Brighton daily, always passing Vine Cottage. Should Mark
be in his garden, the guard would salute him and blow his horn. It
was this coach that the *Punch* staff used for excursions to Brighton
and other seaside resorts.

Of Mark's numerous local enthusiasms, none generated such
excitement as the organization of the fire brigade. For years Crawley
had tried to put out fires with buckets of water, usually with little
success. Finally, after several large houses had burned to the ground,
Mark began soliciting subscriptions for a fire engine. Proceeds from
concerts, readings, and amateur theatricals further augmented the
fund, sufficient for the purchase of the first engine in 1866. Though
a hundred years old, this antiquated Phillips Manual created a sensation. Children flocked around to marvel, the driver kept rubbing the
brass fittings to a high polish, and the newly organized brigade of
thirty, in smart serge coats and helmets, drilled vigorously. Mark
always attended its meetings, but not in uniform. The brigade, he
joked, could not afford a leather strap to buckle round his waist. The
first call for service came when a hay rick caught fire. Having covered
the one and a half miles to the farm in less than a half-hour, the
engine played on the blazing hay as the top layer was being removed.
Afterwards the grateful farmer rewarded the fire-fighters with
quantities of beer, cider, cheese, and bread.

Hoping to raise money for an up-to-date fire engine, the brigade
sponsored a concert. One number featured a song written by Mark:

> We're always pleased to stay the flames,
> And *Omnes sans* a doubt,
> And always very pleased indeed,
> Although we put them out.
> With energy our muscles ply,
> We ne'er from labour shirk,
> And yet our engines always throw
> Cold water on our work.
> Besides, it is a lazy one—
> A strange remark to say—
> We *all* must work so very hard
> To make the engines play.

Mark followed this with a solo rendition of another verse:

> If the house is on fire,
> And the neighbours alarmed,
> He's only a lodger,

KATE LEMON

John Tenniel's model for Lewis Carroll's 'Alice'

MRS. MARK LEMON

VINE COTTAGE. *From left to right, figures in the picture are Betty Lemon (Mark's aunt), Kate Lemon, Mrs. Mark Lemon, Miss Stocker (the governess), Mr. Monkton (her fiancé), Mary Kate Lemon ('Polly'), Tom Smith, Alice ('Lally') Lemon (later Mrs. Timothy Martin), and Betty Lemon (later Lady Romer)*

And cannot be harmed;
At the window he laughs
At the row that is made,
And tells them to send for the Crawley Brigade.[30]

The fire brigade got its new engine. Surmounted by a turret with a large bell for ringing the alarm, this new equipment did away with the hand bell at the fire house.

With Mark constantly seeking new ways to improve Crawley, it is not surprising that a former resident, returning after an absence of a quarter of a century, remarked: 'The town (village no longer) is making rapid advances, and if it continues to advance, as it bids fair to do, it will speedily leave its former prosperity far behind.' Impetus in this direction, continued the visitor, had been given by the 'untiring efforts of one of the most distinguished and popular literary men of the day, who having settled here, has spared no pains in advancing the interests of the place'.

In recognition of his 'untiring efforts' the residents of Crawley gathered at the Station Inn on 7 August 1866 to honour Mark. Characterizing him as 'replete with wisdom, animated with equity and justice, duly exercised in the true and perfect consummation of Christian duties', the county paper reported the event in detail: how the natives had 'hastened to give material proof of the esteem and respect they bear toward Mr. Lemon'; how 'their tribute of regard would have assumed far greater intrinsic proportions' if he 'had not expressed a wish it should be as much as possible confined to the village'; how, in recognition of Mrs. Lemon's 'valuable charitable undertakings', they had produced a silver tea service, one side inscribed 'Presented by the inhabitants of Crawley', the other engraved with 'To Mark Lemon, Esq., as a token of affectionate regard.' Mark had been 'much moved by this acknowledgment of his humble efforts'. He insisted that he valued the inscription 'affectionate regard' beyond silver and gold, 'although the gift was of considerable intrinsic value'. After this the loving-cup, a recent gift from the *Punch* staff to celebrate the fiftieth volume, was filled and handed round the room. So, after 'further speeches, song, jest, and sentiment', ended a memorable evening. Mark had found it heartening, for the villagers had given him proof of their sincerity in repeatedly referring to him during the past few years as the 'Father of Crawley'.

[30] *London Society*, XXVIII (Nov. 1875), p. 413.

10

'SCRIBBLING IS A PLEASURE'

To the peace and seclusion of his 'writing-box', the plain one-room Malthouse on the outskirts of Crawley, Mark retreated whenever he could push aside for the moment his civic and editorial responsibilities. 'I have spent many happy hours there,' he remarked as he pointed out the little building to a friend; 'when one gets fairly started, scribbling after all is a pleasure.' But he confessed that it often took him an hour or more to get into the proper frame of mind for creative work. An established routine preceded composition. A light breakfast or lunch was followed by 'a steady walk to the little cottage-farm'. 'When I get there I unlock my room, put out my paper, nib my pens, and get all in order', he explained. 'Then I go outside, light my pipe, wander into the farmyard, look at the cows, or pigs, or the poultry, or anything else; sit on the gate, perhaps, if I can balance myself, sniff the local perfumes of hay and straw, and presently the fit comes on; down goes the pipe, up comes the pen, and away you go.'[1]

Though writing seemed harder as Mark grew older, it was certainly not from want of practice. In Crawley he merely continued the 'scribbling' that had been going on for over two decades. During his early days at the brewery in Kentish Town, his eleven months at the Shakespeare's Head, his precarious first year with *Punch*, he had held to his hope of becoming an author. Composition he regarded as his highest calling. From his pen had come a succession of plays, songs, verses, sketches, and stories, to be followed in his last decade by six novels. Long since forgotten and patently not in the first rank as literature, his publications deserve consideration, nevertheless, because they reflect his convictions and, at the same time, characterize the temper of the period. Above all, they attest to his remarkable industry.

[1] Hatton, *With a Show*, pp. 73–74.

Concerning his plays (listed in the Appendix) little more need be added to what has already been said in an earlier chapter. The largest body of his work (some eighty pieces, counting his adaptations and collaborations), they are too numerous and, on the whole, too insignificant to warrant systematic examination. Their weaknesses are those of nineteenth-century drama in general. Something further should be remarked, however, about two of the better-known plays.

The first of these, *Hearts Are Trumps*, is a three-act domestic drama which opened at the Strand on 30 July 1849. A personal experience formed the genesis of this piece. Visiting an old actor friend one day, Mark noticed another caller, a shabbily dressed man, yet not undistinguished in appearance. Though he was probably not over fifty, his hair was entirely white. After the stranger had left without being introduced, Mark learned that this was a gambler who had helped the actor through some hard years. Now down on his luck, he came here whenever he wanted a good meal, but was never introduced to anyone. Mark could not dismiss this account from his mind. 'I wondered if he were married, if he had a daughter, and if they knew what his profession was', he explained later. 'Then it occurred to me to build up the story of a gambler who had a daughter living away from town in happy ignorance of her father's career.'[2]

This unforgettable incident, charged with dramatic situations, was translated into a sentimental piece revolving about the dual life of the central character (played by W. Farren). As Mr. Gray he is an affectionate father who safeguards the innocence of his motherless daughter Mary (Mrs. Stirling) by bringing her up in the country. As Ruby, the name he uses with his associates, he is a ruthless professional gambler. A series of tense incidents accomplishes his reformation. About to plunder a young man, Charles Wilmot (W. Forester), Ruby learns from a letter dropped by his intended victim that he is in love with Mary. Meanwhile she has been told by a defecting gambler of her father's dual character. Rushing to London, she arrives at his apartments just in time to see the confirming evidence for herself. In the ensuing scene she nobly forgives her father, accepts her suitor's proposal, and predicts that 'the good the future has in store for us will be sweeter for the bitterness of the past'. Daughter, father, and suitor form a *tableau* and the curtain falls.

For comic relief *Hearts Are Trumps* intersperses some of the more saccharine passages with rollicking episodes. This is managed through

[2] Ibid., p. 49.

a counter plot, in which a Yorkshire footman, Joe Martin (Compton), and a maid, Susan Fletcher (Mrs. A. Phillips), exchange some lively quips. 'It's my belief,' says Joe in proposing to Susan, 'that men and women are like gloves—they're no use except in pairs.' But for all such attempts at wit, the machinery creaks noticeably in this subplot. Eavesdropping, incredible coincidence, and an unexpected legacy from a former employer—all add up to the typical failings of Victorian drama. Particularly inept is the handling of exposition. Too often a character supplies the necessary information by merely reciting it to himself. Thus Joe, speaking solely for the benefit of the audience, summarizes in soliloquy his recent experiences: 'Things be looking up with me at last. For five years I've been slipping down in the world, as though it was all greased over; but this week folks have been taking my pocket for a money box.' And this is followed by a cataloguing of adventures.

Somewhat more skilfully manipulated are the mechanics of the other play to be considered here, *Woman's Suffrage; or, Petticoat Parliament* (Olympic, 26 December 1867). Written during the militant activities of the Suffragettes, it was described by *The Times* as 'a caricature of a state of society which it is supposed might be realised five years hence if the suffrage were conferred on women'. It portrays politically ambitious wives, sisters, and daughters as petty, selfish, and ridiculous in their attempt to govern the nation. Neglecting their household duties, they become a fast and horsy set, with a monopoly on betting and buying. No longer feminine in their pastimes, they take up boat-racing, billiards, football, and cricket. In the Library of the House of Commons the female loungers gossip maliciously about an absent member, only to flatter her extravagantly when she appears. For the official meeting of the Petticoat Parliament the Speaker dons wig and gown. Trivial matters constitute the business of the day. The main petition deals with needles that cut thread, and the tax on rouge is the subject of a heated debate. Unable to agree on anything, the Parliamentarians lose their female charter of supremacy and submit to the males, whom they once held in subjection.

This extravaganza presents the prevailing Victorian point of view on woman's sphere of influence, one that Mark endorsed. Her place, as the Queen herself firmly believed, was in the home. Mark repeatedly took sly digs at feminine demands of equality with men. Hoping to forestall wives and mothers as office seekers, he ridiculed the Suffragettes in the strongest terms. But as dramatic entertainment his hard-hitting propaganda did not come off: discerning critics had little praise for *Woman's Suffrage*. 'It leaves the impression that opportunity for witty and suggestive dialogue has been sacrificed to mere wildness and boisterousness, and that the extravagance is overdone', rebuked *The Times*. 'It might have been expected that there would have been one strong-minded woman who could have been in earnest without losing her temper, and a little more intellectuality would certainly have made the piece a greater success.'

Even as he continued to write for the stage while editing *Punch*, Mark also sent a stream of contributions to various journals (listed in the Appendix). In 1852 his proprietors, under the title *Prose and Verse*, brought out a selection of the earlier pieces. As previously noted, Jerrold facetiously referred to this little volume as 'Prose and Worse'. One of its best sketches is 'The Boys of London'. Of the five boys chosen as representative, the 'Vagabond Boy' gave Mark the greatest latitude for pushing his social protest. Strongly reminiscent of King Lear's 'Take physic, pomp; / Expose thyself to feel what others feel', the opening lines admonish the reader to leave 'his easy comfort' for a look into the 'dens of cheerless squalor', for an excursion into the 'narrow alleys whose atmosphere is laden with foetid exhalations'. Who is to serve as guide through these 'revolting regions.? The Vagabond Boy, 'he who drew his breath in a noisome cellar, and whose swaddling clothes were rags—foul rags'. Denouncing these 'savage dens' as breeding-places of crime, Mark contends that we 'stigmatise Justice with the malignity of Revenge' by sending the victims to 'our penal settlements, to endure suffering the most dreadful'. Like Carlyle and Dickens he deplores the expenditure of 'devoted lives and charitable offerings on the civilisation of the distant savage, whose pagan worship recognises a good and evil', while we 'overlook the savagery and moral insensibility of those who speak our language, and influence our happiness by the daily contact which we and our children have of them'.

Social protest also informs some of the poems included in *Prose and Verse*. Of these 'Spring-time in the Court' is typical. First published in Dickens's *Household Words*—Mark contributed only four pieces to this journal, all of them verse—it is another indictment of the hovels to which the poor are condemned:

> They say the Spring has come again!
> There is no Spring-time here;

In this dark, reeking Court, there seems
No change throughout the year:
Except, sometimes, 'tis bitter cold,
Or else 'tis hot and foul;
How hard it is, in such a place,
To feel one has a soul!

There follows the lament of a distraught father who had once known 'meadows green' and played with flowers, but now must bring up his son in wretched poverty and city filth. Bitterly, almost savagely, he inveighs against the lot of his class.

Why are we housed like filthy swine?
Swine! they have better care;
For we are pent up with the plague,
Shut out from light and air.
We work and wear our lives away,
To heap this city's wealth;
But labour God decreed for us—
'Tis man denies us health!

The piece concludes on a Carlylean note, echoing a prophetic warning found in *Past and Present* (I, 2): 'Judgment for an evil thing is many times delayed some day or two, some century or two, but it is sure as death!' Mark versifies this sentiment thus:

Think you our wrongs
For ever, too, will sleep?
The misery which man has sown
Man will as surely reap!

So, like some of his contemporaries (notably Charles Kingsley), Mark made his publications his pulpit. Whatever the medium—drama, fiction, expository prose, verse—it was often the vehicle for his social gospel. Herein lay his chief weakness as a writer. Time and again he would halt the narrative to let the sermon take over: hence his interpolated remarks to the reader, his personal reflections, his attempts at instruction. But in these practices he was merely following a Victorian pattern: even such a master as Dickens overloaded his early novels with unabashed moralizing. And Trollope, commenting on his responsibilities as an author, insisted in *An Autobiography* that 'the novelist, if he have a conscience, must preach his sermons with the same purpose as the clergyman, and must have his own system of ethics'.

Happily the narratives in *Tom Moody's Tales* are not laden with sermons. Published in 1863 by Bradbury and Evans and illustrated by Hablôt K. Browne (Dickens's 'Phiz' for nearly two decades), it includes some of Mark's contributions under the pseudonym 'Tom Moody' to Surtees's *New Sporting Magazine*. *The Athenaeum* (26 December 1863) described the tales as 'slight sketches, beginning without prelude, contriving to interest without the aid of plot or surprise, and in a few cases terminating abruptly in the manner of narratives which have been described as ending without conclusion'. Woven into the fabric of the stories are the threads of Mark's youthful experiences with country squires, fox hunting, shooting, and riding. There is also a deep-seated hatred of all poachers, at whom Mark was to lash out in subsequent work. A handsomely bound volume, *Tom Moody's Tales* was on display in the bookstalls in time to attract Christmas buyers, its concluding narrative, 'The Adventures of a Christmas Turkey', giving it a seasonal touch.

For many years Mark greeted Christmas with a special poem or tale in the *Illustrated London News*, for which, as already stated, he had prepared the first Christmas supplement. A selection from the narratives was later reprinted as *A Christmas Hamper* (1860). And from 1862 until his death he annually sent a story to the Christmas number of *London Society*. Because the publisher wanted his material early, Mark often worked on his Christmas piece in the summer, under conditions far from conducive to composition, especially if *Punch* business kept him from getting back to his 'writing-box'. So it was that a friend found him one sultry evening in his room at the Bedford Hotel, the lingering aroma of Covent Garden Market drifting in through the open windows. 'I'm glad you are come', Mark greeted his visitor. Removing his spectacles, he complained, 'The muse is a halting faggot tonight; I can do nothing with her.' It was not easy, he continued, to get into the mood for a Christmas story in London on an oppressive summer night. Nor would he have fared better in Crawley. 'It is harder work to cover the fields with snow there than to think of winter here,' he explained. Composition being out of the question for the rest of the evening, he brewed some punch for his guest and himself: claret, soda-water, lemon, sugar, a teaspoonful of brandy, and some ice. 'If we cannot conjure up some snow for "London Society", we can conjure up ice for our cup,' he quipped as he stirred his drink. 'Claret-cup is your only liquor.'[3]

Even without the proper seasonal stimulus, however, Mark always managed to re-create the Christmas scene. The snow-covered streets, the 'grocers' windows, bright with gas-light, and almost bursting with currants, raisins, and citron-peel, garnished all about with holly-sprigs'—all the holiday touches are there. The tales are redolent of roast goose and plum pudding; they teem with Christmas merriment—games, pantomimes, carol singing. Himself a veritable Father Christmas, Mark took an almost childlike delight in the festivities, in the mistletoe, in good eating, in drinking toasts. Would 'that Christmas time came oftener than once a year, and that mince-pies were never out of season', he exclaims in 'Christmas Eve in a Night Train'. Over all hovers an affectionate tenderness. 'Surely it is pleasant to be remembered by those we love,' Mark tells his readers; 'and at Christmas time how many a kind wish and tender thought go forth from hearth to hearth. . . . It is pleasant, surely, to remember the friends and companions of our youth, and by some kindly act or word remind them that they are not forgotten. Bless the Christmas time!'[4]

Such a reminiscent mood releases a host of memories in 'A Christmas Carol'—Mark had no qualms about borrowing his title from Dickens. 'As we sit in our dark and dusty chamber, made bright today by sprigs of holly and mistletoe, we can almost fancy that our grey hair is auburn once again and those rows of dusty books are the bright oak panels of our old country home', he reflects. In retrospect he listens to the carolers of his youth. 'Where are the singers now?' he asks. 'Where the song? Where the love? Gone! But we have been made happy thinking of the old Christmas time.'[5]

Above all, the tales overflow with sympathy for the homeless, the hungry, the lonely. Mark reminds his readers that 'the poor wretches hidden away in those human styes' cannot join in the merriment. 'No! Many sit in hunger and cold, and listen sometimes with anger, sometimes with envy, to the roaring sot proclaiming how the largess has been wasted in horrible excess.'[6] There is indignation, too, for 'the ready-made clothesmen, who had paid starvation prices for the

[3] *London Society*, XIX (Feb. 1871), p. 97.
[4] Ibid., VI (Dec. 1864), p. 4.
[5] *Illustrated London News*, XXVII (22 Dec. 1855), p. 375.
[6] 'Aunt Grace's Sweetheart', *London Society*, XIV (Dec. 1868), p. 26.

garments in their windows [and] had stuck sprigs of holly in button-holes as a sort of Christmas garnish to their non-Christian-paid wares'.[7]

Throughout these Christmas stories the impression persists that Mark has taken his cue from Dickens. There is the same emphasis on merrymaking, on feasting, on charity, on spiritual regeneration. The author's personal interpolations have a decided Dickensian cast. 'I hold it good at Christmas time, despite the sneers of strong-minded critics, to make merry,' Mark declares, 'and encourage all manner of pleasant and innocent devices, to mark the season as one of good will to man, as my father did before me, and as I trust my children and grandchildren will do when I am gone.' Like Dickens, he would have all families 'deck their houses with green holly and mistletoe, and put the latter to its proper use in a modest way'. There should be 'thank-offerings in acknowledgment of the good which has come to them'. Never ought we to let Christmas pass without 'forgiving those who have despitefully used us, [without] seeking a recon-ciliation' with those who have been offended.[8] Though such interpolations often lack Dickens's skill and retard the progress of the narrative, the sentiments are Dickensian.

*   *   *

In 1863, while busily scribbling away at his stories, Mark received a suggestion for quite a different type of publication. 'What do you think of a real *highbred Joe Miller*?' Alexander Macmillan asked him. 'It wants doing. Think of the lot of exquisite stories floating about and getting lost. To pick out the true gems and set them in some proportion and order would be a very fine work.'[9] Mark took to the idea immediately. Was it not a fitting undertaking for the editor of England's leading comic journal? He would advertise in *Punch* for contributions: 'Homeless jokes will find shelter, and have their faces washed and all uncleanness removed.' The product of his labours, some seventeen hundred entries, appeared in 1864 as *The Jest Book*.

In his preface Mark freely admits that he has collected mainly 'old jokes—some older than Joe Miller himself—with a liberal

[7] 'A Christmas Holiday Lesson', *Illustrated London News*, XLVII (23 Dec. 1865), p. 614.
[8] 'A Coat with a Fur Lining', *London Society*, XVI (Dec. 1869), p. 6.
[9] *Letters of Alexander Macmillan*, p. 41.

sprinkling of new jests gathered from books of hearsay'. His investi-
gations have shown him how 'many Jests, Impromptus, and Repar-
tees had passed current, century after century, until their original
matter is lost . . . a Good joke being transferred from one reputed
Wit to another, thus resembling certain rare Wines which are continually being rebottled but are never consumed'. But Mark has
sedulously avoided defining wit as a criterion to his selection. The
results could only have been as inconclusive as any attempt to define
beauty. Without trying, therefore, to find a 'standard of value', he
has merely 'gathered from every available source the old sayings of
all Times', carefully avoiding, however, 'the Coarse and Irreverent,
so that of the . . . Jests here collected, not one need be excluded
from Family utterance'. (They have indeed had 'their faces washed
and all uncleanness removed', as the advertisement had promised.)

The reception of *The Jest Book* was only mildly enthusiastic.
Calling the preface 'a brief and smart essay on wit and wits' and,
therefore, the best part of the volume, the *Athenaeum* (11 June 1864)
objected to the repetition of the same joke on different pages, sometimes with the details only slightly altered. The *Saturday Review*
(23 July 1864), after admitting 'that there should be some honourable
retreat for veteran jests . . . a book which will keep them from
the streets', and recognizing Mark's volume as the 'fullest and best
jest book that has yet appeared', felt that 'it is all very well to give
an asylum to old jokes, but it is quite another thing to open a dead-
house'. Again there was objection to the repetition of similar
anecdotes. The arrangement also came under attack: there should
have been some systematic order, 'if not in the text at least in the
index'. The headings themselves were 'utterly useless'—for example,
'A Sage Simile' to designate Thackeray's 'comparison of a certain
noisy tragedian to "Macready and onions".' Why had Mark thought
it 'necessary to enter into competition' with the jokes he was collecting? Such negative comments notwithstanding, however, *The
Jest Book* was generally commended as a good effort and applauded
for being free from coarseness and profanity, with not a single line
which 'could offend the most fastidious taste'.

Another piece of hack work was *The New Table Book*. Edited by
Mark and brought out by Bradbury and Evans in 1867, it promised
'pictures for young and old parties, with a copy of verses to each
picture, and a page for everybody's favourite'. Addressing his readers
as 'Gentles All', Mark affected an archaic style to explain that,

'although the Pictures speak for themselves, it hath been thought meet to tag them with much reason. There will be many, for certes, inclined to fancy that they could put their pens to better use.' Such persons should inscribe their favourites on these 'fair pages'. 'And when invited to set down their favourite "Book", let us fondly hope thou wilt write in thy best "Roman hand", The New Table Book, and Good Speed to it.'

More ambitious was Mark's next venture, the *Legends of Number Nip*, a rendering of Johann Karl Musaeus' *Rübezahl*. These German tales of the 'turnip numberer' had been translated into English by W. Beckford in 1791, shortly after Musaeus' death. Working from this translation, Mark adapted the legends for youthful readers. When first approached on the feasibility of bringing out this volume, Alexander Macmillan, wondering whether such folk-lore might not be '*too* grotesque and too local for our aim', had suggested as an alternative the compilation of Joe Millers.[10] With *The Jest Book* now off the press, he approved *Number Nip* late in 1864. Charles Keene supplied the illustrations.

In an introductory essay Mark explains why he has occupied himself with these legends in an age when materialism has 'combined to destroy the popular belief in Fairies, Fays, Elves, Trolls, and Dwarfs'. Despite the practical emphasis of recent years, he finds human nature 'in reality unchanged': by seeking pleasure in music, poetry, art, the public still pays 'homage to the Imaginative whilst professing to consider the Material as omnipotent'. On this premise he has concluded that his readers have 'not parted with the Fairies', nor will they be 'willing to cast away the works of those who have recorded their exploits in the wonderful Fairyland, or in the no less beautiful world around us'. He is confident that such legends will continue to delight succeeding generations 'as they have done for hundreds of years'.

A brief historical summary pays tribute to those 'who have thought it worthy of their wisdom to read and write about the Good People and their marvellous doings': Jacob Grimm, Hans Christian Andersen, Thomas Keightley, Crofton Croker. Mark focuses his commentary, naturally, on the 'good Musaeus', who collected stories from old women at their spinning-wheels and even from children in the street, reworking his material with a 'charm of style' which will 'always ensure an immense popularity'. In justifying his own volume

10 Ibid.

as a compilation from a translation of Musaeus, Mark maintains that he has carefully avoided the errors of his predecessor: the introduction of 'much that was extraneous, and more that was very objectionable'.

What errors and extraneous material did Mark find objectionable? The answer is to be found in a comparison of his *Number Nip* with the translation from which he worked, Beckford's complete and exact rendering of Musaeus. With characteristic vigilance Mark has deleted anything even remotely suggestive: 'bastard brood' yields to 'unnatural brood'; 'mistress' in the respectable sense of a beloved succumbs to the obliterating pencil; and 'the abortions of a sick imagination' is emasculated as 'the creations of a disordered imagination'. Slashed ruthlessly is the vivid description of 'a damsel, lovely to behold', as, 'unencumbered with drapery', she emerges from a brook. So is the observation that baths in all ages have been the 'favourite scene of amorous adventures'. Even the blameless injunction of a nymph to her 'virgins to keep strict watch, lest any prying eye should profane their maiden modesty' has been blotted out. Likewise condemned as unfit for youthful eyes is the flippant version of man's original sin: 'The first woman, even in the garden of Eden, could so ill brook her husband's serious turn, that she therefore took up with the serpent as a confidant.' Mark is also careful to soften all references to physical violence, all intrusions of rough language.

What he has accomplished, then, is to condense the original, but too often at a sacrifice of specific detail, concrete images, and earthiness. For the vigour of Musaeus, faithfully preserved in Beckford's translation, he has substituted a bland diet intended for youthful Victorians. That it satisfied at least one critic is attested by the review in the *Athenaeum* (4 March 1865). 'Its usefulness cannot be disputed,' contends the writer, 'and there is no want of dignity in the labour which is directed toward dividing what is hurtful to young minds from that which affords them hearty and refined amusement.'

In addressing young readers, Mark was most successful with tales of his own invention. Here he reached his peak in 1869 with *Tinykin's Transformations*, published by Bradbury and Evans. Handsomely bound in scarlet cloth, embossed in gold with fantastic figures from the story, and liberally illustrated by Charles Green, its attractive format must have appealed to Victorian children. Just as

Mark had dedicated his *Enchanted Doll* to Dickens's daughters in 1848, so he now inscribed this last fairy tale with the names of his six grandchildren: Alice, Daisy, and Ethel [Martin]; and Leslie, Mark, and Ralph [Romer].

Set in the time of King Horsa, Lord of the Saxons, the story relates the adventures of the boy Tinykin, a Sunday child capable of seeing fairies. His four successive transformations as an ouzel, a fish, a fawn, and a mole (all in fulfilment of his own wishes) are accomplished by Titania, the Fairy Queen, who has fallen in love with him. During each of his changes she protects him from danger, always restoring him to his mortal body before his next metamorphosis. In his human form he has no recollection of the experiences just concluded. During his pink-mole stage he climaxes his adventures by rescuing the King's daughter from the land of ugly gnomes, thereby winning her hand. Introduced as minor characters are his mother (Margery), a tender-hearted woman, and his father (Thomas), an ill-tempered verderer assigned to clearing the forest for the King's hunt.

For a children's story the tale gets off to a slow start. The first five pages are devoted to the setting, Tilgate Forest, not far from Crawley. Mark must have credited young Victorians with phenomenal patience. Or he may have intended this localized description specifically for his grandchildren. Once the narrative gets under way, however, it is sufficiently exciting to hold the interest of small readers. The festivities at Titania's fairy court, the suspenseful crises during Tinykin's hazardous transformations, the pathetic account of his slow recovery from illness following a narrow escape—all capture the childish imagination. Compelling, too, is the natural and realistic dialogue. Tinykin actually speaks like a small boy. Asked by his father where Titania comes from, he replies excitedly, 'From Fairyland. I can see bright wings under her rags, and a pretty face through the wrinkled skin that covers it.' To this the father responds roughly, 'What's the boy mean?' His wife has to remind him that their son 'is a Sunday child, and can see fairies'. The conversation is lively throughout.

Much less appropriate is the language of the narrative portions. Either Mark was determined to educate his readers by not writing down to their level, or he just automatically lapsed into his own idiom when, as author omniscient, he turned to his hero's adventures. In any event, the vocabulary is often strangely out of line:

trees are covered with *verdure*, there are *conjectures* about Tinykin's *tribulations*, Tilgate Forest is in a state of *primeval solitude*, and a Fish Baron, by his *necromantic* influence, compels his victims to sacrifice themselves to his appetite. Also sophisticated are the literary allusions: to Bottom, who would in 'after time lay his head in Titania's lap'; and to Sycorax, whose 'dainty spirit, named Ariel, had that day been set free from bondage by one Prospero, much against the will of the old witch'.

Such blemishes are offset, fortunately, by vivid details, imaginative appeal, and sprightly humour, all geared to the tastes of a youthful audience. No children would fail to respond to the account of the kiss Titania plants on Tinykin's forehead, 'to make his eyes feel full of sleep, and a delicious dreaminess to fill his brain, until he sank down upon the green turf'. Nor would they withhold their willing suspension of disbelief when Tinykin, during his metamorphosis as an ouzel, swallows two live beetles and is punished for his greediness: 'Fancy how uncomfortable he must have been, when, as you might have seen by the heaving of his shining black bosom, his dinner was disagreeing with him.' And they would find amusing the grotesque bit about the Fish Baron's wife, a fish so 'singularly beautiful that the Baron preferred marrying her to eating her'.

As for the moral and instructive comments, these, by Victorian standards, have been kept to a minimum and are more often implied than stated. The underlying truth—that difficult and unwelcome experiences give us the weapons and armour through which we later triumph over circumstances seemingly unrelated to our early trials—is so unlaboured as hardly to be evident. But Mark could not altogether resist intrusions aimed at edifying his child readers. Such is the comment that 'our own sorrows and the observance of the sorrows of others correct our selfishness and make us more kind and forbearing. One can hardly understand a proper "love to our neighbour" if we ourselves have no experience of grief and disappointments.' For little girls there is also indoctrination designed to prepare them for their properly subordinate role in womanhood: Margery, who once gives her husband the 'sound drubbing' he deserves, feels remorse 'afterwards, as she thought it was sinful not to obey her husband—all good wives should think the same'.

Mark's tale concludes with a circular device: a return to the locale introduced at the beginning. By referring to actual places near Crawley, the final lines fuse fairy lore with reality and preserve the

spell of enchantment: 'The fairies are said to have left us for good
and aye; but there are some pretty creatures as beautiful as the
fairies could possibly have been, to be seen haunting the margin of
Katrine Lake in Tilgate Forest, and playing under the green oaks of
Brantridge Park.'

* * *

At the age of fifty-four Mark brought his writing career to a
climax by becoming a novelist. On the completion of his first novel,
Wait for the End, published by Bradbury and Evans in 1863, the
Punch Table made a special point of honouring him. Silver noted
the occasion in his diary: 'Pater feelingly proposes Mark's health
and success to his novel—his maiden effort in a new path of penmanship. [Did Silver perhaps regard Mark's new effort as little more
than 'penmanship'?] M[ark] L[emon] replies with tears in his voice—
and hopes his friends will pardon him for any discredit the work may
bring—it was written to relieve him of a temporary distress and not
for any selfish feeling or ambition.' The 'temporary distress' was,
of course, his usual financial embarrassment—by now such an
established pattern as not to be 'temporary' any longer. According
to Mark, 'Pater' had offered him so tempting a sum for his first novel
that, in justice to his children, he was forced to write. Confident that
he could tell a story, he began by sketching the plot: he thought first
of the catastrophe and then of what would lead up to it. Two days
out of every week he wrote, completing a chapter a day, thirty-eight
in all. (He seems to have had the dogged persistence of Trollope.)
As the book grew there was great interest at Vine Cottage in his new
venture. Once, after more than the usual flurry, one of Mark's little
girls exclaimed, 'Mamma, I'm so excited; I feel just as if I'd been
writing a novel.'[11]

Opening with the college days of two brothers, one good, the
other evil, *Wait for the End* takes the reader at a leisurely jog-trot
through some twenty years, introduces the fortunes of a second
generation, and concludes in the third volume by punishing vice and
rewarding virtue. In short, it follows the course of many novels
written in the first half of the century, before George Eliot and
George Meredith had pointed the way to new techniques. Apparently
unaware of recent developments and rising standards in fiction,
Mark seems to have been interested primarily in incidents for their

[11] Silver.

own sake. Of these there is no lack. Thrown in for good measure are robbery, forgery, perjury, swindling, spying, with a cursing father, estranged brothers, and a vindictive wife sustaining the action. In spite of the persistence of danger and violence, however, the reader always knows that all will come out right in the end, for which he is constantly told to wait.

In the next novel, *Loved at Last* (Bradbury and Evans, 1864), Mark again kept the title in view throughout the book, repeatedly thrusting it at the reader with irritating monotony. It applies specifically to the two heroines, who, after the perils and disappointments of three volumes, come to the happy realization that they are 'loved at last'. As in the earlier work, justice is again meted out, as the dishonest head of a firm with the transparent name of Pilcher and Company spends his last days in poverty and blindness.

In 1866 Hurst and Blackett published what is generally considered Mark's best fiction, *Falkner Lyle; or, the Story of Two Wives*, dedicated to the widow of Herbert Ingram. The plot revolves around a man who, disappointed in love, rashly marries someone whom he has known only briefly. She immediately makes his life miserable. Only his devotion to their daughter, once he has rescued her from her mother's criminal neglect, enables him to endure emigration, privations, and persecution. After a span of years all is satisfactorily resolved: his wicked wife poisons herself and he is free to marry his first love, who has secretly nourished an affection for him all these years.

Encouraged by the favourable reviews of this novel, Mark produced two works of fiction the following year. The first, *Leyton Hall* (Hurst and Blackett), is set in the time of Charles I and introduces John Milton as a minor character. The principal narrative revolves around Edward Leyton, a Royalist, who is tricked into believing his wife unfaithful. After years of separation and suffering she at last convinces her husband of her blameless devotion. The story concludes at the end of the first volume with Mark's intrusion: 'Gentle reader! we kiss your hand, and thank you for your patience.' The second and third volumes are made up of tales adapted from his plays and some of his reprinted Christmas pieces. The final, and major, work of the year was Mark's fourth full-length novel, *Golden Fetters*, published by Bradbury and Evans and dedicated to 'my very good Friends and Fellow-workers of Punch'. Its principal characters, all from the lower ranks, include a kindly actor, a slippery schemer, an ambitious mother, her degenerate son, and a tender maiden. The title, again repeatedly called to the reader's attention, emphasizes the thesis that the selfish and grasping are bound by golden fetters which destroy peace and happiness. Only through love can these bonds be severed, in this instance by the devotion of the golden-haired heroine. (At one time Mark had thought of calling the novel *Golden Hair*.)[12]

Mark's last work of fiction, *The Taffeta Petticoat*, was finished a short time before his death. Of the title he remarked: 'I thought it rather novel. The story all turns upon the colour of that particular article of dress.' Originally he had considered *The Blue Petticoat* as a possible title.

Writing in the tradition of the 'instinctive novelist', Mark, like Dickens in his early work, incorporated many features of his own experience. He drew heavily, for example, on his first-hand knowledge of the theatre for glimpses of rehearsals and backstage activity, for portraits of struggling actors, for comments on the declining state of the drama. Introduced at random are hunting scenes with baying foxhounds, sermons against poachers, descriptions of bucolic gatherings culminating in feasting and toasting. The villages and country houses are often modelled on Hendon and Crawley and their environs. Coaching days of a bygone era furnish some happy reminiscences as the traveller whirls along 'through pleasant country scenes . . . silently enjoying the ever changing landscapes, now of broad cultivated places, rich with their promised or accomplished harvests; now of great moorlands, golden with blossoms of the furze, or purple with flowers of the heather; the distance studded with farmers' homesteads or lordly mansions, and changing them to the glorious woodlands, watered by noble rivers or placid streams'.[13] References to London abound: to the Bedford Hotel as 'a favourite resort of country gentlemen', to Covent Garden, to Evans's Supper Rooms. Nor are Mark's friends overlooked in the character studies, Benjamin Webster, for instance, providing the model for an actor in *Wait for the End*. All is faithfully reported.

But like his contemporaries, particularly the early Dickens and Trollope, Mark frequently destroys the illusion of reality by suspending the narrative for his own comment. Repeatedly he intrudes to anticipate a new development or prejudge a character. At every turn the reader must be told in a confidential chat what to expect

[12] Ibid.   [13] *Wait for the End*.

next. 'This will be a very short chapter,' he learns in *Loved at Last*, 'if, indeed, it deserves to be a separate section of our story.' Later, a lull in the succession of adventures demands an explanation: 'We have closed for a time our *confessio amoris*, and opened the ledger— a dull volume enough,—and record therein small profit and loss.' After many more chapters the narrative at last grinds to its conclusion with the promise that 'we must gather up a few tangled threads, and then our task will be done'. But even then the final sentence ('So ends our story') comes only after further tedious interpolations.

The novels are also laden with comments on the writer's craft. 'It is one great privilege of a story-teller that he may spread out his sheet of paper as Prince Hassen spread out his necromantic carpet, and convey the reader backward and forward at will', Mark observes in *Falkner Lyle*. And immediately he exploits this privilege by shuttling between plots: 'It is useful to our story that we leave Bertha, and now follow the fortunes of Falkner Lyle.' Should the reader grow restless as the events run their leisurely course, he is reminded (in *Loved at Last*) that 'the story-teller's quill, like the magician's wand, is potent only by permission of superior agencies and we must wait patiently the coming events, having shown their shadows'. Occasionally, under the pretext of having inadvertently revealed too much, Mark will check himself with 'But we are anticipating.'

When coincidence and unmotivated incident tax the credulity of the reader, Mark pleads for understanding: 'This reads sadly like a romance, but our lives are all made up of unlooked for events' (*Wait for the End*). At times he discreetly refrains, as in *Golden Fetters*, from detailing before 'profane eyes' the amorous raptures of a trysting couple: 'We can record no more. What else was said was only in muttered words and broken sentences, so confused in meaning that to write them down coldly, would be treachery.'

Some of the digressions are clearly personal. 'We have no intention of accompanying them', Mark says in *Golden Fetters* of a couple *en route* to Switzerland, explaining 'that we are somewhat "fat and scant of breath" and have long sought "the shady side of the Mall" for our summer constitutional'. Here he also states his reaction to letters 'precariously crossed . . . a practice which we abominate and condemn, now that the penny post covers such a multitude of words'. Some pages later there is a 'hearty dislike' of the 'little brutes called "pets"', the cost of whose nurture would clothe and feed some neglected child'. (Within a few years George Eliot was to make the same point in *Middlemarch*, Dorothea Brooke referring to Maltese dogs as 'parasitic'.)

Occasionally Mark uses fiction to clarify his position on class distinctions. Like most conventional Victorians, he insisted that everyone stay in his proper sphere. Hence his admiring sketch of Martha Price, a faithful servant in *Falkner Lyle*, who 'would have felt herself scandalized had anyone addressed her as "Miss", or desired her to wait on table without a cap and her back hair done up in plaits and ribbons'. She would have looked with scorn on any housemaid who left her card or headed her 'notepaper with a monogram as large as a shilling'. And Mark interpolates: 'We have received both.' Though Martha has a silk dress, it was given to her as a present from her master on her wedding day, to be worn only on special occasions. Disdaining all social pretensions, she is a credit to her class as the 'best of servants'. She rises early and has her work done 'before many ignorant trollops [think] of leaving their beds'. And she takes pride in her appearance, keeping herself 'presentable throughout the day'. Though her labours in the kitchen necessarily expose her to 'spot and stain', she has always 'transmogrified herself into the neatest handed Phillis with the rapidity of a pantomime change' before carrying the dinner to the table.

As in many of his shorter pieces, Mark's Victorian attitude toward woman comes out in the novels. If she is strong minded, according to *Falkner Lyle*, she is a 'soul misplaced'. A wife can be admired only if she will submit to her husband. At the same time she must assume her share of responsibilities. 'Man and wife, in my opinion, should be a pair of post-horses,' observes a character in *Golden Fetters*. 'The man carries the weight, you know; and she's a bad 'un that won't stick to the collar when there's up-hill work to be done.' Finally, there is the usual emphasis on woman's chastity in preserving the sanctity of the domestic hearth. 'A woman's honour', the reader is reminded in *Wait for the End*, 'is like a polished glass—an infant's breath can cloud it.'

In addition to injecting his personal convictions, Mark occasionally interrupts the narrative flow of his novels with asides directed at his characters. In *Loved at Last*, when two women speculate whether a wealthy farmer will propose to a certain widow, they are reprimanded sharply: 'No! No! good gossips.' Similarly, in *Falkner Lyle* two girls, conjecturing that an acquaintance may have information of

which they are ignorant, are told, 'Very possibly, ladies.' Even a
horse, as it pulls its carriage too slowly, is admonished: 'Skip along,
good horse! there are five miles of straight road before you!'[14] And
Mark goes so far as to address his pen at intervals: 'No, hold back,
good goosequill.'[15]

In keeping with his determination never to let vulgarity disfigure
Punch, Mark's novels are morally irreproachable. Not a word, not
an act of passion dare stain his pages. 'But here we must close the
scene, not follow the devices of an impure imagination and an
unbridled nature to their close', *Falkner Lyle* sternly informs the
reader after a tepid scene. Moreover, profanity is, of course, un-
printable. 'No, the oath must not be recorded', Mark insists in
Wait for the End. If the offending term has actually been uttered, it
is represented by a dash, with an explanation: 'Here followed a
coarse expletive.' On one occasion an admirable character, having
passed the bounds of endurance, is allowed to explode with 'That's
—— nonsense!' This calls for a nudge from Mark. 'It was very
wrong,' he admits, 'but knowing what Jack meant, the Recording
Angel wrote it down beside Uncle Toby's oath.' As a reviewer
pointed out later, this is a slip, for in Sterne's *Tristram Shandy* the
oath is not permitted to remain on the record, but is blotted out by
the Recording Angel's tear.

Like his Christmas tales, Mark's novels condemn social injustice.
The corrupt legal system, the slums, the acute suffering and poverty
in the human warrens of the city arouse his indignation. 'Terrible
expiation for violated laws which have been transgressed as often
from ignorance as intention' is his indictment of transportation in
Wait for the End. 'It will be well if Society, that guards itself so
carefully, can hold up a clean hand and say, "I have done my duty to
these children of sin, and so claim a right to punish the offenders."'
Equally strong is the condemnation of 'dingy swarming alleys
crowded with tattered women and unwashed, lazy men clustering
round the doors of low-browed public houses, or seated in windowed
shops frowsy with piles of rubbish or displaying coarse or greasy
food'. That such misery should be tolerated in London, 'wealthy
beyond count, world-famous, wherein hundreds of churches abound,
and millions of people profess to follow the teachings of the Bible',[16]
is unforgivable. Such sentiments are strongly reminiscent of Dickens,
who made his social criticism an integral part of the novel, however,

[14] *Loved at Last.*   [15] *Falkner Lyle.*   [16] *Loved at Last.*

artistically reinforcing it with symbolism, mood, and prose cadence. By contrast Mark overloads his fiction with repertorial and editorial freightage.

Like Dickens, Mark also exposes religious hypocrisy, his fiction holding up to public scorn canting clergymen and purveyors of sourness and gloom. A preacher in *Falkner Lyle* is presented as 'one of the worst foes of Mother Church, who by arrogance and worldly pride, drove many simple souls away', because they were made to feel 'only rather troublesome poor relations at best'. And in *Golden Fetters* an actor relates how a minister 'preached at us and our profession' and 'took upon himself to be accuser, first witness, judge, and executioner; and the course of his sermon distributed as much red fire as would have served a pantomime'. In the same novel a spinster also disseminates gloom. Of 'very Low Church' persuasion, she feels 'called upon to protest against the beneficence of Providence, which has given us much that is bright and beautiful, and exhilarating, to compensate us for our sorrows and disappointments'.

A further Dickensian flavour pervades Mark's pathos. But the model here is always the early Dickens, who had yet to master his craft. There is the same use of lachrymose detail, of emotionally charged situations. Indeed, Dickens's maudlin account of Smike's death in *Nicholas Nickleby* is matched by a comparable scene in *Golden Fetters*, the death of Mildred. 'Mother, who is that boy standing by my bed?' she asks. 'He has been crying. Now he looks upon me with such a loving face. Ah! I know his name! It is Percy— dear, dear Brother!' Should the reader resist this tug at his heart strings, there is still the final pull: 'Her head sank upon her pillow— her voice was silent. When it was heard again it seemed to be answering the angel calling her to rest.'

*　　　*　　　*

In view of Mark's obvious shortcomings as a novelist, there seems to be much to blame, little to praise. 'We cannot congratulate the author on his performance', declared the *Saturday Review* (17 March 1866) in assessing his fiction. 'Mr. Mark Lemon stands so high in his own peculiar province that we the more regret that he should waste his powers in a line of art for which he is less fitted.' It would be unfair, however, to dismiss his novels as entirely without merit. Repeatedly they illustrate one of his chief virtues as a writer, his powers of careful observation. Whether he describes a rural scene, narrates an episode from theatrical life, or mirrors human idiosyncrasies, his is the fidelity that comes from first-hand knowledge. And the whole is enlivened by forthright humour, especially when pretentiousness and sham come under his scalpel. In *Golden Fetters*, for instance, a hypocritical and designing woman tries to ingratiate herself with a brother whom she has long ignored. Having just learned of his recent prosperity, she affects a show of tenderness by throwing her arms around his neck and trying to weep. 'But hers was a strong nature, and no water was to be found near the surface', Mark observes impishly. Equally pungent is the account of an evangelical spinster who 'swept and garnished her conscience twice every Sunday' and sat down to cold chicken for her dinner, 'tea and potatoes being the only hot items allowed'.

Also worthy of notice are the striking images which occasionally enrich Mark's pen portraits. Such is this simile in *Wait for the End*: 'Mrs. Jellifer moved about her house like an intelligent cat, catching such stray mice as came in her way, rarely showing her claws, and never having scratched [her husband] more than once or twice during the long course of their connubial connection.' (But here, unfortunately, the reader must be told that 'we are pleased with our simile of a cat'.) Even the description of a coffin benefits from a striking comparison: 'It was most respectable, being black cloth, with an angel blowing a trumpet a top and stuck all over with cherubs looking for all the world like apple dumplings with wings.'

In spite of such Dickensian flashes, however, Mark's novels are little more than a pale shadow of the master's. Doubtless no one realized this better than he, for he had no delusions about being a first-rate novelist. According to his own admission, he wrote, not for fame, but in the hope of earning a few additional pounds to leave his children. That he also wrote to escape the harassments of the present by losing himself in fancy is suggested by his confession that 'scribbling is a pleasure'.

11

'IN *PROPRIA PERSONA*'

WHILE augmenting his income by writing, Mark also began wooing his public by presenting himself in his own person. With Dickens scoring triumphs as lecturer and dramatic reader, why should he not make a similar bid for popularity? The public ought to welcome an opportunity to see and hear the editor of England's leading comic journal. He would begin with a venture for which he was admirably qualified: a series of illustrated talks on London and its history, to be delivered early in 1862. 'Just imagine what I can tell in my short time about London,' he told his friends. 'The changes which have taken place within my memory are marvellous.'

Shortly after announcing his plans he met a favourable reaction from the Press. 'He brings to his work the invaluable qualifications with what it is fitting in a literary man to offer and good for an intelligent individual to receive,' commented the *Illustrated London News*; 'and he possesses . . . the physical advantages of a lecturer, a fine voice and a popular manner.' Having already distinguished himself by his performances in Dickens's amateur theatricals, continued the paper, he should be on the best of terms with his audience. As the 'Prime Minister of *Punch* (and "viceroy over him")' he could count on an enthusiastic welcome as he made his appearance 'in *propria persona*'.

With characteristic energy and industry Mark went about assembling his materials from appropriate sources. He began with Fitzstephen for the twelfth century and continued with Stow, Camden, and Holinshed for the sixteenth; Clarendon, Pepys, and Evelyn for the seventeenth; and Charles Knight and John Morley, among others, for contemporary history. Especially useful was a handbook on London by his friend Peter Cunningham, the critic and author, with whom he corresponded regularly. 'In company of these authorities', Mark explained in a prefatory note, 'we propose to walk "up and down the streets of London", chatting as we go, and occasionally detailing some of our experiences—very small change to mix with the golden legends of the old City.'

The material was organized as two separate lectures, each approximately two hours in length: the first, Old London City, with notes on such topics as Old London Bridge, Old Southwark, Paul's Walk, Cornhill on May Day, Bartholomew Fair, Staple Inn, Fleet Prison, and Old Fleet Street; the second, London and West-minster, with concentration on the Temple and Temple Bar, Drury Lane and Covent Garden, the Strand, Old Whitehall, and Ranelagh. Large maps and painted scenery would represent the various places mentioned, with marionettes in the foreground furnishing the animation. As was to be expected, Mark injected some lively asides. Revealing something of his own aesthetic taste, he commented on the equestrian statue of Charles I at Charing Cross as clearly not having 'been erected in honour of the late Mr. Guy Fawkes'. It was 'not a Guy, but a beautiful work of art'. Mark bestowed no such praise on the Duke of Wellington's statue over the arch at the entrance to Green Park: this, he punned, was 'the arch-absurdity'. To Paddy Green, occasionally his host at Evans's Hotel, he handed bouquets for 'having reformed the character of London supper-rooms'. Such digressions helped to offset the general impression that the lectures, because of the very nature of their material, owed more to research than to originality. For whenever Mark had first-hand knowledge of an event or place he introduced details based on observation.

Arranged for the Gallery of Illustration on 6 and 13 January, the Lectures, entitled 'About London', were preceded by elaborate printed programmes. These included, in addition to an itemized summary of the topics treated in the two parts, an inset map of London after the Great Fire, a list of the principal authorities cited, and selections from a 'popular history of England'. Even cab fares from the Gallery of Illustration to various parts of the metropolis were given. As the day of the first lecture approached, Mark became increasingly nervous. 'I'm afraid the subject won't take,' he told his colleagues at the Wednesday-night dinner.[1]

But his fears, happily, were not realized. 'Fashionable and intelligent audiences' listened to him with interest. 'A reference to his programme had led them to expect an exceedingly instructive and

[1] Silver.

elaborate lecture, and not merely a light and sketchy composition intended to amuse and disappoint', reported the *Illustrated London News*. The result 'fully justified' such expectations. *The Times* commended Mark for his industry in collecting a wealth of archaeological information, and promised that 'those who listen to him attentively will learn as much about their forefathers in an hour-and-a-half, as by much thinking over musty volumes. . . . Mr. Lemon not only tells "about London", but he tells his hearers *all* about London.' So successful were his appearances that the *Punch* Table declared, 'Mark should have a brass band to his lectures.'[2]

Encouraged by his favourable reception in London, Mark took his entertainment to the provinces in early spring. He began with Crawley. The proceeds went towards the erection of a large gas lamp in front of the parish church, where at winter evening services the worshippers could hardly enter or leave without jostling each other in the dark. Since the introduction of gas lighting in other parts of the village, reported the local columnist, 'darkness in any place regularly frequented by the inhabitants has naturally enough become intolerable'. At the conclusion of the lectures Mark acknowledged the Reverend John Soper's thanks by assuring the audience that he was ready 'at all times and under all circumstances to render any and every service he could to make Crawley—or rather to keep it—one of the prettiest of places'.

Subsequent engagements took him to Bath, Bristol, Worcester, Nottingham, Wakefield, Birmingham, and Derby. His appearance in Wakefield was heralded by a quotation from one of the London morning papers: 'One can scarcely help regretting that Mr. Lemon has not long ere this given us the benefit of his rich fancy upon the platform as well as in the drama and the pages of *Punch*.' Later his performance was praised for its 'sterling tone of instruction, here and there streaked with flashes of wit'. There was, however, one disturbing note: 'The whole was treated by Mr. Lemon in so superior a style . . . that we regret that, owing to the exceedingly unfavourable state of the weather, but few had the pleasure of witnessing the entertainment.' In Birmingham the reaction was more restrained. 'The effect of his pleasant disquisitions' was felt to result from 'the manner and the man, rather than the matter of his discourse', which was packed with information enough for three, rather than two, lectures. The reviewer in a spate of confused

[2] Ibid.

metaphors offered his opinion that 'the facts tread so closely upon each other's heels that a dripping fire of puns is almost the only palliative treatment admissible'. In Derby, however, there was nothing but acclaim: 'An entertainment more abounding in intellectual wealth and quaint fancy we have not heard or witnessed for a long time past.' It was hoped, moreover, that after the conclusion of his tour Mark would 'give to the world, in the shape of a book, the benefit of his painstaking research'.

This suggestion he carried out eventually, but not until he had once more addressed Londoners for an entire week, commencing 5 May, at the Gallery of Illustration. Following his final engagement he put his manuscript aside, returning to it at intervals for revision and amplification. Early in 1867 the lectures were published as a little book by Chapman and Hall under the title *Up and Down the London Streets*. 'Mr. Lemon lets the reader of his volume understand that he is not chained to a Dryasdust expounder of ancient metropolitan history', commented the *Athenaeum* as it cited examples of his spontaneous humour. But this generally favourable review closed with a slight reprimand: 'A careful revision will indeed benefit the volume, for there are many *slips* which have been overlooked.'

Less than a year after his provincial lecture tour Mark again took to the road, this time with a reading of his drama *Hearts Are Trumps*. Entirely rewritten as a tale, with a generous admixture of pathos and humour, the piece was well adapted for oral presentation. Mark had already tried it out several times at the penny readings in Crawley. Beginning his engagements early in February 1863, he visited Bath, Bristol, Sunderland, Durham, and Newcastle, always interrupting his tour to spend his two days a week at the *Punch* office. At Bath and Bristol he created such a sensation that he had to return for repeat performances, to accommodate those who had been unable to get seats the first time. If he saw the *Western Daily Press* shortly after, he must have been gratified. Predicting that such plays as *Hearts Are Trumps* would eventually supplant Boucicault's 'sensational and non-natural dramas', the reporter applauded Mark's 'natural portraiture of men and women'. (The derogatory reference to Boucicault should not have been unwelcome to Benjamin Webster's old friend.) 'In the grave and in the gay, in the comic and the pathetic', Mark was said to be 'equally at home'. In Sunderland a few days later the *Herald* marvelled both at the dramatic effect achieved without stage setting and the easy 'transition from laughter and mirth to the deepest pathos'. Equally enthusiastic were the reactions to Mark's other provincial appearances. He was usually referred to as the 'genial author' and accorded honour as a great editor.

His next, and most ambitious, public entertainment was one for which he was admirably suited: the dramatic Falstaff readings adapted from Parts I and II of Shakespeare's *Henry IV*. His role as Sir John in *The Merry Wives of Windsor* with Dickens's amateur troupe had convinced him that here was a superbly conceived character. Further study of *Henry IV* and *Henry V* led him to conclude, moreover, that the fat knight had seldom been fully appreciated or properly impersonated. 'Falstaff was a gentleman, fallen away, in the general degeneracy of the times, from the path of rectitude; but, nevertheless, a gentleman', he insisted. 'He was not a buffoon.'[3] Correctly assessing the culture of a knight who could render an extempore play scene in 'King Cambyses' vein', bandy conceits with his Prince, and recognize with envy the latter's ability to quote Scripture, Mark strove to present a polished character, worthy, but for his vices, of a place at court: a man who, however gluttonous, required his capon to be suitably sauced and served. In matters of etiquette Falstaff must be shown as the peer of Prince Hal and Poins, not of the crude ruffians Peto and Bardolph. A courtly comedian—this was the new concept which Mark had already offered in *The Merry Wives* and now planned to re-create more elaborately in the *Henry IV* readings.

The faults of this courtly knight he was either to suppress altogether or render as venial rather than vicious. Sensing that the falsehoods were designed more to entertain than to deceive, he declared them 'mostly white lies'. Such peccadilloes as armed robbery, sponging on friends, and the grossest of war profiteering he disposed of by the sympathetic comment that 'Falstaff was so very hard up!'[4]

How often had Mark himself invented schemes (of a more blameless if less ingenious sort) to find a few more pounds! But this was only one of the parallels that drew him to Sir John: 'Like Falstaff, I am fat and growing old, heaven help the wicked!' he exclaimed. 'I might have as great difficulty in getting up again, being down, as poor Jack had.'[5] Other physical resemblances were the massive white beard, grown only recently, the shock of silver hair—and, of

[3] Hatton, *With a Show*, pp. 17–20.   [4] Ibid.   [5] Ibid.

course, the provocative twinkle in his eye, for as editor of *Punch* he could say with Falstaff, 'I am not only witty in myself, but the cause that wit is in other men.'

His decision to undertake the dramatic readings may have been hastened when in 1864 he attended the superb revival of *Henry IV*, Part I, given at Drury Lane for the tercentenary of Shakespeare's birth. Samuel Phelps's performance as Falstaff he pronounced somewhat 'hard'. (Did he mean that it lacked grace and gentility? Or that it stressed the callousness of the character?) At any rate, his own concept had taken shape, and when Shirley Brooks said, 'But you can play Falstaff better than anyone', Mark may have needed no more encouragement.[6]

After further bouts of study he selected portions from both parts of *Henry IV* and adapted them for the stage with Falstaff as the central character. With Willert Beale (Walter Maynard), the impresario who had tried unsuccessfully to put Dickens under contract for a reading tour, he then booked a series of engagements. Mark was to choose his own cast. As his share for fifty-two appearances, five hundred pounds would be paid down. Profits were to be divided equally.

Though his intimates would have seen his financial need as sufficient motivation for undertaking such a time-consuming and physically arduous venture, Mark promoted it as a vindication of Falstaff, preparing an official statement that promised a fresh view of the character. This interpretation having won 'thoughtful recognition and earnest approval' from those whose opinion he valued, he declared that he could no longer resist the repeated invitations to present his conception of Falstaff 'to a larger audience'. To the announcement was appended the programme of his public appearances.

In adapting his material, Mark used only those portions in which Falstaff figured prominently. From Part I he chose the following: I, ii (Falstaff's intimacy with the Prince and the latter's plot with Poins to play a trick on the highwaymen); II, ii (the robbery near Gadshill, with the subsequent dispersal of Falstaff and his companions); II, iv (a comical tavern scene, highlighted by the rehearsal for Hal's conference with the King); III, iii (Falstaff's charge that his pocket has been picked at the Boar's Head); a telescoping of IV, ii, and V, i (Falstaff's description of his soldiers,

[6] Silver.

followed by his catechism on honour). From Part II Mark took fewer scenes: I, i (Falstaff's address to his page and his encounter with the Chief Justice); II, i (Falstaff's arrest at the suit of the Hostess, followed by his placating her); V, v (Hal's repudiation of Falstaff during the coronation procession). It is significant that Mark omitted all the battlefield scenes. These would have called for more exertion than he felt equal to, especially where Falstaff carries the body of Hotspur on his back. Moreover, some of the episodes would have discredited Sir John, particularly where he offers the Prince a bottle of sack in lieu of his pistol and later stabs the corpse of Hotspur. Throughout, all bustling activity was omitted, so that Mark could usually stand or sit.

A more significant exclusion was that of the coarser scenes in Part II, in which the pox-ridden old lecher becomes at times more repulsive than comical. Rightly assessing the taste of the Victorian audience, and being reluctant to vilify his favourite hero, Mark offered a version in which the Prince's harsh repudiation of Falstaff seemed hardly justified. The adaptation did, however, invite the full luxury of pity for the banished knight, and guaranteed the pathos of Mark's final scene—a sentimental pathos which may have moved its creator more than did the stronger pathos of that episode discreetly omitted: the ageing Sir John, a fifteenth-century 'call girl' on his knee, crying, 'Peace, good Doll! Do not speak like a death's head. Do not bid me remember mine end.'

For this dialogue Mark followed Shakespeare rather closely, except when, for economy, he telescoped several speeches. After the fashion of Thomas Bowdler, he either omitted or altered improprieties of language to conform to the taste of the time. *Whoreson*, *fat-guts*, and *bull's-pizzle* were obvious deletions. But the innocent *belly*, allowed by Bowdler in 1818, was now condemned in 1868, giving way to *body*, thus spoiling the accurate image of 'a decreasing leg, an increasing belly' as symptoms of age. *Wench*, however, was retained (Bowdler had rendered 'most sweet wench' as 'most sweet girl')—and, amazingly, so was Falstaff's boast that he might get a wife in the *stews*.

Deleted were all irreverent mentions of the deity: 'for God's sake' was softened to 'for heaven's sake'; 'may God my girdle break', to 'let my girdle break'. For the milder *damned* and *damnable* were substituted *hanged* and *abominable*. To his friends Mark handsomely absolved Shakespeare of blame 'for making Falstaff use language which we feel called upon to exclude from our drawing-room version'. It was the language of the time, he told them. 'Look in any other playwright's work, and see what others did. They gave you indecency for indecency's sake, lewdness without wit, filth without humour.'[7]

For his production Mark planned no elaborate settings, the stage 'to be hung with tapestry only, as in the days of Shakespeare'. Instead of a curtain to indicate the end of an act, an attendant in Elizabethan attire would hang a placard on the backdrop to announce the change of scene. Furniture, limited to the barest essentials, was to be moved whenever necessary in full sight of the audience.

Assisting Mark would be his son Harry as Bardolph, together with a cast of professionals. These included Herbert Crellin from the Theatre Royal, Queens, as Prince Hal; W. L. Brancombe from the Adelphi, doubling as Poins and Chief Justice; and from the Olympic, Rose Garland as Dame Quickly and John Clarke as Justice Shallow.

Opening at the Gallery of Illustration on 12 October 1868, the entertainment was to run for twelve nights only. Wednesday, of course, would be dark, with Mark attending the weekly *Punch* dinner. As the first night approached he grew impatient with the printers because of their slowness in preparing notices. He hastily dispatched a message urging that 'some fifty on stout board and varnished' be sent him without delay.[8] Like Dickens, instead of delegating responsibility, he tried to take care of everything himself: publicity, tickets, and wardrobe. His own costume, expertly designed by John Tenniel, was completely authentic. From helmet to high boots, from staff to sword and buckler, it omitted nothing. Obviously Mark required little padding. It must have given him some satisfaction that he, like two of the actors mentioned in his *Up and Down the London Streets* ('Fat' Harper and Stephen Kemble), could play Falstaff 'without stuffing'.

Hectic days preceded the first performance. Staying in his chambers at the Bedford Hotel instead of trying to go to and from Crawley, Mark entertained a succession of tailors and painters, all the while trying to meet his editorial responsibilities. Once he cut a ludicrous figure as he dictated with Falstaff's helmet still resting on his head. The dress rehearsal was a fiasco: Mark was nervous, the

[7] Hatton, *With a Show*, pp. 58–59.
[8] P.O. MS.

actors did not know their lines and missed their cues, and the whole performance dragged.

Tense with anxiety, Mark arrived at the Gallery of Illustration for the opening night. Struggling into his costume, he could hear the hum of voices, punctuated by laughter, as the crowd filled the auditorium. Five weeks of favourable publicity had generated considerable interest, the *Gentleman's Magazine* (September) having gone so far as to call him 'the mentor of nearly all the Wits of the Age'.

At the conclusion of the overture (appropriately from Balfe's *Falstaff*) the curtains parted upon a rather bare stage: a table and a few chairs, backed by a tapestry representing a wood. Though there was little action, the players sitting or standing about the table, the entertainment moved rapidly. From the first, Falstaff maintained his superiority over the supporting cast. In spite of his size he carried himself gracefully. His hand lifted in salute or farewell was regal. Spontaneous applause greeted his line 'I am not only witty in myself, but the cause that wit is in other men', its significance being applied to Mark personally as the editor of *Punch*. But the crowning triumph came with Falstaff's disgrace and banishment, when his habitual jauntiness changed abruptly to an attitude of despair and misery. The audience responded with murmurs of pity, then broke into a storm of applause.

The notices were complimentary for the most part. Mark's impersonation was pronounced a 'thoughtful rendering' by a 'living portrait' of Sir John. Because he had 'apparently studied the character more as a critic than an actor', said the *Gentleman's Magazine* (November), his performance had shown more 'intelligence than would otherwise be the case'. The *Athenaeum* (24 October) declared that he had 'the rare intelligence that seizes every point of wit and every shade of character with instant felicity'. *The Times* (14 October) lauded his skill as an actor: 'He does not allow a syllable to drop unheard, and his distribution of emphasis shows the nicest discrimination. By acting instead of reading Falstaff he allows himself freedom of gesticulation that would be denied him on the ordinary platform.' 'The professional actor might indeed learn much from Mr. Lemon,' observed the *Illustrated London News* (17 October), 'for, although always effective, he is always natural and never exaggerates. Every point tells without effort, and all the more because no effort is made to make it tell.'

Impressed by such criticisms, the Prince and Princess of Wales asked to see the production. For them and their party Mark arranged a private performance. The Gallery of Illustration was appropriately decorated, refreshments were provided, and a special band was engaged. In the flurry of seeing after the final arrangements, however, Mark had forgotten to station an attendant in the cloak-room. When the Royal guests arrived there was no one to wait on them. In the nick of time Harry spied the niece of a minor member of the cast and pushed her into the cloak-room. 'Go in there and take off the Princess' shawl,' he ordered.[9]

The selected audience enjoyed the performance immensely, Princess Alexandra laughing heartily during the scene in which Falstaff impersonates the King. Afterwards Prince Edward wished to see Mark, who came to the front of the stage immediately. (Here his behaviour was more compliant than that of Dickens, who, when Queen Victoria asked to see him after a performance of *The Frozen Deep*, excused himself as unwilling to appear in his stage clothes and make-up.) The Prince received Mark cordially, warmly clasped his hand, and thanked him for the pleasure he and the cast had given the entire party.[10]

After the Gallery of Illustration engagements, Mark and his troupe played in St. George's Hall, Langham Place, from 2 to 7 November. In December, with the regular theatres staging the usual Christmas pantomimes and many persons spending their holidays in the country, there were no performances of *Falstaff*. After all, Mark himself so enjoyed the season that nothing, not even the prospect of a few extra pounds, could lure him away from the festivity at Vine Cottage. But early in 1869 all was in readiness for a provincial tour of the North, with Joseph Hatton, impresario and lecturer, as manager. Travelling without a caravan, the players were burdened with numerous boxes containing the costumes and tapestry, all labelled *Falstaff*. The inconveniences of the tour were somewhat relieved, though, by the courteous attention of the railway officials.

En route to Scotland, the players stopped first at Cheltenham for an appearance on 21 January. It was Mark's misfortune to be followed there the next day by Dickens, whose reading apparently overshadowed *Falstaff*, for the Cheltenham *Chronicle* carried a full column under the heading 'An Evening with Dickens', but ignored

[9] Hatton, *With a Show*, pp. 157–8.   [10] Ibid.

Mark, even though it had earlier benefited from his paid advertising.

The first Scottish engagement was at Glasgow, at fifty pounds a night with the company's expenses paid. The natives were friendly, the accommodation excellent. A sumptuous dinner awaited the players after their first performance: thirty different kinds of sandwiches, ham, beef, spiced egg, lobster, crab, anchovy, salmon, potted meats, collops, cock-a-leekie, and a variety of hot dishes. During the day Mark enjoyed his rambles. Through stores, warehouses, shipyards he wandered, stopping everywhere to chat with foremen and workers. Was he tired? No, never, he insisted. He seemed to be finding his youth again, as if determined to relive his frolicsome days with Dickens and the provincial theatricals.

Having struck up an acquaintance with one of the prettiest girls in Glasgow, Harry was also using his leisure to good advantage. But when the young lady saw him on the stage as Bardolph she was shocked. 'I never saw such a dreadful man in all my days as ye were,' she exclaimed. 'Why did ye not tak' the part o' the Prince? I would hae liked ye better. . . . Whatever did ye do to your nose?' Poor Harry! If the papers mentioned his role at all, it was only for his nose—Bardolph's 'burning lamp'. But for this unromantic make-up he might have risked a proposal to the Glasgow lass.[11]

With Edinburgh, his next stop, Mark was enchanted. 'You cannot wonder at the Scotch being a proud race, vain in their country, and Edinburgh in particular', he declared. 'What a great city it is. What rare citizens!' During a sight-seeing tour he stood in front of John Knox's house and tipped his hat.[12] But the city did not reciprocate: it gave him a poor house, not enough to pay his expenses. 'Recently the Music Hall was filled to overflowing to hear Mr. Dickens give readings from his books,' commented the Edinburgh *Evening Courant* (27 January), 'and we certainly expected that Mr. Lemon's "Falstaff" would have proved at least an equal attraction.' (Always it was Dickens who drew the crowds.) Such a small attendance, rebuked the reviewer, indicated either 'a marked deterioration of taste in the Scottish capital' or the absence of an 'appreciative public for the best acting'. As if to make amends for the natives' indifference, the notice heaped extravagant praise on Mark's performance: 'It is Falstaff himself we seem to see, and not any mere image and representation of him; and the Falstaff thus presented is nothing like the vulgar, swaggering, cowardly, and egotistic character

[11] Ibid.   [12] Ibid., p. 35.

generally represented.' The impersonation was also applauded as an intelligent analysis of a 'self-conscious wit and humorist, who knows well what he is saying, and is thoroughly able to estimate its effect on those to whom he is speaking'. The final scene was pronounced 'one of the most perfect embodiments of one of Shakespeare's characters . . . that has ever been presented in this country'.

After a performance in Greenock the troupe left Scotland and began the return journey to London, with engagements at Birmingham and elsewhere. At Bradford there was an excellent house, but with prices considerably lower than any Mark had yet played for. Dismayed at the figure, he was told that even Dickens could not command more.

By now the strain of the tour had begun to tell on him. Financial losses, poor houses, or any hitch in arrangements depressed him. At times he became flustered, once absently inserting a twenty-pound note into an envelope instead of the autograph 'Truly yours, Mark Lemon' promised to a young lady admirer. (Fortunately Hatton, discovering the autograph, retrieved the envelope before it went to the post.)[13] It was no easy matter to cover the miles between engagements and adjust himself to a succession of hotels. For one who always dined well at Vine Cottage and the weekly *Punch* gatherings, the meals were dismal indeed. 'The monotony of English dinners becomes wearisome to us, for go where we will, from town to town every day, and always to the first hotels, the same bill of fare follows us persistently', wrote Willert Beale of a similar tour. 'The same macaroni soup, which makes the Italians laugh, there never being more than a few sticks of macaroni in each plate; the same large boiled turbot, with some pink sauce; the same saddles of mutton, the same boiled fowls, the same cabinet pudding, at which the Frenchman invariably smiles, and identically the same indigestible-looking apple tart.'[14]

Toward the end of the tour Mark began to weary of dressing for the stage. The exertion of lacing his jerkin and getting into his armour winded him, so that he had to go before the footlights short of breath. Often in low spirits, he began to lose his appetite. Since he was constantly on the stage during a performance, to keep going he took a little brandy and water and two glasses of port during the

[13] Ibid., p. 163.
[14] Beale, *The Light of Other Days*, I, p. 97.

interval.[15] Adding to his exhaustion were the constant editorial demands of *Punch*. Though he sometimes delegated Shirley Brooks to take over, whenever possible he returned to London for his two days a week.

Not in good health after the rigours of touring and busy on his next novel, *The Taffeta Petticoat*, Mark played only intermittently after recuperating in Crawley. There were performances in Manchester in late February, Liverpool in March, the Gallery of Illustration and Reigate in May. Though *Punch*, true to its editor's 'no puffing' policy, published no accounts of these dramatic activities, it did on one occasion (22 May 1869) take its cue for the Large Cut from his Falstaff impersonation. The subject was Sumner's speech demanding that the United States be paid a half million pounds for alleged damages by the *Alabama*, the Southern cruiser built at Liverpool during the American Civil War. The Tenniel drawing features a meeting of Jonathan Falstaff (in stars and stripes) and the Prince of Wales:

PRINCE OF WALES Sirrah, do I owe you a thousand pound?
SIR JONATHAN A thousand pound, 'Al?—Four hundred million! Thy
love is worth four hundred million: thou owest me thy love.

In June *Falstaff* was at the Olympic in a benefit performance for the Printers' Orphans. In September followed another benefit at the Gallery of Illustration for the widow and children of W. B. Clarke, Mark's secretary and dresser for years. His sudden death during the first provincial tour had contributed to Mark's growing depression. Because the players were now appearing irregularly, sometimes after an interval of several months, they became rusty. 'It is to be regretted that so many of the cues were not forthcoming at the proper time,' complained the *Era* after the Clarke benefit, 'and that, to speak technically, there were so many "sticks" on the stage of the little theatre.'

Late in September a series of engagements took the troupe to Wolverhampton, Shrewsbury, and again to Birmingham. Scheduled for November were Torquay, Exeter, and Plymouth. At Exeter, Mark was called 'the best Falstaff of his time' and honoured at an elaborate corporation dinner. But in Plymouth the next day minor embarrassment marred his triumph: the lessee of the theatre brought charges against him for playing in an unlicensed building, the Royal

[15] Hatton, *With a Show*, pp. 53–56.

Hotel Assembly Rooms, even though a barrister, consulted before the performance, had declared it legal. Mark was asked to pay a token fine of one pound. An Exeter editorial deplored this action: 'Mark Lemon has been through life so excellent a friend of the whole body of dramatic artists, and has done so much, in connection with the Dramatic Authors' Society and otherwise . . . that most actors and patrons of the drama will regret that he was not permitted to give his representation of Falstaff without being made an example in defence of that profession. We are glad to say that the same course was not followed in this city.'

Annoyances like the Plymouth experience must have convinced Mark that he had been right in discouraging Thomas Hardy from considering a dramatic career. In 1867 the young Hardy, to acquire some technical skill before trying to write plays in blank verse, had thought of going on the stage for six or twelve months. He had, accordingly, called at the *Punch* office to get the opinion of 'an ardent amateur-actor'. Mark had told him that the elder Mathews had once declared himself unwilling 'to see a dog of his on the stage' and that he himself, 'much as he personally liked the art of acting, would rather see a daughter of his in her grave than on the boards of a theatre'.[16]

Concluding *Falstaff* at Brighton in December, where he also read from *Pickwick*, Mark could congratulate himself on the reception that had generally been given him in *propria persona*. To be sure, there had been some unfavourable notices, but on the whole his interpretation of the fat knight had been hailed as the best of the century. Henceforth his name would always be associated with that of Falstaff. But he had less reason to rejoice over his financial returns. Heavy losses at Edinburgh and at St. George's Hall, London, had not been balanced by the proceeds from other places. Expenses had been great: professional actors, railway tickets, and hotel accommodations were a constant drain on funds, with the troupe idle for a day or two each week while Mark was in London looking after *Punch*. The final reckoning showed that the *Falstaff* venture, complicated by inefficient book-keeping, had resulted in alarming losses. Instead of a legacy, Mark would leave his family only unpaid bills. He might possibly have wiped out these deficits by taking his entertainment to America, where some attractive offers had been made him. Though he could not expect to clear

[16] F. Hardy, *The Early Life of Thomas Hardy*, p. 71.

twenty thousand pounds in six months as Dickens had done—there were always the expenses of a supporting cast—he might have made a respectable profit. But he rejected this tempting possibility. His first duty was to *Punch*: a prolonged absence from his editorial post was unthinkable.

12

'UNDER THE DAISIES'

WHILE Mark was exhausting himself by shuttling between his provincial *Falstaff* engagements and his editorial duties in London, he endured again the misery of seeing his first-born drift toward ruin. Unable to adapt himself to the climate of India, young Mark had returned to England, ambitionless, shifty, insolent, with gambling and drinking his chief diversions. When in need of money he plagued his father. Shirley Brooks's diary records how Mark, having been called from the office one morning, returned shortly with instructions to the boy at the door: 'When my son comes again he is to be told I am engaged.' Then he broke down and wept. 'His cub is more of a nuisance than ever,' observed Brooks. 'Everyone wishes he were dead, but such beasts never die. It were a good deed to keep him supplied with money, that he might go harder at the brandy, and be done with it.' Some days later, calling on Nelly Lemon at the Bedford Hotel, Brooks met 'young Mark at the door, looking beastly'.[1]

Worse was yet to follow. 'Odd story from M[ark] L[emon]', Brooks confided to his diary. 'This accursed son is said to be father of an illegitimate son. Later he [Mark, sen.] had reasons to doubt so much about the matter that it did not much annoy him, or rather, this small crime was merged in the impression made by others.' Less than a week later Brooks, noting that young Mark had been getting into 'new scrapes' at Birmingham, commented indignantly: 'I said insanity, and wished he could be locked up.' The next report had the wayward son imprisoned in the country for swindling, a 'most venomous account of the proceedings, with names', having been published. 'What a curse this young ruffian is!' Brooks ex-

---

[1] For the details of young Mark's behaviour as presented in this paragraph and the two following, I have drawn on the following entries in B.D.: 9 Jan. 1869, 12 Sept. 1869, 22 Sept. 1869.

claimed. Later Mark himself reported that the 'illegitimate business' could not be proved and that the swindling charge had been dismissed. He was still greatly distressed, however, having only just learned of the boy's recent abominable behaviour toward his mother. 'Had I been there,' Mark declared, 'I would have kicked him out of the house.' Whether his behaviour had been anything more than churlish insolence is not made clear. In any event, he 'had fulfilled the promise of his youth', as Mark had once remarked of a blackguard son in *Golden Fetters*, by repaying 'his mother's fondness with disrespect, contumely, and ingratitude, and bitter were the tears shed by the strong-loving woman'.

For Nelly, Mark always showed tender affection, and nothing so aroused his wrath as their son's impudence to her. More than ever she seemed to inspire the sentiments expressed nineteen years earlier in one of his poems for *Household Words* (20 July 1850):

> I would not have thee young again
> Since I myself am old;
> Not that thy youth was ever vain,
> Or that my age is cold;
> But then upon thy gentle face
> I see the shades of time,
> A thousand memories replace
> The beauties of thy prime.
>
> Though from thine eyes of softest blue
> Some light hath passed away,
> Love looketh forth as warm and true
> As on our bridal day.
> I hear thy song, and though in part
> 'Tis fainter in its tone
> I hear it not, for still thy heart
> Seems singing to my own.

Little wonder that, by his own admission, Mark had lost all feeling for his elder son. His only hope was to get the boy out of England; and his sons-in-law, Timothy Martin and Bob Romer, now explored that possibility. Young Mark eventually emigrated to Australia and became a respected citizen, though not, unfortunately, in his father's lifetime. But by his great-nieces, who never knew him, he is still spoken of as 'wicked Uncle Mark'.[2]

[2] Information furnished by Miss Phyllis Matthews, Crawley.

If Mark ever felt that he had failed as a father, he should have been heartened by the growing esteem for his younger son. 'Notwithstanding the heavy claims on the time of Harry Lemon, Esq., we are to be favoured fortnightly with an original narrative from his humorous pen', reported the Crawley columnist. Using a 'quaint and singular imitative delivery', he amused large audiences with the 'private and confidential confessions' of one Miss Phoebe, which he dedicated to the ladies of Sussex. Nor was his reputation confined to Crawley. His dramatic pieces frequently appeared on the London stage. Scarcely a Christmas, Boxing Day, or Easter passed without one of his burlesques or pantomimes at such places as Astley's, the Crystal Palace, and Sadler's Wells. 'It is a great satisfaction to many persons here', boasted the Crawley reporter, 'that our young townsman, Mr. Harry Lemon, has made a hit in his new piece at Astley's. *Mazeppa* and the burlesque *Blue Beard* have drawn crowded houses.' The young man had also made himself useful as his father's assistant at the *Punch* office. 'I presume there would be no objection to Harry taking a place and weekly guinea?' Mark asked his proprietors. 'I wish to have him always with me.' At such a modest wage Harry would be the cheapest editorial assistant in town, according to his father.[3]

But even at the well-regulated *Punch* office there were vexations. 'A paragraph has been going the round saying that W. Agnew, of Manchester, has become the proprietor', Brooks recorded in his diary on the twenty-eighth birthday of *Punch*. It was rumoured that the journal had been sold for seven thousand pounds. Having advised Mark 'to notice this', Brooks seized the initiative and wrote a paragraph 'plainly denying the change of hands'. It appeared in various newspapers, including the Sussex *Advertiser*:

31 July 1869. The meddlesomeness of some ill-informed busy body has made it necessary to announce that *Punch* is not sold. Of course not; and only a profane and un-English mind could have mixed up the two notions. *Punch* is no more sold than the Archbishop of Canterbury, or the Poet Laureate, or the British Neptune, or Gog and Magog, or any other undying representative of the power, the truth, the wit, the quietness of old England. The irreverent inventor of this fiction should have a care, or he may find himself writing flat blasphemy before he has done.

In spite of his exasperations and griefs, Mark had the faculty of

[3] P.O. MS., Lemon to Bradbury and Evans, 15 Mar. 1869.

MARK LEMON
IN HIS
'WRITING-BOX'

MARK LEMON
IN HIS
'CHAPEL OF
EASE'

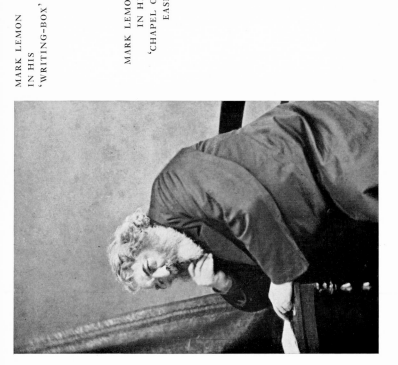

JOHN TENNIEL'S
DRAWING OF MARK
LEMON AS FALSTAFF
From the Illustrated
London News

MARK LEMON AS
FALSTAFF

casting off despondency by helping others out of the slough. One of these was Louise Romer, wife of his nephew, Frank Romer, jun. ('a cub of a husband', Brooks called him). This talented young woman, who had once joined the Lemons on a holiday in Wales, now needed to support herself. Having a flair for art and lyric verse, she was able to do initials and carry out small assignments for *Punch*.[4] 'The deuce is that in helping her one helps her husband, but it can't be helped,' complained Brooks.[5]

For his mother, housebound now and almost blind, Mark also showed every consideration, visiting her for an hour every day. Sometimes he read to her: the working drafts of his own novels, the papers, the Bible. Though living conveniently next door, she was careful not to demand unnecessary attention from the Lemons. A great knitter, she passed the solitary hours with her needles. Her son may well have had her in mind when he characterized Mrs. Masham in *Loved at Last* as 'a model mother-in-law, never intruding troublesome advice, or endeavouring to retain a dictatorship. . . . There were times when [she] felt lonely enough in her little parlour. . . . The remembrance of old days, with their busy tasks and anxious sorrows, would come back to her, so softened by time that they begat momentary regrets they were hers no longer. . . .'

Much as Mark tried to lose himself in concern for others, however, the chaotic state of his own finances could no longer be ignored. The losses incurred by the *Falstaff* readings had added to the mountain of unpaid bills until there seemed no way out of the canyon of gloom in which he found himself. Yet there was one escape: when hounded by collectors he could always borrow money to repay old debts. So it was that he turned to his friends: Brooks, 'Ponny' Mayhew, and the *Punch* proprietors. That 'Ponny' may have responded generously is suggested by his wife's story that Mark owed him a thousand pounds.[6] And documents preserved in the *Punch* Library show that Bradbury and Evans were repeatedly appealed to for ready cash, either as outright loans or advances on salary. Pathetic were Mark's entreaties to his proprietors: 'I am sorry to trouble you, but I am very, very short'; 'I really blush to be so troublesome, but things are so bad'; 'I had hoped that by this affairs would have been settled so far that I should have known what my means of support for the future wd be, but as such is unhappily

[4] Louise Romer is better known by her later name, Mrs. Jopling-Rowe.
[5] B.D., 13 Jan. 1867.   [6] Ibid., 16 Apr. 1873.

not the case I am obliged to apply to you again as my store is quite exhausted.'

If embarrassed about the repeated appeals to his friends, Mark could always turn to the loan sharks. He soon knew the 'multifariousness of their dealings' and in *Loved at Last* drew on his experiences for a pen portrait of a bill discounter:

The dingy hangings of rich brocade—some spendthrift's purchase, the sooty Turkey carpet 'of noble dimensions', the faded morocco chairs and tomb-like sideboard proclaimed that men were eaten there—needy fathers, thoughtless sons, struggling traders. The ogre himself sat in an adjoining room. . . . An elegant writing-table with a silver inkstand was the altar of sacrifice; and the sacrificial priest, arrayed in a furred dressing gown (although it was summer), played with an ivory paper knife, as though there could be no danger in approaching him. There was a forced smile upon the fellow's face . . ., but the greed of gain instantly dispelled it, and left the upper lip ruled as if it were with the lines of a ledger.

When really desperate Mark tried yet another expedient, the pawnshop. Not until after his death were the unhappy details brought to light. Bob Romer told the *Punch* proprietors, who in turn passed the information on to Shirley Brooks. 'Towards the end poor M[ark] had recourse to the "Mount of Piety" ', Brooks confided to his diary. 'I did not guess this. In the eventide there was not "light" for him.' At one time it was even feared that Mark might have pawned the silver tankard presented to him on the twenty-fifth anniversary of *Punch*. According to Mrs. Clarke, the widow of his secretary, he had given her a cup to dispose of. Did Brooks wish to redeem it? But it turned out to be a 'mean looking, battered affair—I don't know how L[emon] got it—not from Punch, as had been supposed', Brooks noted.[7]

How was it that Mark, the highest-paid editor of his time, could not live within his income? With two of his daughters married and Harry earning his own spending money, the family responsibilities certainly had been lightened. Of course, young Mark was still a financial liability, and there is a theory, currently advanced by the Lemon descendants, that this profligate, bearing his father's name, was able to write cheques on his account. Even so, this abuse could have been halted before it went too far. More credible is the belief that wildcat schemes and disastrous speculations were the chief

[7] Ibid., 27 June 1873.

cause of Mark's indebtedness. Unable to resist the lure of investments with specious promises of quick returns, he was too often taken in. His first-hand knowledge of shady deals and swindles came to be reflected in his later novels, like this realistic account in *Golden Fetters*: 'The company about to be launched was promising enough—and of course [he] was to be secretary, with four hundred pounds a year, and other advantages, and all that he was to do in return—at least just at present—was to place at the embryo company's backers eight hundred pounds, taking [a] note of hand for the amount, to be recouped out of the first payment of calls.' Painful, indeed, must have been Mark's recollections of the fiasco that inevitably followed such speculations: 'It would be useless to describe the progress of this bubble from its blowing to its bursting; for burst it did. . . .'

In addition to falling an easy prey to slippery promoters, Mark was unrealistically generous. As long as he had cash on hand, he would cheerfully part with a five-pound note to a superannuated actor in distress, underwrite civic improvements in Crawley, and shower his friends with gifts. Brooks recorded in his diary how Mark had brought him a cast of 'the pleasing devil in Lincoln Cathedral' and had presented him with a pianoforte.[8] All this in the face of impending disaster, when the 'dread of dependence became day by day more intolerable', to quote *Golden Fetters* again. But Mark was inordinately optimistic. Like Dickens's Micawber, he looked hopefully to the future: some unexpected good fortune, some unforeseen windfall would yet free him of his troubles. Meanwhile the *Punch* proprietors were instructed to make yearly deductions from his salary, 'to meet certain claims upon me'. And to provide for Nelly and his minor children in the event of his sudden death, he insured his life for six thousand pounds. But it is doubtful whether there was anything left for his beneficiaries after his creditors had been satisfied.

However ominous the threats of ruin, however frequent the recurring periods of depression, Mark was extraordinarily resilient. 'I never saw him in better spirits', remarked Brooks at a time when the financial situation and young Mark's behaviour were at their worst. 'He had had just enough wine and fun to make him, what he can be, about the pleasantest table companion in the world.'[9]

What kept Mark going through all his troubles may have been

[8] Ibid., 28 July 1869.　　[9] Ibid., 2 June 1869.

his ability to relax. On a brief late-summer holiday at Bognor with his son-in-law (Timothy Martin), young Fred Evans, and a few others, he found complete freedom from care and luxuriated in his idleness. To Brooks he sent an idyllic account:

Dear SB, I vow this is the drowsiest place in the world—Sleepy Hollow not excepted. I thought of writing yesterday but I had not energy to begin especially as I have nothing to say. No nice excursions as you have—and don't want them, having seen mountains and lakes and sunsets for sixty years, so that I have but to close my eyes and recall all the beauties you are now admiring—provided I do not go to sleep—a state impossible to avoid at Bognor. . . . I breakfast and smoke—drag my slow length along to the pier, smoke and read and refresh myself with cold tea. Stay there till I am called for and urged home to dinner. So, *die per diem.* BUT I have thoroughly enjoyed the rest and shall go to London tomorrow a new man.[10]

Back at the *Punch* office two weeks later Mark was still in the same high spirits as he wrote to Brooks again. Full of choice Crawley gossip, his letter concluded with a bit of doggerel on Harriet Beecher Stowe's airing of Lord Byron's incest with Augusta:

> When scandal Mrs. Beecher Stowe
> Pours out upon our Poet
> I feel that if she were a man
> I would her breeches toe it.[11]

*   *   *

Because Mark had suffered bouts of illness for years, few of his friends realized how fast he was failing in the late 1860s. As early as 1848 Jerrold had quipped to Forster, 'Lemon has been at death's door,—but has kept on the outside.'[12] And in 1854, according to Dickens, he had a condition resembling gout.[13] Bulletins on his health were to appear at intervals in Silver's diary. In February 1859 he was reported unwell at Crawley, so that Brooks had to 'take over the inkstand'. In April 1860 he had himself steamed for a bad cold. A few months later he was ill again, but managed to attend the *Punch* dinner. In April 1863, while finishing his first novel, he had

[10] Hunt. MS., Lemon to Brooks, 27 Aug. 1869.
[11] Ibid., 11 Sept. 1869.
[12] V. and A. MS., Jerrold to Forster, 25 Aug. 1848.
[13] Nonesuch, II, p. 561, W. Collins, 7 June 1854.

neuralgia in his eyes—from overwork, according to his doctor. So it went—colds, aches, stiffness. In a letter to Peter Cunningham he complained, 'I am getting very rusty and rheumaticy and church-yardy.'[14] At the beginning of his *Falstaff* readings, however, he seemed to enjoy a resurgence of health and vigour. 'Mark never better. Falstaff agrees with him', Silver noted on 2 December 1868. But after months of intermittent touring it was another story. 'Mark looks pale and seedy. Wants rest', Silver observed on 26 July 1869. A few days later he took to his bed. Then came periods of partial recovery, when he would alternate trips to the *Punch* office with confinement at his home. At the end of August, Nelly sent word that he was 'suffering terribly again'.

As his health declined Mark often appeared lost in thought. Though still contributing his share of banter whenever he could attend the weekly *Punch* dinners, he always seemed conscious of the broken links in the fraternal chain that he had helped to forge. Five of his colleagues had fallen from the ranks in little more than a decade, all of them in their prime: Gilbert à Beckett in 1856, Douglas Jerrold in 1857, Thackeray in 1863, John Leech in 1864, and C. H. Bennett in 1867.

A stunning blow had been the sudden death of Thackeray, only thirteen months after the completion of his handsome new house at 2 Palace Gardens, Kensington. He was found in his bed on the morning before Christmas, his limbs 'fearfully contorted', but his 'features calm'. His end was thought to have been 'instantaneous'.[15] Deeply moved, Mark at first could not get through the night without dreaming of him. 'Poor man, sleeping all these years alone!' he lamented as he reflected on the insanity which had robbed Thackeray of his Isabella early in their marriage and now kept her confined in a private asylum. And he recalled how only the previous year Thackeray had written the Lord's Prayer in the size of a threepence and had drawn a crown and '3' in the centre, with an inscription to Mark on the border: 'Dear Friend, I've writ this little page / When I and 50 is my age.'[16]

As Thackeray's Table companions sadly contemplated his empty place at the first dinner following his death, 'Ponny' Mayhew had an inspiration. 'I'll tell you what we'll do,' he suggested; 'we'll sing

[14] Ed. U. MS., Lemon to Cunningham, 7 Feb. 1867.
[15] Silver. See also Ray, *Thackeray. The Age of Wisdom*, p. 416.
[16] Ibid.

the old boy's "Mahogany Tree"; he'd like it.' The men arose, some
with tear-stained faces, most with a catching of the breath, and,
without any attempt to hide their emotions, sang the words Thackeray had written twenty years earlier:

> Evenings we knew,
> Happy as this;
> Faces we miss,
> Pleasant to see.
> Kind hearts and true,
> Gentle and just,
> Peace to your dust,
> We sing round the tree.[17]

'Thank God, we shan't have to go round with the hat!' exclaimed
John Leech as the Table discussed Thackeray's estate after the
funeral. 'His daughters will have one thousand between them.' Little
did anyone suspect that within the year Leech himself would be
gone and that at the death of his widow in 1868 only his house would
remain, all her money having been lost in bad investments.[18]
Always morbidly sensitive to street noises, especially barrel
organs, Leech had suffered acutely in his last years. 'They're killing
me!' he would complain of the organ men. Forced to listen to their
renditions of 'The Rat-Catcher's Daughter', 'Annie Laurie', and the
serenade from Verdi's *Il Trovatore*, he sometimes spoke of a haunting
fear that, in a fit of desperation, he might murder one of them. Even
when he took refuge in the country he found no peace, for he could
not endure the grating of the roller over the gravel walks.[19]
When Michael Bass, M.P., introduced a Bill in the House of
Commons to control street music (1863), Mark gave it full support.
'I am so greatly interested in the success of your measure,' he
assured Bass, 'that I am desirous of strengthening your hands by
putting you in possession of some facts within my knowledge.' And
he explained how the 'continual visitation of street bands and organ
grinders' had caused Leech's health to decline 'alarmingly'.[20] The
first reading of the Bill was frequently interrupted by laughter.
Reprinting part of *The Times* report in *Punch* (25 July 1863), Mark
added: 'And so the subject was dropped, and the "Laughing Jack-

[17] Spielmann, *History of Punch*, p. 87.   [18] Silver.
[19] Vizetelly, *Glances Back*, p. 137.
[20] Lady Nevill, *My Own Time*, pp. 265–6.

asses" (may they eat dirt!) are to have their long ears tickled by the maddening music of the street.'

Before long, however, Mark was forced to the conclusion that no legislation could save Leech, who had begun to complain about the 'open-air preaching nuisance'. 'Finds a nuisance everywhere, poor devil!' observed Silver. Lately he had 'let out his hate' on pet dogs. The Table felt that he should take a rest, but, according to Mark, he would be annoyed 'to think that *Punch* could go on without him—even for a month'. How unfortunate that his great gifts had not made him a happier man! A half-year later his suffering ended. 'John Leech *obit aetat* 46', recorded Silver. 'Special meeting at the Bedford on Tuesday to consider what is to be done.' From Millais, who had visited Leech as the end approached, came the particulars: 'Ill in the morning with a spasm. Went to bed at six, another spasm: "If I have another it will kill me"—another came at seven: "I'm going" and so died.'[21]

On a chill November morning Mark and his colleagues, the rosettes on their arm bands stamped with the letters 'J.L.', gathered in the chapel of Kensal Green Cemetery. According to Silver, Burnand was 'loud in nose blowing—snivelling infectious—not affected, God knows'. A plain black hearse without feathers or ornament and drawn by only two horses, the same that had borne Thackeray to his grave, carried Leech to a neighbouring plot. In a voice faltering with emotion, Canon Hole, a close friend, read the service. 'When the coffin was lowered', du Maurier recalled thirty years later, 'John Millais burst into tears and loud sobs, setting an example that was followed all round; we all forgot our manhood and cried like women!'[22] Mark threw a wreath into the grave; the others followed with immortelles.

The thinning of the ranks had continued with the death in 1865 of Joseph Paxton, one of Mark's closest friends. 'Another *Punch* diner gone!' Silver noted in his diary. 'Only aged 62. His broad shoulders looked as if they would have borne 30 winters more.' He was followed in 1869 by the elder William Bradbury, one of the old *Punch* proprietors. Asked by Mark to write a tribute for *Punch* (24 April), Brooks emphasized Bradbury's 'brotherly sympathy' and declared that the Table would 'not soon forget the good man, and good friend'. Little more than a month later Mark lost another intimate, Peter Cunningham. For years they had carried on a lively

[21] Silver.   [22] Whiteley, *George du Maurier*, p. 48.

correspondence. 'I hear of you now and then and often think of you and the pleasant times which are gone', Mark had written in one of his last letters. 'I hope we shall foregather again some day.'[23]

*   *   *

With too many of his old friends he would not 'foregather' again, Mark reflected sadly as the year 1870 dawned. Meditating on how these companions had slipped away one by one, he composed his last song:

> Forth we went a gallant band—
> Youth, Love, Gold, and Pleasure.
> Who, we said, can us withstand?
> Who dare dances measure?
>
> Round about the world we went;
> Ne'er were such free lances
> Victors, in each tournament
> Winning beauty's glances.
>
> Gold at last his prowess lost,
> And when he departed,
> Pleasure's lance was rarely crossed,
> Pleasure grew faint-hearted.

Still exhausted from his last *Falstaff* appearances in December, Mark felt more 'churchyardy' than ever. In the latter part of January, according to Silver, he had a sore throat. On 2 February he was reported 'sad and semi-speechless from cold'. Later that month he was still hoarse—the aftermath of his reading exertions, he thought. The 'Falstaff throat' persisted well into March. Whenever he felt able he still came to town for his two days weekly at the *Punch* office, though Brooks frequently took over now.

Between his periods of illness, with their attendant fits of depression, Mark appeared to be quite himself. He worked on his last novel, spoke with conviction on political and social developments, and kept his companions chortling at the Wednesday-night dinners. At home in Crawley he was still full of promotional schemes. He planned to buy the square opposite the entrance to St. John's Church, demolish the small shops and houses, and build a town hall

23 Ed.U. MS., Lemon to Cunningham, 7 Feb. 1867.

on the site.[24] And in the centre of the village he hoped to sink a well and erect a pump and drinking fountain.

On 3 May he and Nelly were gladdened by the marriage of their third daughter, Helen, to Frank Topham, called by the local reporter 'a rising young artist of considerable celebrity'. For this occasion St. Margaret's Church in Ifield had been 'tastefully decorated'. After the ceremony, performed by the Reverend R. N. Blaker, the guests 'in the most quiet and unostentatious manner partook of the *déjeuner* in a marquee erected on the croquet ground' at Vine Cottage. During the meal there were 'excellent speeches', such, perhaps, as Mark had described in *Wait for the End*: 'The [wedding] oratory was rather discursive, and the metaphors somewhat mixed, but the hearts of the speakers were in their words; and where that is the case, any one, to our thinking, is a Demosthenes.' As the festivities wore on Mark may well have been reminded of another observation in that novel: 'Matrimony is considered by the highest authorities epidemical; and such whisperings and smilings, such daring attempts at pressing fingers, and, in one or two instances, of waist encirclings, that one might have surmised that more than a dozen couples, strolling about, had taken the infection that happy morning.' After all the toasting and dining, Frank and Helen bade their many well-wishers farewell. According to the local columnist, 'The happy pair departed for Italy amid the legendary shower of old slippers.'

A few days after the wedding Mark took to his bed. No one thought his condition alarming: he would get up at intervals, entertain visitors, read and write. Never did his sense of humour fail him. When, for example, Macdonald, a young custom clerk who had played a minor part in *Falstaff*, came for a brief visit and blundered with the inner and outer doors to the room, Mark laughingly chided him for his awkward entrance: 'Surprised at your stupidity, Mac; *you* certainly ought to understand double entry.'[25] On Saturday, 21 May, he wrote a short piece and got into a lively discussion over it with a caller. Sunday night he was in exceptionally good spirits as he joined friends in the drawing-room. When he became tired and spoke of returning to his bed his visitors offered to carry him. As they laboured under their burden, his convulsive laughter made

[24] Information supplied by Miss Daisy Warren, Arundel. Today this is a car park.
[25] *London Society*, XXVIII (Aug. 1875), p. 156.

their undertaking doubly difficult. He was highly amused that it took four strong men to support his Falstaffian figure.[26]

His slumber was peaceful that night. Occasionally he fumbled with the sheets and babbled some indistinct snatches—was it of the green fields outside his window? Or was he jockeying once more with the agile wits of the *Punch* Table, pleased with his own *bons mots* and outrageous puns? Towards morning he spoke briefly. At his bedside sat Annie Duffell, the faithful servant who had spent many years with the family. As she watched him he went quietly back to sleep. There followed some minutes of deep breathing, then silence. The physician who signed the death certificate gave as his medical opinion 'Obscure disease of the larynx and pharynx, probably malignant.'

Children on their way home from school that 23rd of May paused before Vine Cottage and wept. And Ye Old Time Coach, put back into service between Brighton and Crawley through Mark's efforts, was said by the local reporter to pass 'in a manner most reverential to him who was now silent unto death.'[27]

Shirley Brooks, the first *Punch* colleague to be notified by the family, went immediately to Crawley. 'I saw Lally, Betty, and Polly, and they seemed—no, they *were* comforted in a measure by seeing me', he wrote in his diary. 'Then I went into the drawing-room, in which lay, in an oak shell, the remains of my dear friend—very noble in death.'[28] To Leigh, Brooks addressed a brief note: 'It is not easy, it is hardly possible to realize what has occurred, or that we shall not hear the genial voice again—here—but the impression deepens painfully every hour.'[29]

With Brooks came an artist to take a cast of Mark's face. But how would the family react? Would the women want their 'sacred dead touched'? Brooks decided to risk it. 'The cast was taken tenderly, rapidly, reverently', he recorded in his diary for 24 May. 'All vestiges of the work were cleansed utterly away, and for the last time, having touched head and brow, I looked at my friend of 29 years, my faithfullest friend, and left the dead. . . .'[30]

Later the Reverend R. N. Blaker called, and on Polly's suggestion

[26] As reported by Mrs. Sidney Matthews, Crawley.
[27] *Sussex Express*, 31 May 1870.
[28] As quoted in Layard, *Brooks*, p. 397.
[29] P.O. MS., Brooks to Leigh, May 1870.
[30] As quoted in Layard, *Brooks*, pp. 397–8.

he and Brooks went to St. Margaret's Churchyard in Ifield to select a site for the grave. They chose a spot a few paces to the south-east of the church. Here on bright afternoons the simple stone building, where Mark had made his last public appearance at the marriage of his third daughter, would cast its shadow. Brooks and Blaker then returned to Vine Cottage, to ask Polly to confirm their choice. Brooks's favourite, she found his presence comforting. To the grieving widow, Blaker spoke of the 'enormous good Lemon had done in the two parishes—much more than money could do'. Back in London that evening, Brooks concluded his diary entry for the day: 'So for the last time I left Mark Lemon in his much-loved home.'[31]

As soon as word of Mark's death reached the public flowers began to arrive from various parts of England, Scotland, Ireland, and Wales. They decked the coffin and filled the drawing-room, where the body lay in state. Messages of condolence poured in. Among them was one from Dickens to Harry. 'Circumstances divided me from your father for some years,' the note said, 'but there was never any serious estrangement between us, and I am glad to remember now that we embraced affectionately when we met at Stanfield's grave.'[32] Acquainted with Mark's insolvency, Dickens thought immediately of a Civil List pension for Nelly and her un-married daughters.[33] But before he could initiate the necessary steps —he wished to take sole charge—his own death on 9 June shocked the English-speaking world.

Among the many Press tributes to Mark Lemon, perhaps that in the *Athenaeum* (28 May) best caught the essence of the man. Calling him chief of the 'writers and artists who have been shooting folly on the wing', it continued:

He had fun in him; his was a merry eye and a laughing lip; but there was a fine warm fibre underlying all, and holding the man together. It was by this element in him that he succeeded in holding satirists and humorists and caricaturists together. Appointed navigator in troubled waters, he poured out the oil of his gentle nature without stint. His approach brought sunny weather; his voice was balm to the angry; he loved the quiet, orderly, becoming way.

Commenting on his attributes as an author, the *Daily Telegraph*

[31] Ibid., p. 409.   [32] Nonesuch, III, p. 780, H. Lemon, 25 May 1870.
[33] B.D., 11 Mar. 1871.

(24 May) declared: 'If none of his productions were in the highest class, many of them were very good of their kind, have afforded much merriment in thousands of homes, and have not left one stain behind.' In *Notes and Queries* (28 May) he was applauded for waging through *Punch* an 'unsparing war against humbug and immorality, whether in high or in low places'. And from Crawley (*Sussex Express*, 31 May) came a tribute to the beloved first citizen of the village: 'Far more valuable to us than his greatness and popularity in letters were his numerous little acts of kindness and sympathy outside the gaze of the stormy world.'

On Friday, the 27th, all business houses in Crawley were closed. As the bells of the two parish churches began to toll, villagers, hushed and reverent, lined the street in front of Vine Cottage. From there the funeral cortège proceeded to Ifield, a distance of two miles. Seventeen carriages holding the immediate family, the entire *Punch* staff, and the proprietors followed the plain black hearse. Behind them came a long file on foot. At St. Margaret's Church, Blaker and Soper, the rectors of the two parishes, took over. Hundreds of spectators stood respectfully apart. 'I am the Resurrection and the Life . . .': as the solemn words rose from the graveside on this bright morning it seemed as if nature were giving her benediction. Beyond the low stone walls of the churchyard stretched the lush fields and flowering meadows, dotted by dense woods. Occasional bird songs blended with the voice intoning the ritual of commitment. It was the lovely and tranquil countryside that Mark had cherished during the last twelve years of his life. At the conclusion of the service two young girls whom he had often befriended stepped forward and placed their home-made wreaths on the coffin, its brass plate simply inscribed 'Mark Lemon, Esq., Editor of *Punch*, died May 23, 1870, aged 60 years.'[34]

Like Dickens, Mark had often expressed a distaste for public monuments. Like Dickens, moreover, he needed no such testimonial, for he had left behind a living memorial in *Punch*. He had, as Gladstone remarked two years later in awarding Nelly a Civil List pension, 'raised the level of comic journalism'.[35] Yet, had he not kept the paper going during its beginnings by using the proceeds from his plays to defray printing costs, had he not shrewdly judged human

[34] This account of the funeral is based on the Crawley column in the *Sussex Express*, 31 May 1870.
[35] Hatton, *With a Show*, p. 1.

nature and recognized talent in selecting his staff, had he not united these turbulent intellects as a loyal working team, there might be no *Punch* today.

Mark used to say that he believed in one God, one woman, one paper. It was fitting, therefore, that the low marble coping enclosing the burial plot should be inscribed with this witness to his simple faith: 'I look for the resurrection of the dead.' It was fitting, also, that space should be provided inside the coping for the wife who had shared his fortunes for nearly thirty-one years and would be buried beside him in 1890. It was fitting, finally, that the coping, bearing their names and dates, should be contributed by Mark's *Punch* associates.

To this day only the plain stone border marks the grave of the first editor of *Punch*. He once told his family that he wanted no elaborate tombstone, no imposing obelisk. He hoped, rather, to sleep 'under the daisies'.[36] His wishes have been respected. Each summer a heavy turf of daisies blankets the grave.

[36] The *Bookman*, Nov. 1909, p. 69.

APPENDIX

1. PLAYS AND OPERAS (listed in chronological order, with the date and place of earliest production and the type of drama)

P.L.; or, 30 Strand. 25 Apr. 1836. Strand. Farce.

Arnold of Windkelreid; or, The Flight of the Sempach. 27 July 1836. Surrey. Drama.

The Pacha's Bridal. 2 Sept. 1836. English Opera House. Opera.

The Ancestress; or, The Doom of Barostein. 27 Mar. 1837. City of London. Melodrama.

The Avenger. 27 Apr. 1837. City of London. Tragedy.

My Sister Kate. 1 Mar. 1838. City of London. Farce.

Love and Charity. 3 May 1838. St. James's. Burletta.

Rob of the Fen. 7 July 1838. English Opera House. Opera.

The M.P. for the Rotten Borough. 27 July 1838. English Opera House. Operatic farce.

The Grey Doublet. 28 Aug. 1838. Lyceum. Farce.

Self-Accusation; or, A Brother's Love. 10 Sept. 1838. Lyceum. Melodrama.

Pupil of da Vinci. 30 Nov. 1839. St. James's. Burletta.

A Familiar Friend. 8 Feb. 1840. Olympic. Farce.

The Ladies' Club. 25 Feb. 1840. Olympic. Burletta.

Lost and Won. 24 Mar. 1840. Olympic. Drama.

Gwyneth Vaughan. 1 Apr. 1840. Olympic. Drama.

The House of Ladies. 25 Apr. 1840. Olympic. Burletta.

A Captain pro tem. 18 May 1840. Olympic. Farce.

The Three Secrets. 9 June 1840. Olympic. Drama.

Ins and Outs. 26 June 1840. English Opera House. Burletta.

The Demon Gift. 29 June 1840. English Opera House. Drama.

Out of Place. 19 Oct. 1840. Haymarket. Farce.

Fashionable Arrivals. 29 Oct. 1840. Covent Garden. Farce.

Fridolin. 26 Nov. 1840. Prince's. Burletta.

Bob Short. 5 Dec. 1840. Haymarket. Farce.

A Gentleman in Black: or, The Loves of Devils. 9 Dec. 1840. Olympic. Farce.

The Deer Stalker: or, The Outlaw's Daughter. 12 Apr. 1841. English Opera House. Drama.

Domestic Economy. 12 Apr. 1841. Adelphi. Extravaganza.

The Good for Nothing. 4 Feb. 1841. Haymarket. Farce.

The Little Gipsy. 12 Apr. 1841. Olympic. Burletta.

The Silver Thimble. 12 Apr. 1841. Strand. Domestic drama.

Punch (renamed *Star of the Street*). 17 Sept. 1841. Strand. Farce.

What Will the World Say? or, Captain Taradiddle. 25 Sept. 1841. Covent Garden. Comedy.

My Man Tom. 27 Jan. 1842.

Robinson Crusoe. 21 Mar. 1842. Olympic. Burletta.

Dick Whittington and His Cat. 28 Mar. 1842. Olympic. Burletta.

Robert Burns. 31 Mar. 1842. Strand. Burletta.

Wax and Wonders. 1 Aug. 1842. Strand. Burletta.

Grandfather Whitehead. Adapted from the French. 31 Aug. 1842. Haymarket. Comedy.

Adventures of a Gentleman. 3 Oct. 1842. Olympic. Drama.

The Turf. 31 Oct. 1842. Covent Garden. Comic drama.

The Lady of the Lake. 31 Jan. 1843. Covent Garden. Opera.

The Bashful Irishman. 20 Apr. 1843. Haymarket. Farce.

The Yellow Husband. 17 May 1843. Haymarket. Farce.

Old Parr. 9 Oct. 1843. Haymarket. Drama.

The Chimes; or, A Goblin Story of Some Bells that Rang an Old Year out and a New Year in. With Gilbert Abbott à Beckett. A dramatization of Dickens's 1844 Christmas book. 19 Dec. 1844. Adelphi. Drama.

Ali Baba; or, Harlequin and the Genii of the Arabian Nights. With Gilbert Abbott à Beckett. 8 Apr. 1844. Lyceum. Pantomime.

Open Sesame; or, A Night with the Forty Thieves. With Gilbert Abbott à Beckett. 8 Apr. 1844. Lyceum. Burlesque.

The Sempstress. 25 May 1844. Haymarket. Drama.

Don Caesar de Bazan. With Gilbert Abbott à Beckett. 8 Oct. 1844. Princess's. Drama.

Knight and the Sprite; or, The Cold Water Cure. With Gilbert Abbott à Beckett. 11 Nov. 1844. Strand. Extravaganza.

Grandmother Browning. 1844. A skit in *The Quizziology of the British Drama* by Gilbert Abbott à Beckett.

St. George and the Dragon. With Gilbert Abbott à Beckett. 24 Mar. 1845. Adelphi. Burlesque.

The Old Soldier. 18 June 1845. Haymarket. Drama.

Peter Wilkins. With Gilbert Abbott à Beckett. 9 Apr. 1846. Adelphi. Domestic drama.

Sister and I. 25 May 1846. Lyceum. Farce.

Honesty the Best Policy. Adapted from French opera. 15 June 1846. Strand. Operatic farce.

The World Underground; or, The Golden Flute and the Brazen Waters. With Gilbert Abbott à Beckett. 27 Dec. 1847. Haymarket. Extravaganza.

The Haunted Man; or, The Ghost's Bargain. A dramatization of Dickens's 1848 Christmas book. 30 Dec. 1848. Adelphi. Drama.

Hearts Are Trumps. 30 July 1849. Strand. Drama.

The Dumb Bedouin; or, Arabs of the Desert. 29 Sept. 1849. City of London. Drama.

The Loving Woman. 17 Dec. 1849. Haymarket. Drama.

Jack in the Green; or, Hints on Etiquette. 23 May 1850. Adelphi. Farce.

The School for Tigers; or, The Shilling Hop. 28 Oct. 1850. Adelphi. Farce.

A London Fog. 10 Apr. 1851. Adelphi. Farce.

O Gemini; or, Brothers of Coarse. With Gilbert Abbott à Beckett. 22 Apr. 1851. Haymarket. Burlesque.

Mind Your Own Business; or, The Man of Tact. 24 Apr. 1852. Haymarket. Drama.

Sea and Land. 17 May 1852. Adelphi. Drama.

Keeley Worried by Buckstone. With Benjamin Webster. 12 June 1852. Haymarket. Farce.

Slave Life; or, Uncle Tom's Cabin. With Tom Taylor. A dramatization of Harriet Beecher Stowe's novel. 27 Nov. 1852. Adelphi. Drama.

Webster at Home. 28 Mar. 1853. Adelphi. Farce.

The Camp at Chobham. 30 June 1853. Adelphi. Farce.

Sardanapalus, the 'Fast' King of Assyria. With Gilbert Abbott à Beckett. 20 July 1853. Adelphi. Burlesque.

Number Nip and the Spirit Bride. 26 Dec. 1853. Adelphi. Drama.

The Begging Letter. 31 Dec. 1853. Drury Lane. Melodrama.

Paula Lazarro; or, The Ladrone's Daughter. 9 Jan. 1854. Drury Lane Drama.

A Moving Tale. 7 June 1854. Adelphi. Farce.

Hopes and Fears. 4 July 1854. Adelphi. Drama.

The Railway Belle. 20 Nov. 1854. Adelphi. Farce.

ML–P

The Slow Man. 20 Nov. 1854. Adelphi. Farce.
Welcome Little Stranger. 30 Mar. 1857. Adelphi. Comedy.
Destiny; or, The Broken Heart. 30 Jan. 1860. Victoria. Drama.
Petticoat Parliament; or, A Woman's Suffrage. 26 Dec. 1867. Olympic. Extravaganza.

2. PERIODICAL PUBLICATIONS (a selected list)

A. Contributions to the *New Sporting Magazine* (under the pseudonym 'Tom Moody'): 'Dick Hyperbole', Feb. 1834; 'Anacreontic' (verse), Mar. 1834; ' "The Marquess of Lansdowne." A Character', Apr. 1834; 'A Monody on the Death of John Mytton, Esq.'. Jan. 1835; 'My Grandfather's Boots. A Familiar Epistle' (verse), Feb. 1835; 'An Extraordinary Adventure', May 1835; 'Accidental Stanzas, Written in a Sick-Bed, after Three Months' Confinement from Accident', Oct. 1835.

B. Contributions to *Bentley's Miscellany:* 'Some Passages in the Life of a Disappointed Man', Sept. 1837; 'The True History of the Celebrated Wedgewood [*sic*] Hieroglyph, Commonly Called the Willow Pattern', Jan. 1838; 'The Song of the Fire-King' (verse), July 1838; 'Horrible Delusions' (under the pseudonym 'Sydney Bywater'), July 1848.

C. Contributions to *Punch*:
  1841. 'The Heir of Applebite' (in ten chapters), I, 73, 89, 97, 109, 121, 146, 171, 182, 194, 206; 'Songs for the Sentimental' (verse), I, 8, 22, 37, 49, 81, 85, 123, 143, 149, 202, 233, 252, 262, 267; 'Songs for the Seedy' (verse), I, 93, 155, 167, 179, 184, 251.
  1842. 'Songs for the Sentimental', II, 20, 32, 51, 77; 'Songs for the Seedy', II, 97, 123, 203, 215, 224, 233, 248, 257—III, 2, 26, 38, 66, 74, 95, 101, 138, 167, 172, 182, 198, 202.
  1843. 'Literary Intelligence', IV, 105; 'Punch's Phrenology', IV, 115, 160; 'Moral Reflections', IV, 120; 'Philosophy Outdone' (verse), IV, 124; 'A List of Wants', IV, 129; 'Epigram' (verse), IV, 160; 'Substance and Shadow', V, 22; 'Important to Cricketers', V, 96; 'Madness', V, 113; 'Famine and Fashion', V, 203; 'The Pauper's Christmas Carol' (verse), V, 269.

1845. 'A Ballad for the Delectation of All True Sportsmen', VIII, 58; 'The Imaginative Crisis' (verse), VIII, 105; 'A Contribution by Cobden' (verse), VIII, 126; 'Young England's Lament' (verse), VIII, 127; 'Courtship and Matrimony' (verse), IX, 32; 'The Exiled Londoner' (verse), IX, 147.

1846. 'The Farmer's Corn Law Song' (verse), X, 15; 'The Land of Bulls' (verse), X, 204; 'Sonnet', XI, 237; 'Reflections on a Tea-Table' (verse), XI, 263.

1849. 'What's in a Name?' XVI, 157.

1862. ' "Sensation" Advertising', XLIII, 10; 'Where's Your Ticket?' XLIII, 59; 'A Question of Political Economists', XLIII, 80; 'Good News for the Whiskerless', XLIII, 96.

1863. 'Extraordinary Annihilation of Space', XLIV, 83; 'Jokes for Laughing Jackasses', XLV, 39.

1864. 'Shakespeare Tercentenary', XLVI, 175.

1866. 'A Dose for a Doctor', L, 44.

1867. 'A First-Rate Game To Be Played by All England', LII, 34; 'Word Splitting', LII, 144.

1868. 'A Puff Direct', LV, 208.

1869. 'A Supplementary Paragraph', LVII, 269; 'The Pope and Dr. Cumming', LVII, 96.

1870. 'Not a Puff Really!' LVIII, 136.

D. Contributions to *Household Words*: 'Spring-Time in the Court' (verse), 25 May 1850; 'All Things in the World Must Change' (verse), 10 Oct. 1850; 'Gentle Words' (verse), 28 Sept. 1850; 'The Emigrant's Bird' (verse), 28 Sept. 1850.

E. Contributions to the *Illustrated London News*: 'Who Brings the Bride Home?' (verse), 27 Dec. 1851; 'Christmas Day' (verse), 22 Dec. 1855; 'Bringing in the Boar's Head', 22 Dec. 1855; 'A Christmas Carol', 22 Dec. 1855; 'Cold Without' (verse), 22 Dec. 1855; 'A Spanish Gipsy' (verse), 23 Aug. 1856; 'The Old Bell-Ringer's Story', 20 Dec. 1856; 'The Arrival of Uncle John', 20 Dec. 1856; 'The Christmas Hamper', 20 Dec. 1856; 'The Christmas Errand: Fanny's Story', 19 Dec. 1857; 'The Unexpected Guest', 19 Dec. 1857; 'A Christmas Carol' (verse), 25 Dec. 1858; 'Snapdragon', 25 Dec. 1858; 'The House on Fire on Christmas Eve', 23 Dec. 1860; 'Aunt Sally's Christmas-

Boxes', 20 Dec. 1862; 'Flowers and Thorns', 24 Dec. 1864; 'Page of Nonsense for Christmas', 24 Dec. 1864; 'A Christmas Holiday Lesson', 23 Dec. 1865; 'Ragged Tom's Christmas-Box', 22 Dec. 1866; 'How We Decorated Granvale Church', 18 Dec. 1869.

F. Contributions to *London Society*: 'In Kensington Gardens', Aug. 1862; 'Christmas Charades', Dec. 1862; 'The Pilgrims of the Rhine', Dec. 1863; 'A Christmas-Day in a Jew's House', Dec. 1863; 'Christmas Eve in a Night Train', Dec. 1864; 'What Came of Killing a Rich Uncle One Christmas Time', Dec. 1865; 'The Small House over the Water', Dec. 1866; 'An Actor's Holiday', Dec. 1867; 'Aunt Gracie's Sweetheart', Dec. 1868; 'A Coat with a Fur Lining', Dec. 1869; 'What Might Have Happened One Christmas Time', Dec. 1870.

G. Contributions to *Once a Week*: 'The Two Hands' (verse), 1 Dec. 1860; 'Look after Brown', 23 Mar. 1861; 'The Whip and the Night-Hunters', 8 Feb. 1862; 'Lorelei' (verse), from the German of Heinrich Heine, 16 Nov. 1867.

H. Contributions to the *Gentleman's Magazine*: 'The Two Pensioners' (under the pseudonym 'Tom Moody'), June 1868; 'Alone' (verse), Jan. 1869.

3. BOOKS

A. Tales, verse, and miscellaneous prose: *The Enchanted Doll*, Bradbury and Evans, 1849; *Prose and Verse*, Bradbury and Evans, 1852; *The Heir of Applebite* and *Our Lodgers*, Bradbury and Evans, 1856; *Betty Morrison's Pocket-Book*, Bradbury and Evans, 1856; *A Christmas Hamper*, Routledge, Warne, and Routledge, 1860 (containing 'The Old World and the New', 'The Christmas Errand', 'Jacob Sharp's Game of Snapdragon', 'The Old Bell-Ringer's Story', 'Uncle John's Christmas Visit', 'News from Home', 'A Christmas Carol' [verse]); *Tom Moody's Tales*, Bradbury and Evans, 1863 (containing 'The Whip and the Night-Hunters', 'The Martyr Post-Boy', 'The Riders! The Riders!', 'What Firkin Picked up on the Road', 'Recollections of a Retired Butler', 'The Rotten Borough', 'A "Run" with the Smugglers', ' "Fly" Hunting', 'How I and Davy Handey Lost Our First Loves', 'A Bull-Fight at Bayonne', 'A Little about Poaching and Poachers', 'Never Won till It's Lost', 'The Monster Nugget', 'The Adventures of a Christmas Turkey'); *The Jest Book*, Macmillan, 1864; *The Legends of Number Nip*, Macmillan, 1864; *Up and Down the London Streets*, Chapman and Hall, 1867; *Fairy Tales*, Bradbury and Evans, 1868 (containing *The Chronicles of the Three Sisters* [from the German] and *The Enchanted Doll*); *Tinykin's Transformations*, Bradbury and Evans, 1869.

B. Novels: *Wait for the End*, Bradbury and Evans, 1864; *Loved at Last*, Bradbury and Evans, 1864; *Falkner Lyle*, Hurst and Blackett, 1866; *Leyton Hall, and Other Tales*, Hurst and Blackett, 1867 (containing 'Hearts Are Trumps', 'Mind Your Own Business', 'The Talking Shell', 'Flowers Are Thorns', 'What Came of Killing a Rich Uncle', 'A Christmas-Day in a Jew's House', 'A Christmas Holiday Lesson', 'Christmas in a Night Train'); *Golden Fetters*, Bradbury and Evans, 1867; *The Taffeta Petticoat* (not published).

BIBLIOGRAPHY

(Unpublished sources are listed in the Key to Abbreviations)

À Beckett, Arthur W. *The À Becketts of 'Punch' : Memories of Father and Sons.* London: Constable and Co. Ltd., 1903.
Recollections of a Humorist. London: Sir Isaac Pitman and Sons Ltd., 1907.

À Beckett, Gilbert Abbott (ed.). *Scenes from the Rejected Comedies.* London: *Punch* Office, 1844.

Altick, Richard D. *The Cowden Clarkes.* London: Oxford University Press, 1948.
The English Common Reader. Chicago: University of Chicago Press, 1957.

Barham, R. H. *The Garrick Club.* London: privately printed, 1896.

Barham, R. H., *et al. Personal Reminiscences.* ed. Richard Henry Stoddard. New York: Scribner, Armstrong, and Co., 1875.

Beale, Thomas Willert [Walter Maynard]. *The Light of Other Days.* 2 vols. London: Richard Bentley and Son, 1890.

Boas, Guy. *The Garrick Club, 1831–1947.* London: The Garrick Club, 1948.

Boase, George C. *Collectanea Cornubiensia: A Collection of Biographical and Topographical Notes Relating to the County of Cornwall.* Truro: Netherton and Worth, 1890.

Bourne, H. R. Fox. *English Newspapers.* 2 vols. London: Chatto and Windus, 1887.

Brooks, Shirley. 'The Late Mark Lemon', *Illustrated London News,* LVI (4 June 1870), pp. 573–4.
'Lecture on *Punch*', Reported in the Durham County *Advertiser,* 27 February 1863.
'Mark Lemon', *Punch,* LVIII (4 June 1870), p. 219.

Browne, Edgar. *Phiz and Dickens.* London: James Nisbet and Co. Ltd., 1913.

Bunn, Alfred. *The Stage: Both Before and Behind the Curtain.* 3 vols. London: Richard Bentley, 1840.

Burnand, F. C. 'Mr. Punch: His Predecessors and Contemporaries', *Pall Mall Magazine,* XXIX (January–April 1903), pp. 95–105, 255–65, 390–7.

Records and Reminiscences. 2 vols. London: Methuen and Co., 1904.

Carroll, Lewis [Charles Lutwidge Dodgson]. *The Diaries of Lewis Carroll.* ed. Roger Lancelyn Green. London: Cassell and Co. Ltd., 1953.

Chadwick, George F. *The Works of Sir Joseph Paxton, 1803–1865.* London: Architectural Press, 1961.

Clarke, Mary Cowden. *Recollection of Writers.* New York: Charles Scribner's Sons, 1878.

Cooper, Leonard. *R. S. Surtees.* London: Arthur Barker Ltd., 1952.

Cooper, T. Sidney. *My Life.* 2 vols. London: Richard Bentley and Son, 1890.

Crowe, Joseph. *Reminiscences of Thirty-Five Years of My Life.* London: John Murray, 1895.

Dickens, Charles. *The Letters of Charles Dickens.* ed. Walter Dexter. 3 vols. London: The Nonesuch Press, 1938.

Mr. and Mrs. Charles Dickens. His Letters to Her. ed. Walter Dexter. London: Constable and Co. Ltd., 1935.

The Unpublished Letters of Charles Dickens to Mark Lemon. ed. Walter Dexter. London: Halton and Truscott, 1927.

Dickens, Henry F. *The Recollections of Sir Henry Dickens, K.C.* London: William Heinemann Ltd., 1934.

Dodds, John W. *The Age of Paradox.* New York: Rinehart and Co., 1952.

Doyle, Richard. *Bird's Eye View of Society.* London: Smith, Elder, and Co., 1864.

A Journal. ed. J. H. Pollen. London: Smith, Elder, and Co., 1885.

Du Maurier, George. *The Young George du Maurier. A Selection of His Letters, 1860–67.* ed. Daphne du Maurier. Garden City, N.Y.: Doubleday and Co. Inc., 1952.

Fielding, K. J. 'Charles Dickens and His Wife: Fact or Forgery?' *Études Anglaises,* VIII (July–Sept. 1955), pp. 212–22.

Forster, John. *The Life of Charles Dickens.* ed. J. W. T. Ley. London: Cecil Palmer, 1928.

Friswell, J. Hain. *Modern Men of Letters Honestly Criticised.* London: Hodder and Stoughton, 1870.

Frith, W. P. *A Victorian Canvas.* ed. Nevile Wallis. London: Geoffrey Bles Ltd., 1957.

'Funeral of Mark Lemon, The', *Illustrated London News,* LVI (4 June 1870), p. 574.

'Funeral of Mark Lemon, The', *The Times*, 30 May 1870, p. 14.

Glover, William. *Reminiscences of Half a Century.* London: Remington and Co., 1889.

Graves, Charles L. *The Life and Letters of Alexander Macmillan.* London: Macmillan and Co. Ltd., 1910.

Mr. Punch's History of Modern England. 4 vols. New York: Frederick A. Stokes Co., n.d.

Greville, Charles C. F. *The Greville Diaries.* ed. P. W. Wilson. New York: Doubleday Page, 1927.

Guthrie, Thomas Anstey [F. Anstey]. *A Long Retrospect.* London: Oxford University Press, 1936.

Halliday, Andrew (ed.). *The Savage Club Papers.* London: Tinsley Brothers, 1867.

Hannay, James. *Satire and Satirists.* London: David Bogue, 1854.

Hardman, Sir William. *A Mid-Victorian Pepys. The Letters and Memoirs of Sir William Hardman.* ed. S. M. Ellis. London: Cecil Palmer, 1923.

Hardy, Florence Evelyn. *The Early Life of Thomas Hardy, 1840–1891.* New York: The Macmillan Co., 1928.

Hatton, Joseph. *Club-Land.* London: J. S. Virtue and Co. Ltd., 1890.

In Jest and Earnest. A Book of Gossip. London: Leadenhall Press, 1893.

'In Memoriam. Our Christmas Contributor', *London Society*, XIX (February 1871), pp. 97–98.

Reminiscences of J. L. Toole. Related by Himself and Chronicled by Joseph Hatton. 2 vols. London: Hurst and Blackett Ltd., 1889.

'The True Story of *Punch*', *London Society*, XXVIII (July–December 1875), pp. 49–56, 152–61, 237–46, 341–51, 408–15, 511–17; XXIX (February, March, May 1876), pp. 127–32, 253–60, 438–42; XXX (July, December 1876), pp. 57–63, 554–62.

With a Show in the North. Reminiscences of Mark Lemon. London: W. H. Allen and Co., 1871.

Hodder, George. *Memories of My Time.* London: Tinsley Brothers, 1870.

Hole, Samuel R. *The Memories of Dean Hole.* London: Edward Arnold, 1893.

Hood, Thomas. *Memorials of Thomas Hood.* ed. by his daughter.

Preface and Notes by his son. 2 vols. Boston: Ticknor and Fields, 1860.

Horne, R. H. 'Bygone Celebrities', *Gentleman's Magazine*, VI (February, May 1871), pp. 247–62, 660–72.

Horsfield, Thomas W. *The History, Antiquities, and Topography of the County of Sussex.* London: Nichols and Sons, 1835.

Hudson, Derek. *Charles Keene.* London: Pleiades Books, 1947. *Lewis Carroll.* London: Longmans, Green, 1958.

Jackson, Mason. *The Pictorial Press.* London: Hurst and Blackett, 1885.

Jerrold, Blanchard (ed.). *The Best of All Good Company.* London: Houlston and Sons, 1871.
The Life and Remains of Douglas Jerrold. Boston: Ticknor and Fields, 1859.

Jerrold, Douglas. *Facts and Fancies.* London: Hunt and Clarke, 1826.

Jerrold, Walter C. *Douglas Jerrold and 'Punch'.* London: Macmillan and Co., 1910.
Douglas Jerrold: Dramatist and Wit. 2 vols. London: Hodder and Stoughton, 1914.
Thomas Hood: His Life and Times. New York: John Lane Co., 1909.

Johnson, Edgar. *Charles Dickens: His Tragedy and Triumph.* 2 vols. New York: Simon and Schuster, 1952.

Kitton, F. G. *Charles Dickens, His Life, Writings, and Personality.* London: T. C. and E. C. Jack, n.d.

Knight, Charles. *Passages of a Working Life.* 3 vols. London: Bradbury and Evans, 1865.

'The Late Mr. Mark Lemon', *The Times*, 24 May 1870, p. 11.

Layard, George S. *A Great 'Punch' Editor. Being the Life, Letters, and Diaries of Shirley Brooks.* London: Sir Isaac Pitman and Sons Ltd., 1907.
The Life and Letters of Charles Samuel Keene. London: Sampson Low, Marston and Co. Ltd., 1892.

Ley, J. W. T. *The Dickens Circle.* New York: Dutton, 1919.

Lower, Mark Antony. *A Compendious History of Sussex.* 2 vols. London: John Russell Smith, 1870.

Lucas, E. V. *Reading, Writing and Remembering.* New York: Harper and Brothers, 1932.

Lucy, Henry. *The Diary of a Journalist*. London: John Murray, 1920.

Sixty Years in the Wilderness. London: Smith, Elder and Co., 1909.

Mackay, Charles. *Forty Years' Recollections of Life, Literature, and Public Affairs: from 1830 to 1870*. 2 vols. London: Chapman and Hall, 1877.

Macmillan, Alexander. *Letters of Alexander Macmillan*. ed. George A. Macmillan. Glasgow: The University Press, 1908.

Macready, William Charles. *The Diaries of William Charles Macready, 1833–1851*. ed. William Toynbee. 2 vols. New York: G. P. Putnam's Sons, 1912.

Maurer, Oscar. ' "Punch" on Slavery and Civil War in America, 1841–1865', *Victorian Studies*, I (September 1957), pp. 5–28.

Mayhew, Athol. *A Jorum of 'Punch'*. London: Downey and Co., 1895.

Mayhew, Henry. *Mayhew's London*. ed. Peter Quennell. London: Spring Books, n.d.

'Mr. Mark Lemon', *Athenaeum*, 28 May 1870, pp. 708–9.

'Mr. Mark Lemon', *The Times*, 14 October 1868, p. 5.

'Mr. Mark Lemon as Falstaff', *Illustrated London News*, LII (17 October 1868), p. 384.

Morley, Henry. *The Journal of a London Playgoer. From 1851 to 1866*. London: George Routledge and Sons, Ltd., 1891.

Morris, Helen. *Portrait of a Chef: The Life of Alexis Soyer*. Cambridge: Cambridge University Press, 1938.

Nevill, Lady Dorothy. *My Own Times*. London: Methuen, 1912.

Nicoll, Allardyce. *A History of Early Nineteenth Century Drama, 1800–1850*. Cambridge: Cambridge University Press, 1955.

A History of Late Nineteenth Century Drama, 1850–1900. Cambridge: Cambridge University Press, 1959.

Odell, George C. D. *Shakespeare from Betterton to Irving*. 2 vols. New York: Charles Scribner's Sons, 1920.

Patmore, Coventry. *Memoirs and Correspondence of Coventry Patmore*. ed. Basil Champneys. 2 vols. London: George Bell and Sons, 1900.

Pearson, Hesketh. *Gilbert, His Life and Strife*. New York: Harper and Brothers, 1957.

Planché, J. R. *Recollections and Reflections*. 2 vols. London: Tinsley Brothers, 1872.

Price, R. G. G. *A History of Punch*. London: Collins, 1957.

Quennell, Peter. *Victorian Panorama*. New York: Charles Scribner's Sons, 1937.

Ray, Gordon N. *Thackeray. The Uses of Adversity, 1811–1846*. New York: McGraw-Hill Book Co. Inc., 1955.

Thackeray. The Age of Wisdom, 1847–1863. New York: McGraw-Hill Book Co. Inc., 1958.

Redesdale, Algernon Bertram Freeman-Mitford. *Further Memories*. New York: Dutton, 1916.

Renton, Richard. *John Forster and His Friendships*. New York: Charles Scribner's Sons, 1913.

Rose, R. N. *The Field, 1853–1953*. London: Michael Joseph, 1953.

Rowell, George. *The Victorian Theatre*. London: Oxford University Press, 1955.

Sala, George Augustus. *The Life and Adventures of George Augustus Sala*. 2 vols. London: Cassell and Co. Ltd., 1895.

Things I Have Seen and People I Have Known. 2 vols. London: Cassell and Co. Ltd., 1894.

Scott, Clement. *The Drama of Yesterday and To-day*. 2 vols. London: Macmillan and Co. Ltd., 1899.

Semmel, Bernard. *The Governor Eyre Controversy*. London: Macgibbon and Kee, 1962.

Smith, Albert, ed. *Sketches of London Life and Character*. London: Dean and Son, 1959.

Spielmann, M. H. 'Mark Lemon', *Bookman*, XXXVII (November 1909), pp. 77–86.

The History of 'Punch', New York: The Cassell Publishing Co., 1895.

Stevenson, Lionel. *The Showman of Vanity Fair*. New York: Charles Scribner's Sons, 1947.

Stirling, A. M. W. *Victorian Sidelights*. London: Ernest Benn Ltd., 1954.

Stirling, Edward. *Old Drury Lane. Fifty Years' Recollections of Author, Actor, and Manager*. 2 vols. London: Chatto and Windus, 1881.

Strauss, Gustav L. M. *Reminiscences of an Old Bohemian*. 2 vols. London: Tinsley Brothers, 1882.

Taylor, Bayard. *At Home and Abroad*. New York: Putnam, 1891.

Thackeray, William Makepeace. *The Letters and Private Papers of*

William Makepeace Thackeray. 4 vols. ed. Gordon N. Ray. Cambridge, U.S.A.: Harvard University Press, 1946.

Tinsley, William. *Random Recollections of an Old Publisher.* 2 vols. London: Simpkin, Marshall, Hamilton, Kent and Co. Ltd., 1900.

Tisdall, E. E. P. *Queen Victoria's Mr. Brown.* New York: Frederick A. Stokes Company, 1938.

Tolles, Winton. *Tom Taylor and the Victorian Drama.* New York: Columbia University Press, 1940.

Tomlins, Frederick G. *A Brief View of the English Drama.* London: C. Mitchell, 1840.

Vizetelly, Henry. *Glances Back through Seventy Years.* 2 vols. London: Kegan Paul, Trench, Trübner and Co. Ltd., 1893.

Walford, Edward. *Greater London.* 2 vols. London: Cassell, 1885–7.

Wallack, Lester. *Memories of Fifty Years.* New York: Charles Scribner's Sons, 1889.

Ward, Henrietta M. A. [Mrs. E. M. Ward]. *Memories of Ninety Years.* ed. Isabel G. McAllister. London: Hutchinson and Co., 1926.

Watson, Ernest Bradlee. *Sheridan to Robertson.* Cambridge, U.S.A.: Harvard University Press, 1926.

West, Sir Algernon. *Recollections: 1832 to 1896.* London: Thomas Nelson and Sons, 1899.

Whiteley, Derek Pepys. *English Masters of Black and White: George du Maurier, His Life and Work.* New York: Pellegrine and Cudahay, 1947.

Williams, S. H., and Madan, Falconer. *The Lewis Carroll Handbook.* Being a new version of *A Handbook of the Literature of the Rev. C. L. Dodgson (Lewis Carroll).* Now Revised, Augmented and brought up to 1960 by Roger Lancelyn Green. London: Oxford University Press, 1962.

Woolf, Maurice. 'Origin and Lemons', *The Jewish Chronicle,* 15 August 1958, p. 3.

Worth, George J. *James Hannay: His Life and Works.* Lawrence, Kansas: University of Kansas Press, 1964.

Yates, Edmund. *Fifty Years of London Life: Memoirs of a Man of the World.* New York: Harper and Brothers, 1885.

INDEX